Heated Pleasures

A Sassy, Down to Earth Reference Guide on Sensuality, Sexuality, & Self-Discovery

Ella Patterson

Heated Pleasures

A Sassy, Down to Earth Guide on Sensuality,
Sexuality, Sex and Self-Discovery
By Ella Patterson

Knowledge Concepts Publishing
P. O. Box 973 * Cedar Hill, Texas 75106 - 0973

Library of Congress in Publication Data has cataloged this edition as follows
Heated Pleasures
A Sassy, Down to Earth Guide on Sensuality, Sexuality, and Self-Discovery
Ella Patterson - 1st. Edition 2015
1st printing 2014
p. cm.

1. Health: information. 2. Self-esteem: mind. 3. Body improvement. 4. Sexuality: knowledge for women. 5. Relationship enhancement techniques. 7. Sex-Esteem: feeling better. 8. Resource: glossary, contacts, experts. 9. Psychology. 10. Education. 11. Tips, treats and techniques. 12. Pleasure. 13. Beauty.

I. Ella Patterson. II. Title.
ISBN: 978-1-884331-71-8 CIP: 95 - 94105
LCCN: 2009011518 SAN: 257 - 6163

10 9 8 7 6 5 4 3 2
USA $25.99
Canada $35.99

Manufactured in United States of America
Published by Knowledge Concepts Publishing

This book includes ...
*Index. *Questionnaire. *Resource. *Reference.
*Helpful Websites.*Order Form. *576 pages

PRINTED IN THE UNITED STATES OF AMERICA

Table of Contents

What People Are Saying 5
Heated Shorts 7
A Note from Ella 8

Preface Finally, an Adult Book for Adult Women 14
Intro Your Portal to Pleasure 24

Part 1 **In Pursuit of Heated Pleasures 46**
Chapter 1 Why Heated Pleasures 47
Chapter 2 The Woman's Body 64
Chapter 3 The Man's Body 86

Part 2 **Improve Your Personal Profile 101**
Chapter 4 Improving Your Feminine Hygiene 102
Chapter 5 Improving Your Appearance 114
Chapter 6 improving Your Sexual Radiance 150
Chapter 7 Improving Your Mental Foreplay 156
Chapter 8 Improving Your Conversations 160

Part 3 **Enhance Your Sensuality 171**
Chapter 9 Enhancing Your Touch 172
Chapter 10 Enhancing Your Sexual Rhythm 181
Chapter 11 Enhancing Your Kisses 194
Chapter 12 Celebrating 'Us' Time 202
Chapter 13 Bringing the Heat to Your Bedroom 208

Part 4 **Incorporate Stimulating Pleasures 225**
Chapter 14 Giving Yourself Stimulation 226
Chapter 15 Man Stimulating the Woman 237
Chapter 16 Woman Stimulating the Man 249
Chapter 17 Stimulating with Pleasurable Hand Treats 261
Chapter 18 Stimulating with Pleasurable Oral Sex Treats 287
Chapter 19 Pleasurable Tune Ups (aka Quickies) 325
Chapter 20 Getting Stimulating, Pleasurable Good Sex 332

Chapter 21 Pleasurable and Heated Sexual Treats 352
Chapter 22 Stimulating Places, Games, and Fantasies 369
Chapter 23 Having the Most Pleasurable Orgasms 380

Part 5 Pleasure Containers / Sexual Supplies 395
Chapter 24 Using Containers and Sex Supplies 396
Chapter 25 Using Vibrating Sex Toys 407
Chapter 26 Using Sensuous Clamps 449
Chapter 27 Using Cyberskin Toys 451
Chapter 28 Using Lubricants, Gels, Oils and Creams 456
Chapter 29 Using Electricity 467

Part 6 Indulging In Sensuous Foods 470
Chapter 30 Pleasure Foods 471

Part 7 Protecting Yourself 500
Chapter 31 Safe Sex Reminders 501
Chapter 32 Understanding Sexual Diseases 514

Afterword: Ella's Final Note 529
Appendix A: Questions for Women Who Read This Book 533
Appendix B: Helpful Resources 538
Appendix C: Organizations Dedicated To Sex Ed 539
Appendix D: Legal and Sensuous Internet Sites 540
Appendix E: Weights for Vaginal Exercises 540
Appendix F: Recommended Reading 541

Space for Notes 542
Acknowledgements 544
Index 548
About the Author 572
Books by Ella 573
Order Form 574
More from Ella 575

What People Are Saying About Heated Pleasures

"Heated Pleasures is a BLOCKBUSTER all day long. The need is overwhelming for this material. OH MY GOD!!!!!!!!!!!!!! I'm getting every one of my girlfriends this book."

~ Karen Sessoms PR - Atlanta, GA.

"Heated Pleasures to me... is filled with reasons why I should make love with my partner. I'm learning so much about myself each day. I can't wait to introduce the new me to him. This book is a great resource guide for me."

~ Venita McFadden, - Ft. Worth, TX.

"Ella gives women additional reasons to accept their sexuality. This book helps women open their minds to great times, and great experiences. It has helped me make important adjustments in my attitude and sensual techniques so that I can be happy in my relationship in and out of the bedroom."

~ Bettie Jones, - San Diego, CA.

"This book is so mentally and physically stimulating ... Heated Pleasures surely awakened my sexuality. It gave me the perfect excuse to be the Diva that I am. This is my passport to be sexy".

~ Denella Ri'chard, - Miami, FL.

"As I read Heated Pleasures, I discovered that this is really a great book. It's filled with lots of educational resources and is a great Rite of Passage for women who are between stages of wanting to be grown and need to be grown. It has been my personal guide. I love it."

~ Pamela Kennedy, - New York, NY

Also by Ella Patterson

Will the Real Women Please Stand Up?
Will the Real Men Please Stand Up?
1001 Reasons to Think Positive
Sexual Healing
Pampering Pleasures
Higher Expectations
Moving In the Right Direction
Successful Things That Successful People Do
Stupid Things Men Should Never Say To Women
Life Lines
Life Goes On
Life Lessons
Celebrations
Smart Moves
For Women Who Live Alone
For The Sake of Women
Lasting Values

This is another Ms. Real book!

Heated Shorts

Each chapter contains boxes that provide interesting and helpful information.

You Should Know
These boxes mention important things that every woman should know.

Watch Out
These boxes provide warnings and cautions.

Heated Pleasures
These boxes present facts about sex and sensuous information.

Ms. Real Suggests
These boxes feature tips and suggestions by Ms. Real.

Heatology
These boxes present facts that help open your mind to new things.

A Note from Ella

Dear reader, this sassy down to earth reference guide on sensuality, sexuality, and self-discovery presents couples with ways to enrich their relationships through intimacy and sexual loving. It's an easy to understand guide that's written for contemporary adult women.

Before I completed this book I found myself interviewing every woman who would speak with me and before our conversations concluded they asked me "*When is the next book coming?"* I was embarrassed to say that I didn't know. So, for the past few years I've been working intensely on a collection of new books and now that you're reading one of them I hope you like my style. The writing of this book has been one of the most difficult, wildest, wackiest, exhilarating and fulfilling adventures that I've experienced. It is organized like a sensuous walk through life. Use it as you discover new ways to gain knowledge, incorporate intimacy, enhance romance, embellish beauty, and pursue individual goals that will bring you great moments of joy and happiness.

Some chapters are purposefully super short so that you can put this book down, practice the techniques, and then go back to where you stopped. Each activity is bulleted or numbered so you can easily find your way back to the place where you left off.

If you are new to this kind of guide its best that you read it to gain sensual knowledge and understanding. If you feel that you're already informed, I suggest you read this guide to enhance what you already know. It's a great guide for women who want to step their game up and become more sensuous. I welcome you as you absorb this information. You'll find that you haven't read anything quite like this and your relationship will definitely be better by the time you reach the end of this book. (Which is why you bought this book, right?) Many women who are really smart and conscious human beings feel like complete idiots when it comes to getting earthshaking, write-home-about-it kind of intimacy. They want their partners to love them in ways that they can be sure each loving moment is theirs alone. Women want more hands-on passion, commitment and pleasure from their relationships, but they aren't always sure how to get it or give it. They want the kind of intimacy that's bonding, romantic and offers a taste of divine peace of mind. They want great feelings that are solid and true!

For example; when a woman has to experience intimacy before she's ready she doesn't always know what she wants nor is she sure how to get what she wants. The beauty of Heated Pleasures is that it makes the secrets of intimacy and sexual loving common knowledge. Written in everyday language it offers couples a manual for navigating the myriads of questions, and confusion in intimate relationships. You are definitely embarking on a fun journey, but before we begin, here's the formula for getting into your sensuous zone.

Helpful Instructions before Reading

Have a friend that you trust take your children to the mall or movies for a few hours. Once the children are gone, put on your favorite lounge wear; prepare your favorite drink, switch the ringers off on your phones and then find a quiet, cozy and comfortable place where you can read. I like to refer to it as “a place that you can call your space.” Here, you'll abandon inhibitions and create your own inventive nature.

To help you smoothly transition from one page to the next here are some tips that will help you along your way.

1. You can read this book from cover to cover, or dip in and out of different sections for tasty treats whenever the mood strikes.
2. You might want to read this book alone at first so that each surprise will unfold in your own time, naturally and spontaneously - not because it’s what your partner expects you to do.
3. If some of the ideas are exciting, but seem too heated for you - don't worry, move on and then return to the more tantalizing treats at a later date - when you are ready.
4. If you find something particularly delicious that you want to try but are a little nervous about trying it, share your desire with your partner and then let nature take its course.
5. Include your own treats as you advance your knowledge. There’s some space in the back of this book for your notes.
6. Take deep breaths often - inhale slowly, then exhale. Let go of any negative feelings, thoughts or

moods that might be complicating your life. Focus on the positive reasons that you're seeking to live a more sensual life.

7. Know and understand that you don't have to perform sexually in order to become a luscious goddess of love because you're already one.
8. As you read, circle at least fifty things you would like to do. Now, try to create a few more of your own. Again, use the spaces in the back of the book to jot them down.
9. Be sure to read all directions before using any of the toys, props, or supplies and be sure to check with a professional health expert before attempting any skills that this book has to offer.

I hope that these pages through their wisdom, and comfort - help you discover the sensuous woman that you were born to be and I hope that this information will bring you great happiness and joy.

Sit back, relax and enjoy your moments as you read. Let's raise our glasses and toast together as I humbly present "*Heated Pleasures: A sassy down to earth reference guide on sensuality, sexuality, sex and self-discovery*.

Now let's get started.

Preface

Finally, an Adult Book for Adult Women

Love is not a feeling; it's a wonderful state of MIND!”

Yes! Finally; a female sexuality guide that's wholesome, educational, sensual, down to earth, and sassy enough to help the contemporary adult woman. Every growing, maturing and exploring woman should have a copy of this book. It endorses the power of female sensuality and is for women who believe that healthy sexuality is a woman’s friend, not her enemy. It also encourages a positive healing force for women rather the promotion of anger, destruction, danger, depression and disease.

You Should Know
Sexual exercises can help you achieve heightened sexual pleasure so that you can achieve greater levels of sexual confidence.

This book will provide information that's helpful for women. It's fun and written in an easy-to-read, easy-to-follow style and it's endorsed by women who believe in these particular methods.

It's rare to find a book such as this one - one that provides quality advice on how to incorporate sensual pleasures into your relationship. Included are topics on sensuality, sexuality, sex, self-esteem, personal appearance, sex talk, sex games, sexual hope chest, sex toys, sexual lubricants, safe sex habits, and much more. There's also advice and sexual exercises that will help women achieve heightened intimate pleasure so that they can gain greater levels of sexual confidence.

This is a healthy and nurturing sensuality guide that presents plenty of fun-loving tips and techniques for grown women. Every adult woman will enjoy the benefits of this book long after they have finished reading it.

Why Women Need This Guide

Shortly before I began writing this book something inside of me was stirring. I was restless and wanted to create intimate and wonderful ways that women could reconcile their authentic sexual selves. It was a personal challenge for me because I knew that most women wanted to have more enjoyable sex as they enhanced their sexual aptitude even though they didn't always admit it.

Ms. Real Suggests
When you're finished reading this book you might want to read Appendix B "helpful Resources and Appendix C "Organizations dedicated to sex education.

The information in this book is valuable, but it isn't always easy for women to talk about sex. It's a sensitive conversation, especially when sex games, toys and sexual interludes are a part of the subject. Many bad people have given good sex a sour reputation, so it's important for me to communicate the positive side of intimate female sexuality.

This reference guide is my attempt to provide answers to tough sexual questions and give solutions to difficult sexual situations. It should assist women on their journey to understanding encounters, which might include sexual etiquette, sexual pleasures, and sexual desires. It helps women incorporate sensuous ideas into their intimate relationships too. I will tell you most everything important that will help improve most any sexual interlude you encounter. I will hide nothing from you – my readers.

The techniques in this book are so easy to use that women can make the personal adjustment from a drab and uneventful life to a sensuous one in a matter of hours. It includes creative tips and techniques that will help most every woman evolve sensuously.

While many of the current sexuality books focus on the mechanics of sex, this book addresses how women can improve their sensuality and sexuality and how they can have some really great sexual experiences with the person they love.

Men are grateful when women learn this information and as a woman learns more she begins to experience confidence that brings happiness in and out of her bedroom. Quite frankly, a woman tends to smile often; she's more relaxed and has less frustration when she

You Should Know

The techniques in this book are so easy to use that women can make personal adjustment from a drab and uneventful life to a sensuous one in a matter of hours.

You Should Know
This is not a book that seeks to pacify women into believing they should agree with everything I say.

is sensuously in tune with her sexual wants, needs and desires. When she is sexually fulfilled she is happy, satisfied and her personal relationships embody it.

There are many books out there that focus on a woman's body; few address her unique emotional and sexual needs. This book does. Every woman needs this book; and with it they will learn how to become more alluring and super sexy. Along the way they will enjoy some really good sexual tips, techniques and treats to use when they are ready.

Things You Should Always Do

1. Love your body.

This is important. When you learn to love and honor your body you are able to enjoy intimate pleasures and fulfilling sensations.

2. Appreciate your unique differences.

Adore every bump, mole, scar or imperfection. When you feel good about your physical self, you won't mind coming from under the covers, turning on the lights and gazing into your partner's eyes. When you begin to understand that there is no perfect body on this earth you will begin to accept your good and imperfect parts too.

3. **Discover what you like.**

   Take responsibility for your own pleasure and really find out what you like. You have to be the one who discovers what turns you on.

4. **Share what you learn.**

   Once you discover what turns you on, share it with your partner. If you don't know what you want, how on earth would you expect him to know? Communicate with your partner so that he can share in the journey.

5. **Relax and then receive.**

   While sharing intimate moments with your lover relax your mind and body so that you can better receive his love and affection.

Worry no more… here's your chance to become the sensuous woman you are meant to be and along the way I offer you an exciting and relaxing journey.

Share This Book with Him

If a woman suggests to a man that he read this book, it is important that she provide him loving attention and a sense of care that gives him the message she wants to improve their sex life. It should not sound too serious to him and she should not make him feel that he isn't good enough or that he needs to improve in this area. He'll feel insulted and might shut down if she approaches him in this way. Instead she should ask him to read this book with her or she can read it to him. She should tell him how much fun the two of them would have, and mean it. If a woman wishes, she may also take turns reading certain parts to him and he should do the same for her.

> **Heated Pleasures**
> A man responds eagerly if he feels that the woman really wants to improve her sex life with him.

A man responds eagerly if he feels that the woman really wants to improve her sex life with him. Once he sees the sex is improving and she's having fun doing it he'll want to participate in the reading and learning process. He'll want to help her improve.

If a man doesn't seem interested, simply leave the book lying around in strategic places that he will visit. His curiosity will motivate him to begin reading. Reading together can help each partner become more open when communicating about sensuous things they would like to try.

Watch Out
As you gain more knowledge you began to open your mind and try new things. Be prepared to become more exciting.

Another suggestion is that both partners take their own time reading parts of the book they like separately from one another and coming back to explore what they have read with one another.

This book is educational and is greatly beneficial to couples if they continue to discuss sex after reading it. For passion to grow, it is important that women do not feel that they are being judged, criticized or analyzed for their sexual desires.

I'll Always Be Honest with You

If you're the kind of woman that thinks she knows everything I suspect that this might not be the book for you. You won't be able to absorb the knowledge I'm bringing to you. Put it down or gift it to someone who wants to enhance their love life. If you are inhibited or feel a little intimidated then some of the treats, tips and techniques in this book might not be easy for you to digest. I understand and must be honest with you … this is not a book that seeks to pacify women into believing they should agree with everything I say. It is a book filled with sensual and sexual knowledge. You can decide whether or not you are ready.

My goal is to provide a resource of truthful information. And isn't that what we as women have always wanted… truthful, honest, and upfront information that can help us. Haven't we wanted the right to make our own choices about what we will and will not need?

If you prefer to take baby steps and soak in a little of this information at a time that's fine by me. Or maybe you would prefer the element of surprise where you explore and then discover another sensual treat each day. It's up to you. Enjoy the treats without guilt, shame or intimidation at your own pace. It is a book that you can share or choose to keep to yourself. This is a girlfriend's book, but it is written with grown women in mind.

Take a moment and figure out if this is the book for you, and then answer the following questions.

1. Do I enjoy making love?
2. Am I open enough to try new thing with my lover?
3. Do I feel sensuous and pamper myself daily?
4. Do I know how to pamper myself?

5. Am I ready for an intimate and sexual relationship?
6. Am I ready to be sexually committed to my partner?
7. Do I connect with him in ways other than sex?
8. Do I possess positively sensuous attributes?
9. Do I practice non-sexual intimacy regularly?
10. Do I maintain my sexual ethics?
11. Do I bring spirituality into my intimate relationships?
12. Does my lover see me as a sensuous person?
13. Do I create sensuous moments for my partner?
14. Are my bedroom activities boring and nonsexual?
15. Do I practice feminine hygiene on a daily basis?
16. Do I work diligently to enhance my appearance?
17. Do I judge people because of their sexual practices?
18. Do I combine sensuality with safe sex?
19. Do I practice mental foreplay?
20. Do I know how to add spark to my conversations?

These are powerful questions that need to be considered before any woman can begin to understand her sensual self. Heated Pleasures actively encourage both partners to communicate and help each other create the best loving and sensual experiences with each other.

This Is a Book for Adult Women

We know moving forward means that every adult woman must do something to keep her relationship positive, hopeful and continuously developing. Every woman is responsible for setting up a personal relationship mechanism that will be effective for her - now and in the future. By beginning to make progress and get the wheels moving there will be relationship efficiency. Here are some Heated Pleasures benefits you might need. You will ...

- Take responsibility for your happiness.
- Accept love, give love, share love and believe that love is your friend.
- Learn to express your feelings ways.
- Feel new, alive, and whole and then improve what you know by making things better.
- Enjoy making love and enjoy the pleasure of love.
- Become sensuously attractive.

What Heated Pleasures Is Not

It is not judgmental!

There is always something positive you can do that will enhance your relationship.

Introduction

Your Portal to Pleasure

Good sex awakens sexuality and defuses sexual tension.

Women long for sexual understanding even more than they desire sexual intercourse. They want their sexual heat to come from a partner who understands their emotional and sexual needs and who genuinely cares about them.

The fact of the matter is good sex has positive effects on women. Good sex promotes a sense of intimacy and care; and can improve human growth and development. Good sex works wonders for reducing stress and enhancing a woman's psyche. Research has proven over and over

Watch Out

Sometimes a woman can become so desperate that she seeks answers from people who don't know the truth and many times these same people won't tell her the truth when they know the truth.

again that positive sexual activity promotes a healthy wellbeing.

As a degreed health educator, and nationally published author, I have had the opportunity to speak with individuals and couples who are disheartened or discouraged by their lack of intimacy and sexual gratification. Some women remain *'virgin wives'* because they fear vaginal penetration. Women who are embarrassed and depressed by their husband's inability to achieve and maintain erections have lost the closeness and intimacy that they once shared. For these women the road ahead is bumpy and they don't know which way to turn. They need advice and help. Their road to passion is bumpy.

Your Bumpy Ride Stops Here

A woman's life is filled with so much drama that sometimes she doesn't know how to handle the situations she encounters. She's hungry for answers and is often worried about finding solutions. Sometimes she becomes so desperate that she seeks answers from people who don't know the truth. These same women often become workaholic's, stressaholic's, and careaholic's who are judged by society's standards of what it should take to make them happy. Searching for the best answers can cause a woman's emotions to be up one minute and down the next, creating an emotional roller coaster. The bumpy ride stops here. It's time to make the sensuous ride smoother. This book will certainly do that for you.

Your Time Is Now

These are great times for women. These are great times for dating, laughing, having fun and being adventurous. It's time to let go of inhibitions and experience good love, but first, let's answer a few sensuous questions:

1. Are you ashamed of your body? If so, why?
2. Is your ideal body image a short term or long term project, or no project at all?
3. Is it difficult to express your feelings about sex?
4. Are you a sensuous person?
5. Are you a romantic?
6. What kind of home would others say you have?
7. Does your home denote cleanliness, a welcome feeling, peacefulness, freshness, or pleasantries?

8. Is your home junky, cluttered, dirty, smoke filled, odor filled, dusty, or have allergens?
9. Does your home have a sense of sensuality?
10. Does your bedroom have an intimate, cozy, feeling?
11. Do you accept how your body feels during sensuous times?
12. Do you know the difference between sex and sexuality?
13. Do you understand your sensuality? Your sexuality?
14. Do you try to make your relationships more sensual than sexual?
15. Are you comfortable having sex with your mate?
16. Can you come up with 10 creative ways to enhance your own sensuality? If so, what are they? List them in the back of this book or in 'Your Heat Journal'.
17. Do you long to experience more heated pleasures?
18. Do you ever get sensual massages?
19. Do you give yourself love at least 5 times a week?
20. Do you long for the simple or fancy things in life?
21. Are you sensual, but haven't felt sensuous lately?
22. Are you yearning to feel good about your sexuality and your power to be a sensuous woman?
23. Has it been a long time since you felt truly rested?
24. Has it been more than a week, a month or a year since you felt love and concern for a lover?

25. When was the last time you read a good book?
26. When was the last time you walked barefooted outside?
27. Do you want your spirit and attitude to be better?
28. Does your lovemaking moments need a boost to become more of what you want them to be?
29. Do you yearn for a quickie, but can't get one?
30. When was the last time you had a romantic dinner?
31. When was the last time you cuddled with your lover?
32. Do you yearn for a long sex session with all the bells and whistles, but can't pull it together when the time comes?
33. Does your partner need encouragement to become sexually motivated?
34. Do you feel happy, sad, good or bad when you think about sex? Why do you feel the way you feel?
35. Are you ready to try new things and become more sensuous?

If you answered yes to any of these questions you probably need this guide. It will help you start enjoying pleasure today? What follows are loads of solutions, tips, techniques and treats that will help enhance your sex life, improve your understanding and make you feel better about indulging in heated pleasures.

Why Women Need Pleasure

Let's face it. Sexual exchange between loving couples creates great levels of pleasure. It builds self-esteem, promotes feelings of well-being, and sustains a sense of self-sufficiency. For women, pleasurable sexual exchange has been known to provide relief from loneliness, decrease in depression, and distraction from pain. It relieves tension, reduces anxiety and reinforces positive feelings about being a sensuous female.

Heated Pleasures

Sex is best when there are no expectations or actual goals of achievement.

For women, "sex is more than an act of pleasure, its' the ability to be able to feel so closely connected and comfortable to a person, that it's almost breathtaking and to a point you feel you can't take it. At this moment you're a part of one another."

We want an extraordinary holistic experience with an attentive, perceptive, and expressive partner who is willing to delve into the depths of our soul, sharing absolute bliss in our sexual union. Is that too much to ask?

That's a pretty tall order to fill for the average man, who gets an erection from a split-second glance at a quasi-sexy image and then goes through a nearly automated sequence of simple physical motions which culminates in ejaculation.

Women are different - more complex. She needs various forms of physical stimulation as well as energetic and emotional connection. She wants her lover to make love to her mind. She wants to feel a sense of recognition, value, and appreciation. If men only knew how much better their sex lives could be with an empowered woman who feels confident, sexy, and passionate. If they knew, then they would certainly be willing to consider what women truly want in bed. Guess what, ladies—it's up to us to lead the way.

You Should Know

Pleasure takes the bitch out of women, even if only for a short while. It softens her and makes her calm down and become mellow.

Accept Your Pleasures

To accept pleasure you have to enhance your ability to receive pleasure, compliments, and affection by letting go of inhibitions and expectations. Get out of your heads and into your hearts, so that you can relax and empty your minds. By evoking a state of reverent meditation during lovemaking, your sensitivities will be enhanced, making a deeper, more profound experience possible for both partners.

Your conscious awareness is a meandering personal discovery of what you take pleasure in, gradually surrendering into pure instinct and intuition with every breath. It is essential to allow plenty of time and space to sensuously explore, with genuine curiosity and a playful attitude. You can gently guide and direct your man's attention with subtle body language and responsive gestures. The more you respond in a positive and engaging way, the more aroused you both become - building energy and excitement.

You Should Know

We have the ability to set the tone with every movement, expression, and reaction.

Sex is best when there are no expectations or actual goals of achievement. Allowing the pleasure of lovemaking to gently unfold, whether it's the first time together or the five hundredth time is best. We have the ability to set the tone with every movement, expression, and reaction. To achieve optimum orgasm, simply focus on the physical sensations, feeling fully present in the moment—in the body. The currents of our life force surge through our bodies, revitalizing every cell, removing blocks and balancing the body, mind, and spirit.

And finally, we can learn to ride our sexual energies into our inner world, the world of the soul, as well as outward into relationship. We can practice lovemaking as a form of meditation—opening our hearts to love, enabling us to have more intense and momentous orgasms while sharing mystical bliss with our partner. A healthy sex life can improve all other areas of our lives, as we expand our mind and feel a deeper connection with who we truly are.

You Should Know

While women have been having lots of sex, many of them aren't feeling the level of pleasure they would like to feel.

The Benefits of Sexual Pleasure

Women want, need and desire pleasure. Pleasure leads to laughter and rejuvenation; intimacy and engagement; and it will definitely present a sense of satisfaction in most all relationships - even when many things in life are going bad. Pleasure takes the bitch out of women, even if only for a short while. It softens her and makes her calm down and become mellow. She smiles more and is less offensive when pleasure is in her life; especially sexual pleasure.

A woman looks forward to having private yet special ways to feel good about whom she is. She wants to have the kind of memories that she can refer to when she needs to feel good. Great sex should be one of them. It makes a woman feel good physically and emotionally and boosts her spirit.

Women love to be loved and they like satisfying mind blowing sex. They want to define it and seek it without restrictions. There's so much evidence that proves good sex lengthens life and makes a woman's bodies feel alive and happy.

> **You Should Know**
> Many women appear to be happy and lead such fulfilling lives - where others are so unhappy, bitchy and seemingly unfulfilled.

Studies prove that women are less likely to experience a heart attack when they experience good sex with a person they care for. Other studies show that quality sex is great for a woman's health, not to mention it is very satisfying.

While working as a contributing writer for Essence, Jet, Upscale, Today's Black Woman, Cosmo, and Eclipse Magazine I received thousands of letters and emails from women who wanted more information about sex and the pleasures of sex. Some women only knew the most basic information about sex even though they had been indulging in sexual activity for decades. I have traveled the globe speaking to women about the important factors of mutually satisfying sex.

> **You Should Know**
> Contrary to what your mama always said, you should become a woman who appreciates your own sexuality.

I discovered that while women have been having lots of sex, many of them aren't feeling the level of pleasure they would like to feel. They want more than the bumping and grinding kind of sex. They want to experience intimacy that brings magical satisfaction. They want heated pleasures.

Your Pathway to Heated Pleasures

Many women express an inner sadness because they cannot achieve complete satisfaction. They feel sexually inadequate. The bedroom pressures are overwhelming and the lack of adequate performance has caused them to be unfulfilled. Many are unhappy and won't be happy until they are sexually satisfied. They want multiple orgasms too. They want orgasms every time they have sex and feel that if they don't have them they have been cheated. They feel that they should know every sexual trick and technique that will make their partners beg for more.

Pleasure is not about performance or reaching goals. When you judge performance you are setting yourself up to fail long before sex can begin or end. Pleasure will come when you are relaxed, confident, and comfortable with you and your partner's performance. There is not one way to achieve orgasm. There is no wrong or right way either. You are the CEO of your satisfaction and you alone define the kind of pleasure you need. Even though your partner helps you get there, it is you who ultimately decides what feels good and what makes you desire him more.

You Should Know
Exploring your own sexual attitudes can help clarify your personal values.

Check Your Attitude about Sex

Many women adopt attitudes and values about sex without thinking about whether they truly believe and accept them. This might cause confusion and guilt when what they want doesn't agree with what they believe morally. Exploring the sources of sexual attitudes can help clarify values.Keep your mind open, explore your desires, get to know how your body works and be sure to know your partners body.

Learn to enjoy the human body and you will not only enjoy what you read, you will understand how to make your body feel better than it has ever felt. That's what this book is really about.... That's the real message! FEELING GOOD INSIDE AND OUT!!!

You Should Know
I began this mission by asking women some of the simplest sexual questions and then the most difficult sexual questions.

Stumbling Blocks to Avoid

Like any other self-improvement process, pleasure seeking has some stumbling blocks you should be aware of. Contrary to what mama always said, you should become a woman who appreciates your own sexuality. You'll need to learn to love the woman you are and look forward to becoming the woman you want to be.

Since you will be promoting yourself, it is up to you to let everyone know how great you feel about yourself. You must invest in you. You should be willing to devote time and effort into your self-improvement. There's no getting around the fact that to have a dynamic you, you must spend time improving, revising, and updating yourself.

Take Time for Yourself

There are times that women get so caught up in taking care of their partners that they neglect taking care of themselves. Oh, they find time to treat themselves to nice dinners, buy new clothes or go the beauty shop, but they aren't very kind to their inner selves. They don't always pamper and indulge in the things they enjoy. More often than it feels comfortable to admit there are women who give so much to others that they become withdrawn and angry at the universe because of what is missing from their own lives. It's time for women to receive the kind of sexual pampering that can heal and thrill a woman's soul. It's time for women to take care of number one.

You Should Know

We can program our subconscious to bring about something we genuinely want. Program yourself for happiness.

Connect the Dots

Before pulling everything together for this book the dots had to be connected. I needed to find out why women desired heightened sexual pleasure and what kind of pleasure they wanted. Also, why did so many women appear to be happy and lead such fulfilling lives - where others were so unhappy, bitchy and seemingly unfulfilled? After long-term observation I found out that women are usually pretty happy, but their true happiness came when they were being true to their sensuous self. The happier the woman, the more sensuously satisfied she is.

You Should Know

You must invest in yourself in order to improve yourself.

I began this mission by speaking to women of all races, creeds and colors. I asked women some of the simplest sexual questions and then the most difficult sexual questions. As I observed and spoke to them I wrote; and as I wrote I evolved. I began to gain better understanding of my own gender. As the days passed I wrote and then the better parts of me began to surface. My most spiritual and sensuous self-began to awaken. I realized that … like most women - I too was a woman in desperate need of heated pleasures.

I had to take stock of what women really wanted and what they needed to do in order to find their authentic sexual fulfillment. I had to also figure out why some women didn't want to have sex with the men they confess to love. Was it the woman or the life the woman was living? Perhaps for the first time I had to be honest with myself both inwardly and outwardly.

During this time of profound introspection, four practical and creative principles were incorporated in my life, they are…

1) Set goals
2) Get in tune with my own sexuality
3) Make better life choices and
4) Open my mind.

These principles have become the catalyst, which helped me write the book that I now present to you. These principles will become an important part of your life and help you define your authentic sexual self.

Set Your Goals

Before you move ahead on your sexual self-improvement venture, establish concrete goals. Over and over, it has been proven that those who take the time to think and write down specific steps are those who achieve success. Experts tell us that we can program our subconscious to bring

Heated Pleasures
It's important that you lay out a sexual plan of action. Begin your plan of action today.

about something we genuinely want.

There are three things you must do to reach your sexuality goals. First, clearly identify and quantify your goals. Second, write down each goal as if they exist. Third, affirm them by writing them down and/or state them repeatedly aloud; sincerely believing they have already been accomplished. You can do this before you've reached your goals.

Your affirmation might go something like this: "I have learned to do vaginal exercises that will help tighten my vaginal muscles by June 1." Or you might say, "I have improved my relationship by leaps and bounds and feel very good about my accomplishments." *"I am improving my relationship each week."* By expressing your desired outcome in the present tense, you condition your subconscious mind to accept it as fact.

You Should Know

If you find yourself feeling a little shy about trying new things... remember that you do have a choice in your own happiness.

Once you set your sexuality goals decide what steps you should take to help get you there? It would be wise to read this whole guide before you map out the route that will lead to your long-range destination. You may decide that learning more about the male and female anatomy provide

Heated Pleasures

It's normal to go slowly before trying new sexual treats and its okay to feel a little shy at first.

the best results for you. Improving your personal profile could be a great start. Or maybe improving your sensuality will get you there the fastest. Could updating your home; the style and mood get you there? Perhaps the section on sexual toys and props and supplies is your 'open sesame.' Choosing to become the woman you want to be is up to you, as long as it brings you the desired results.

It's important that you lay out a plan of action. Write the steps involved. Break down the overall process into easily digestible chunks. Get rid of what doesn't work. Take more generous bites of those that work and are satisfying. Set your goals, and plan carefully for your successful journey. As you embark on learning more about your own sexuality, you should consider the best way to also get in tune with what you want sexually.

Get In Tune with Your Sexuality

While many of the principles in this book are obvious to some women they are quite absent to others. I suggest you keep them in mind when striving for your own sexual satisfaction. These principles will add years of happiness to your life and that alone makes them well worth knowing. Along the way there are some sensuous treats that will help you get in tune with your own sexuality.

Because this is a very sensuous book, I suggest you keep it in your lingerie drawer. It is a grown woman's book that you can safely indulge in at any time you need. If any of the treats surprise you and some of them probably will - try your best not to become intimidated. Be a grown ass woman and open your mind. It's normal to go slowly before trying new sexual treats and its okay to feel a little shy at first. Consider that you are reading this book to gain insight and knowledge on how to get in tune with your personal self, your inner diva, and your own sexuality.

You Have a Choice... Make It!

Don't get bent out of shape or worry that you're not ready for this kind of book. Most women who want to learn new things are a little hesitant at first, but as time goes by you'll start to feel more comfortable in your own skin. You'll want to learn new things and explore new pleasures. It's the normal order of

Ms. Real Suggests

This is your time – enjoy it. Take the time to adopt a wholesome and healthy attitude toward your own sexuality.

You Should Know
It's important that you lay out a plan of action. Write the steps involved. Break down the overall process into easily digestible chunks.

growing into a sensual woman. If you find yourself feeling a little shy about trying new things, please understand that you do have a choice.

Let's face the facts: there's no reason you should feel guilt or shame for what you like to do sexually with your lover. If you want to be sensuous and have fun while doing it, you'll have to learn how to add the kind of heat that will bring sensuous spice into your relationship.

You do not have to indulge in any of these treats if you don't want to, but imagine how learning these new things will spice up and strengthen your love life. Work to understand that trying new things with your lover will help make your time together much more rewarding and fun.

Open Your Mind

As you read the pages that follow I want you to free your mind of any negatives and open your mind to your ability to become more sensual and enjoy the idea of having good sex.

Toss away any mental blocks that might be keeping you from enjoying your sex life. Some mental blocks that you might experience are: guilt, fear, shame, pain or false expectations. Maybe you're holding on to resentments or anger with your current partner or because of past partners.

If you've had negative feelings due to past sexual experiences it might be difficult to get past them. You will need to work through those emotions in order to truly free yourself so you can have the kind of love life you truly desire.

Work toward enhancing your sexual experiences with him. He needs to feel your enthusiasm. Men are like that. They tend to seek the things they need in someone else if they can't find it in you. I suggest that you share these tips and techniques intimately and verbally. Please keep in mind that this is not a contest.

> **Ms. Real Suggests**
>
> Consider that you are reading to gain insight and knowledge on how to get in tune with your personal self, your inner diva, and your own sexuality.

Gain wisdom and knowledge and then become the woman you truly want to be. You can have a wonderful relationship with self and with him. This is the key to and living a good life, one that is full of joy and completeness from inside out.

Accept the Challenge

Get a medical checkup before participating in any of the suggested tips, treats and techniques. Always do what's best for you and pass on any information you get that can help others.

While exploring Heated Pleasures you might find that you are being challenged on different personal and sexual habits. I must admit that when I first began writing books about female sexuality, I was too. Take your time and move at the rate you feel comfortable. In my travels, many women have asked me to write more about becoming a real woman. They wanted something spicier than my book Will the Real Women Please Stand Up. Heated Pleasures is my answer to those requests. It has been a labor of love and I hope you enjoy reading it as much as I have enjoyed writing it. I wish you happiness, excitement, satisfaction and many heated pleasures. Now, if you really want to get things heated with your special someone; take this book, go to your special place and let's get started.

You can always feel more than you can see.

In Pursuit of Your Own Heated Pleasures

Why Heated Pleasures

Sexual pleasure is relaxed and balanced and nurtures your life and well-being.

Ummmm, heated moments. Exciting moments filled with love, romance, intimacy, communication, and sensuous adventures. Private moments filled with fun, laughter, and excitement. Sensuous moments filled with exploration, rejuvenation and the kind of attention women long to experience. All of these moments can make you feel very good!

The words heated pleasures should bring great thoughts to your mind and a smile to your face. In my mind, when I hear the word pleasure I immediately think of sensual gratification, sexual indulgences and great moments of wanted and needed sexual happiness with the person I love.

What Are Heated Pleasures?

Heated pleasures are those moments that include a spectrum of pleasurable feelings from satisfaction to indescribable ecstasy. For some women it might be that familiar embrace or touch received from a lover. To others it might mean a woman's lover does sensuous things that he knows she wants, needs, and desires. To some; heated pleasure might be the excitement she gets from a new sexual position, new experience, or sensual experiment. To others it might be his passionate tongue flirting from top to bottom on both pairs of her lips or maybe it's the twinkle in his eye when he's caressing her clitoris with gentle palms. Whatever the case may be heated pleasures are as individual as the woman who is giving or receiving it. Think for a moment; what moments of heated pleasures have you experienced?

Heated Pleasures

You'll never learn new ways that will enhance your love life unless you try new things. Try to incorporate a few sensual treats of your very own.

Preparing For Heated Pleasures

Maybe getting into new erotica isn't quite your style. Maybe you don't think your man would like to indulge in the kind of pleasures that cause the both of you to get naked and make love on the patio or in the backyard. Or maybe, just maybe after years of doing things a certain way you feel that you are ready to try new things. Yes, maybe it sounds like fun, but you just can't imagine doing it. You can't seem to get pass "the nice girl's don't do that" thinking.

Ms. Real Suggests
A great way to feel more comfortable about trying new things is to read this book and learn more about the things you're interested in.

A great way to feel more comfortable about trying new things is to read this book and learn more about the things you're interested in. You can share some of these sensuous ideas with your partner and then you can incorporate some of the intimacies that follow:

- Indulge more by creating your own games.
- Become intuitive about what makes your body happy.
- Do sensuous things he'll enjoy.

- Notice when he's hinting and ready to try new things.
- Catch his messages of what he likes and dislikes.
- Talk to him about sex in a fun and relaxed tone.
- Smile when discussing sex.
- Enjoy being sensual by initiating sex.
- Open your mind to new sexual adventures.
- Suggest fun activities that will encourage him to participate.
- Communicate what you want clearly.
- Listen to his fantasies and enjoy instead of rejecting.
- Relay your fantasies to him with an open mind.

If you slowly began to incorporate these things you'll improve your romantic style. And because you're reading this book several other things will happen.

- Your thinking will become more sensuously tuned.
- Your sensuality will become enhanced.
- Your sexual aptitude will increase.
- Your pleasure zone will flourish.
- Your attitude about what good sex is will heighten.
- You will become more open minded about your own desires.

You don't have to be a sexual expert to want more knowledge and information about your own sexuality. And you don't have to feel like a nymph just because you enjoy sexual pleasure.

It's Time to Celebrate

Even though some women would like to say they don't need to learn more about pleasure, the truth is - we all do! We need to celebrate our pleasurable experiences, especially those that are authentic healing experiences.

Who you really are is your authentic self -- the self that you are meant to be. It's the core of your emotional and spiritual self. As a woman learns more about who she is she should also celebrate her discovery!

"Wisdom is a continuing process." It's similar to the human life cycle -- constantly growing, changing and forever improving. So, rather than mark this celebration with a collection of sexual antidotes, I offer you wisdom that has worked for centuries!

Heated Pleasures

Beginning today, train yourself to accept gifts when offered and compliments when given as a natural part of being a woman.

Time Brings About Changes

There will be times in your life when sex will not be as fulfilling as you want. Your desire may deplete or you may find it difficult to become aroused. Your vagina may not be ready when your mind is and it may be difficult to achieve the level of sexual pleasure you have been accustomed. Over time, you may experience pain or completely lose interest in sex.

Sexual pleasures can go downhill because of medications, relationship problems, or life altering problems that get in the way. The good news is that there is help for almost every sexual problem or dysfunction.

> **Ms. Real Suggests**
> Seek professional help if you experience any prolonged problems that cause you not to want sex, lack of desire or if you have encounters of sexual related pain.

How Sexual Women Are Judged

Some women feel left out if they can't find the man of their dreams. Even when they are deeply involved with a man and having sex their minds are sending messages that haunt them during their sexual journey.

If a young woman in high school enjoyed sex it meant she was the school slut. In college she was considered the campus whore and in her grown up life she's considered a nymphomaniac. Women have been bombarded with so many negatives messages about sex that the bad overrides any good she wants to feel. Today we're going to change this way of thinking.

Are You Emotionally Vested?

Many women think sex is better if they are emotionally connected to the person they have sex with. The fact of the matter is … her partner must be just as committed to her emotional needs in order for the fireworks to go off. Sex can be good if there is no emotional connection, but let's face it in order for sex to be the bombshell kind of sex - you have to be emotionally vested. Only when the feelings are safe, honored, and complete is the sex quality. There's exciting pleasures ahead when you open your heart to the person you're sharing your loving emotions with.

Heatology

Let's face it; in order for sex to be the bombshell kind of sex women dream about - you have to be emotionally vested

Ask yourself if you are you emotionally connected and invested. Can you say that you are in it 100%?

Giving and Getting Pleasure

Sexual pleasure is a two-way street that must be actively shared. You have to be able to give it as well as receive it. This seems so simple, but for many women it's a difficult path to follow.

> **You Should Know**
> You can experience breathtaking ecstasy and still not be sexually satisfied.

Some women find it difficult to open up enough to accept wholesome pleasure that is rightfully due to them. Some of them find it difficult to accept a simple compliment for a job well done or for looking good, and being good. Think about it, when someone tells you that they like your new dress, your new shoes or even your hairstyle, instead of accepting it graciously with a smile do you deflect the compliment and find fault with yourself? If you can't accept simple compliments you probably find yourself deflecting opportunities of deeper pleasures of intimacy as well.

Beginning today; train yourself to accept gifts when offered and compliments when given as a natural part of being a woman. Be willing to accept compliment and enjoy them without reservation.

If It Feels Good To You

Today, for many women and men orgasm has become the epitome of mind-blowing sex. We have been trained to think that if we don't have an orgasm we are not having satisfying sex. When we don't reach orgasm we add it to our list of personal failures. We blame something... our bodies, ourselves, our partners, our jobs our families, whatever comes to mind. We lose so much of ourselves for the 'O' word and if we don't experience orgasm we resent, fear and shut down certain parts of our sexual spirit.

Heated Pleasures

Let's face it; sometimes you won't be able to see your lover when you want and you'll have to accommodate yourself.

Let's face it; sometimes you won't be able to see your lover when you want and you'll have to accommodate yourself. Self-pleasuring is one of the simplest forms of gratification. It can be as personal and as private as you like. Women indulge in self-pleasuring through masturbation and many have decided to use sex toys or fantasizing for pleasure. (See Chapter 15 and Chapter 25)

When making love try not to hold your breath as you approach an orgasm. When you tighten up, an orgasm might happen, but it should happen while surrendering, losing control so that pleasure can have its way with you. The more relaxed you are while having an orgasm the more gratifying the orgasm will be. When you ask people how they describe great sex many will close their eyes and imagine a satisfying love making session; foreplay, oral sex, intercourse and finally orgasm. That's what some say it's all about. Personally, I don't describe oral sex as my indicator of great sex. It's possible to experience intense multiple orgasms without feeling satisfied. You can even experience breathtaking ecstasy and not feel satisfied.

> **You Should Know**
>
> To achieve the ultimate pleasure; focus on enjoying all of the physical and emotional sensations that you and your partner create when you're together

To achieve the ultimate pleasure; focus on enjoying all of the physical and emotional sensations that you and your partner create when you're together. Imagine fulfillment, and then savor how he looks, how his body feels, how he smells, and how he moves toward you. Capture the things

Heated Pleasures
A sensuous woman shares her ideas with her partner and tunes in to what he wants while still working to achieve what she wants.

you like most in him. Think about how he feels when you are holding him. Can you feel the electricity? Relax, and release. Have wonderful orgasms. Come at your own pace. Now let it be you who decides when, where and how many.

Do You Know What Turns You On

Maybe your turn-on is an indulgent warm bath with water that envelops your body letting the ripples of water rubs against your nipples. It might become a much-needed ritual that you look forward to when alone in your bath, or consider water flowing from a removable showerhead being used to hit against your clitoris while showering. You might even enjoy walking around in the nude after a long day at work glancing often at your body as you pass the mirror. Does it excite you?

Being able to give yourself moments of sensual freedom is no one's business but your own, so why not indulge in feel good pleasures without anyone ever knowing. To bring your mind to an area of pleasure, ask yourself these questions then answer them. (See Chapter 15 for more details)

1. What are ways you indulge in pleasurable moments?
2. What are some of your personal fantasies?
3. What is it that makes you feel more sensuous on some days and not so sensuous on others?
4. Do you consider yourself a sensuous woman?
5. Do others consider you sensuous?
6. What would it take to make you more sensuous?

Become a More Sensuous Woman?

Are you a sensuous woman? Do you even know what makes a sensuous woman? Maybe you're not sure of yourself. Just in case you're wondering, here are several sure fire ways you'll know if you are. Are you…

- The kind of woman that does not mind letting your sexuality shine through?
- Resourceful and feel powerful about who you are and how you look?
- Coming across as sleazy or trampish when you feel you are sexy?
- Feeling in tune with living a life of happiness?
- Who is sensuous and admires things that appeal to your senses?

- Feeling good about all parts of your life?
- Confident and comfortable in your own skin?
- A woman that has that so-called "thing" that makes you feel sexy?
- A woman who possess sensuous quality?
- Who knows how to use your gift of sensuality?

Most all women are committed to finding ways that will enhance their sexuality. It's an important and time-consuming quest. Working to become a sensuous woman is a valuable part of what a woman considers quality time. Because I work daily to enhance my own personal sexuality, I have found that the best way for any woman to improve her sexuality is to begin with first - who she is!

Sensuous Women Are Different

Sensuous women are definitely different than other women. They think, act, and treat themselves differently than non-sensuous women. Their differences help them discover new and better ways to express themselves. They find it pleasurable to discuss their sexual desires with their

> **Ms. Real Suggests**
> A woman wants to feel sexy, sensuous and special all the time, not only when the man is fired up and sexual.

partner and they find ways to please themselves.

She pays close attention to his subtle clues about what turns him on and then sends him easy messages about what she likes. Are you the woman who's having problems feeling sensuous? Here are some important questions you should ask yourself.

1. Is it simply dinner, and back home - feeling distant from your lover?
2. Are most of my evenings spent watching reruns?
3. Am I feeling lonely?
4. Am I bored with my partner?
5. Am I bored with sex?
6. Is my love life frustrating and lack-luster?
7. Am I feeling neglected in my relationship?

If you answered yes to any of these questions you might need sensual adjustment.

What a Woman Wants

Even though women are working to become sensuous and trying their very best to incorporate more heated moments they sometimes feel that the world is against them.

Many men are so eagerly consumed with getting sexual pleasure from women that they forget the fact that

> **You Should Know**
> Men equate sex with intimacy whereas women equate intimacy with sex.

their relationships require work. They start to regret being in their relationships and in turn they begin to reject their partner's sexual advances. In many cases the woman feels neglected by the person she cares for the most - her partner. Her reoccurring concern is: "Why is it so difficult to feel good about my sexuality?" Her biggest complaint is: "Men don't try to understand a woman's needs, or her sense of sexual prowess." Men equate sex with intimacy whereas women equate intimacy with sex.

What a woman really wants is a loving, caring, and attentive partner in her life - one that shows support, love, and affection during her good and bad times. A woman wants to feel sexy, sensuous and special all the time, not only when the man is fired up and sexual.

A Change is Coming

Women are changing and it's been a long time coming. Women have been changing for the past thirty years while men have looked on. They have changed how they think, work, have fun and how they make love. These changes are helping women make positive strides in their lives and part of this change has included her sensuality.

Women are seeking and incorporating techniques that help them become more sensual, but many of them have become so career and goal oriented they've forgotten how to be successfully sensuous. Don't get me wrong, women are doing things to look sexier; like buying sexier clothes, reading sexier books, and buying sexier products, but that doesn't make them more sensuous, they're simply sexier … and there lies the problem.

Quite frankly, we all need to work on our sensuous attributes. We work on looking sexy, but we don't work enough on becoming sensuous. Women are definitely sexier, but they have not adjusted to becoming more sensuous along with their sexy. They admit that their sensuality needs a little polishing and they're desperately working to get more in tune with the new changes they are making. Those who have read my books have already benefited from these sensuous ideas. The change is working in their favor for sure.

> **Heated Pleasures**
> Today's women are definitely sexier, but they have not adjusted to becoming more sensuous with their sexy.

Write Your Own Script

Women who have read my books have only been married a few years, but some have been married more than twenty years and some have never been married. Each group of women enjoyed what they read. I offer this book, as a reminder of things you should know.

You'll find tips, techniques, treats, positions, exercises, games, toys and all kinds of suggestions and ideas to try. Know that any of the treats are as individual as you are. Don't try to keep up with how your friends are doing it.

> **Heatology**
> Your personal treats are as individual as you are. Don't try to keep up with how your friends are doing it.

Don't try to measure your sex life against anyone else's. Don't use movies, soaps, romance novels, or TV shows as your sexual indicator of what sex should and should not be. Orchestrate your own heated pleasures and see how delicious your own sex can become.

Every woman has a sexual aptitude.
All she has to do is use it.

Chapter 2

The Woman's Body

This chapter will help you love and understand your body.

Because you are on an intimate pleasure journey you should willingly explore your own sexual anatomy. And because sex is more than putting his pole into your hole you need to understand how your sex organs work and how to get your body to respond the way you want it to.

This chapter covers some of the basics of how you can enhance your sexuality by understanding your sex organs. I will give you a road map and guided tour of your body. You will explore your anatomy, especially your sexual

Ms. Real Suggests

Explore a on your own in the beginning. Learning about your body can be just as much fun for you as it is for your lover.

anatomy. Your exploratory journey is really a private journey just for you and you alone. Find a private place where you won't be interrupted and get totally comfortable. It's time for exploration.

Relax: Get yourself a glass of wine or your favorite beverage. Start reading the remaining parts of this book and as you read, you'll start relaxing.

Breathe: Take your time, feel your entire body move into a relaxed state. Breathe, get comfortable and clear your mind for your new education.

Read: Concentrate on what you are reading. Give yourself some time to really indulge and enjoy what you are learning. Don't go too fast or rush through these lessons. Soak in the information and enjoy the knowledge you are gaining.

Think: When you are ready spend time trying each new treat. Don't be afraid or ashamed. This is a book for grown women. You're ready for this so I know you can take it. You know you need it, so enjoy it in your own time and privacy.

Apply: Put the games, toys, techniques and lessons to use. Use them and then experience them as often as you feel the need. Think of new ways to add your own tips, techniques and heated pleasures, then incorporate them in your very own grown folk's games. A woman's body is unlike any other on this planet so this particular journey will be unique. I'll tell you what and where, but you'll have to look and touch in order to discover your most personal and sensuous self.

Because this is an exploratory journey, you'll have to decide whether you want to take this trip alone or include your partner. It's up to you.

What Is It That Works For You

What works sexually for one woman might not work for another. What feels good to one woman sexually might feel totally ridiculous to another woman. Some women might love being naked, but another woman might feel a little shy about the very thought of being unclothed. Your

You Should Know

Maybe you've heard a few names for the vagina: punanny, private, snatch, snapping turtle, pussy, poopoo, down there, coochie, cock, and cunt, as if it's true name is not enough.

ideas of passion can be very boring to other women, yet very exciting to you.

The best way to discover your own sexual pleasures is to experiment with your own body, releasing your inhibitions about sexual fulfillment and learning what feels good and what doesn't. You'll have to open your mind, heart and body. Remember it's all about you because what **you** like is what works best for you!

Every woman deserves a love life that is full, nurturing, wholesome, gratifying, fun, passionate, thrilling, and sensual. Believing that you are worthy is the first step to getting there. It only takes a little practice, some encouragement, and the desire to get it done. It's that simple.

Take a Private Parts Journey

When we speak of a woman's sexual anatomy it's sometimes referred to as her vagina, but there are many other names women use when it comes the description of her vagina. Maybe you've heard of a few of them... punanny, private, snatch, snapping turtle, pussy, poopoo, down there, coochie, cock, and cunt, as if it's true name is not enough. Part of the reason we have so many names for it is because of the desire to keep it a secret.

As we uncover its true identity, we find that the vagina is a very intimate, yet complicated part of a woman. So popular women were afraid to play with it or touch it. Let's explore it in more detail.

The vulva refers to the external sex organs: the clitoris, the labia, vaginal opening, and the urethra opening. Inside, the parts include the vagina, the cervix, the pubic bone, and the urethra.

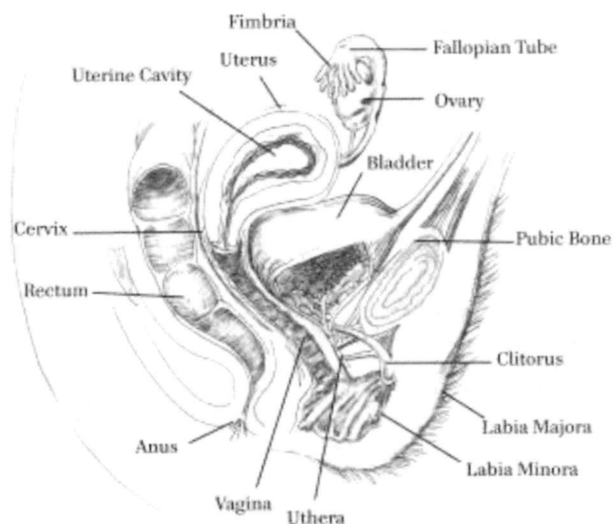

FEMALE INTERNAL ANATOMY

Your Mons

The first part of your vulva that you will most likely see is called the mons. The mons is a cushion of fat that sits over the pubic bone and is covered with hair. The skin covering the mons contains many nerves. Touching, licking and stroking this area can be quite pleasurable. It tends to give you a calming feeling.

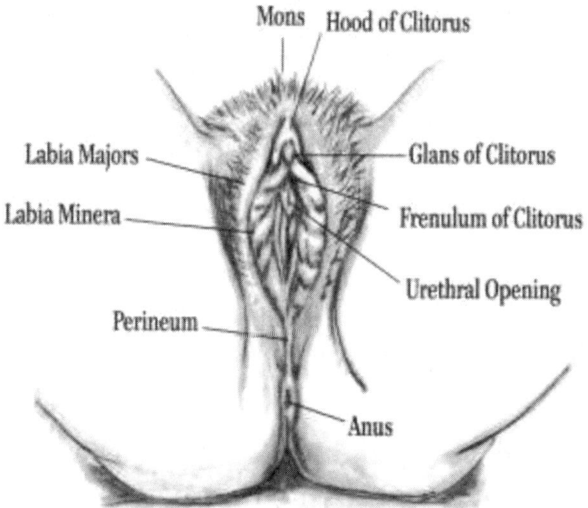

The Vulva

Your Outer Lips (labia majora)

These are the fatty areas on both sides of the vulva that are covered with pubic hair in mature women. They perform a protective role, securing the sensitive structures of the clitoris and vulva that are nestled between the lips. Using a vibrator here is exhilarating and provides wonderful feelings of pleasure. Shaving the labia majora and the mons is a common activity performed for both hygiene and cosmetic reasons.

An extreme form of cosmetic surgery is gaining popularity in which liposuction is used to reduce the labia majora so as to open the vulva and leave the inner genitals exposed.

You Should Know

Shaving the labia majora and the mons is a common activity performed for both hygiene and cosmetic reasons.

One theory is that this ensures the clitoris is exposed to direct stimulation during intercourse increasing the likelihood of an orgasm. I don't know if this is true. Haven't tried it and haven't found anyone that has.

Your Inner Lips (labia minora)

Labia minora are the flaps of delicate flesh that meet the hood of the clitoris at the front of your vulva and run down either side of the vaginal opening. They are nestled between the labia majora, which protect them. Nipping and biting this area can become so thrilling that it can cause a woman to ooze into sleep.

Size and color vary enormously from woman to woman. Some have labia that hang down five or more centimeters from between their labia majora, others have labia minora that are tiny and are little more than creases between the inside surface of their labia majora and their vulva. Color is not just race related. Your labia can be any shade from light pink to dark brown to deep dark brown, looking almost black no matter what their race is. The more activity, the darker it gets.

You Should Know

When a woman gives birth and during sexual intercourse, the vagina widens and lengthens up to 2-3 times its normal size.

Wearing jewelry on the labia minora is increasingly popular, though piercing must be done by a labia minora expert to reduce the risk of infection. Cosmetic surgery on the labia minora is also increasing, though from a low level. The most common procedure is the reduction of larger structures or the evening out of asymmetric pairs of lips. The labia minora is not especially sensitive though pulling and stretching it can provide a variety of sensitivity during masturbation. How sensitive is yours?

Your Clitoris

What is it? The clitoris is a small bud like formation situated where the top of the inner vaginal lips meet. Normally it hides under a small hood of skin, but when sexually aroused it expands and emerges peeking out like a bright little light in the dark. It is a primary source of erotic stimulation for women. Most women can gain orgasms by gentle massaging of the clitoral area.

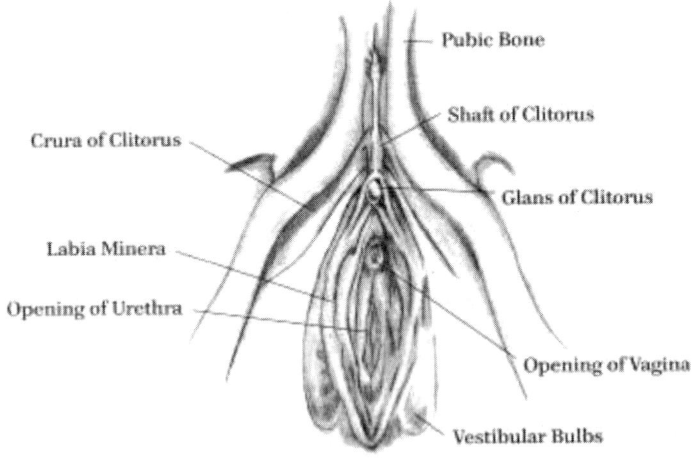

The Clitoris

How Big Is The Clitoris?

It's not very big. While working on this book I have been privileged to see the genitalia of literally hundreds of women while they were both sexually excited and unexcited.

The vast majority of women have an excited clitoris glans (i.e. the visible part of the clitoris at its maximum size is about one eighth of an inch across, to about three eighths of an inch across (i.e. 3mm to 8mm across).

Biologically, it is directly equivalent to the male penis. Indeed, for the first few months after conception the genitalia of male and female fetuses appear to be identical. It is this equivalence that is a direct cause of much misunderstanding.

Your Urethra

The urethra is a tube, which connects the urinary to the outside of the body. The urethra has an excretory function in both sexes, to pass urine to the outside, and also a reproductive function in the male, as a passage for sperm.

Your Vagina

The vagina is an elastic muscular tube about 4 inches (100 mm) long and 1 inch (25 mm) in diameter that connects the vulva at the outside to the cervix of the uterus at the inside. If the woman stands upright, the vaginal tube points in an upward-backward direction and forms an angle of slightly more than 45 degrees with the uterus. The vaginal opening is at the back (caudal) end of the vulva, behind the opening of the urethra. Above the vagina is Mons Veneris. The inside of the vagina is usually pink, as with all internal mucous membranes in mammals.

Length, width and shape of the vagina may vary. When a woman gives birth and during sexual intercourse, the vagina widens and lengthens up to 2-3 times its normal size. Vaginal lubrication is provided by glands near the vaginal opening and the cervix and also seeps through the vaginal wall (which does not contain any glands).

Your Hymen

The hymen is a membrane situated behind the urethral opening—partially covers the vagina in many organisms, including some human females, from birth until it is ruptured by sexual intercourse, or by any number of other activities including medical examinations, injury, certain types of exercise, introduction of a foreign object, etc.

The Functions of Your Vagina

The vagina performs the following functions:

- Providing a path for menstrual fluids to leave the body.

- Giving birth.
- Admitting the male penis for sexual intercourse.

Your Perineum

In anatomy, the perineum is the region between the genital area and the anus of both sexes. It's considered one of the most intimate parts of the body. Common nicknames for the perineum area include banus – choad – chode – gooch – gouch – grundel – grundle – and taint.

Your Anus

The anus is often considered a taboo part of the body, and is also known by a large number of slang terms, which are generally considered vulgar and not used in polite speech. The human anus is situated between the buttocks, which is posterior to the perineum. It has two anal sphincters, one internal, the other external. These hold the anus closed until time to defecate. One sphincter consists of smooth muscle and its action is involuntary; the other consists of striated muscle and its action is voluntary.

You Should Know
Anal intercourse can be pleasurable for both the inserting partner and the receiving partner.

The Anus and its Role in Sexuality

The anus has a relatively high concentration of nerve endings and is an erogenous zone. Sigmund Freud's theory of psychosexual development, for example, described an anal stage, hypothesizing that toddlers derive pleasure from retaining and expelling feces. This is the source of the derogatory term anal-retentive.

Anal intercourse can be pleasurable for both the inserting partner and the receiving partner. For females, pleasure from anal intercourse is related to the shared wall between the rectum and the vagina as well as the G-spot.

You Should Know

Anal intercourse can be pleasurable for both the inserting partner and the receiving partner.

For males, the tightness of the anus is often said to be a source of pleasure in penetrative anal sex, while the presence of the prostate gland near the rectal wall is generally seen as a source of pleasure during receptive anal intercourse. Other animals have also been observed practicing anal intercourse.

Female Ejaculation Body Fluids

Before discussing female ejaculation let's address female body fluids in general. Our society as well as most others views all forms of liquid that are produced by the female body with great disdain. Women are not permitted to openly perform most normal bodily functions; it is not seen as feminine or proper etiquette.

Female Fluids and Our Society

Female body fluids are considered harmful by some societies. There are societies in which menstruating women are thought to cause crops to fail and livestock to die. This myth creates a problem with sexual pleasure for women in several cultures.

Women are expected to maintain a dry pristine appearance regardless of their current physical activity. Mothers once told their daughters it was unwise to engage in sports, as boys would see them sweaty and disheveled and this was seen as unattractive. Deodorant and antiperspirant ads drive home the phrase, "Never let them see you

You Should Know
Give yourself permission to get wet and messy. Have fun and enjoy sex.

sweat." Women are told they need special stronger deodorants made just for them. Tampon and sanitary napkin advertising stresses the products ability to conceal a woman's menstruation from others more than their primary task of absorbing menses or any feminine moistures.

> **You Should Know**
> Women are expected to maintain a dry pristine appearance regardless of their current physical activity.

Most women would prefer to have their fingernails ripped out one by one than be seen having a "menstrual accident;" menstruating in public. There are women who learn to dislike the idea of urinating in a public bathroom, holding their urine all day until they get home. Perhaps they are afraid to be seen as less than pure by others?

Men Fluids versus A Woman's

Sweaty men are seen as sexual and virile. Their manhood is measured by their ability to produce large quantities of semen. They write their name in the snow with their urine and see who can piss the furthest. Men making a mess with their ejaculate are seen as unavoidable, normal, and are never questioned. It is even idolized in adult movies.

Watch Out

Men making a mess with their ejaculate are seen as unavoidable, normal, and are never questioned. It is even idolized in adult movies.

Men can ejaculate on the face, in the mouth, on hair and in the body of their partner and it is seen as normal. If a woman gets her body fluids on her partner that is another story, she has made a dirty mess. This is an interesting double standard. If a man can cover his partner with his body fluids, a woman should be able to do the same.

Vaginal Lubrication

Female sexuality is marred by these unwritten laws. It is hard to relax and enjoy sex if you arc worried about sweating heavily or producing too much vaginal lubrication. Women who produce large quantities of vaginal lubrication, sweat, and who ejaculate have been known to avoid sex rather than expose their partner or themselves to these fluids.

`Though a woman's desire for sex may increase during her menstrual period she may not engage in sex during this time because she fears she will make a mess and is inherently undesirable. Social stigmas concerning female body fluids can significantly restrict female sexuality and pleasure.

You Should Know

If a woman squirts urine at the moment of orgasm, she should not worry, it happens to many women

These fluids are a normal and natural part of women's lives. There is nothing that is inherently bad about them. A woman cannot allow herself to ejaculate and experience potentially earth-shattering orgasms if she cannot let go when the pressure or urge to ejaculate arises. Give yourself permission to get wet and messy. Have fun and enjoy sex.

As a result of the taboos concerning female body fluids, the main motivation behind the studies into female ejaculation appears to be the determination of whether or not the expelled fluid is urine. Some believe that if a woman ejaculates any liquid that is not urine like a man, it is normal and she cannot help it. If she ejaculates urine they suggest she has a medical problem and is not normal.

Do we mean to take this pleasure away from her? If you squirt urine at the moment of orgasm, don't worry. If you ejaculate uncontrollably, so be it. It is not another person's place to judge how your body reacts during sexual pleasure.

Your Cervix

The cervix is actually the lower, narrow portion of the uterus. It joins with the top end of the vagina. It is cylindrical or conical in shape and protrudes through the upper anterior vaginal wall. Approximately half its length is visible with appropriate medical equipment; the remainder lies above the vagina beyond view. It is occasionally called "cervix uteri", or "neck of the uterus".

Your Uterus

In most females the hollow muscular organ in which the fetus develops and from which it is delivered at the end of pregnancy is the uterus. The human uterus is pear-shaped and about 3 in. (7.6 cm) long (it expands greatly during pregnancy); it normally lies in the pelvis, where it's supported by a ligament on either side and extends to the pelvic wall. The body of the uterus tapers down to a neck like structure (cervix) that leads into the vagina. On either side of the uterus is an oviduct (called fallopian

You Should Know

Fertilization occurs in the oviduct; the fertilized ovum then continues into the uterus, where it becomes implanted in the lining of that organ, also known as the endometrium.

tube, or uterine tube, in humans) from 3 to 5 in. (7.6–12.7 cm) long, one end opening into the uterus and the other, wide-mouthed, ends in close proximity to an ovary.

You Should Know

In vertebrate animals the ovary also secretes the sex hormones estrogen and progesterone, which control development of the sexual organs and the secondary sexual characteristics

These oviducts serve as passageways for the ova to reach the uterus. Fertilization occurs in the oviduct; the fertilized ovum then continues into the uterus, where it becomes implanted in the lining of that organ, also known as the endometrium.

Your Fallopian Tubes

Either of a pair of tubes extending from the uterus to the paired ovaries in the human female also called oviducts, technically known as the uterine tube. At one end the long, slender fallopian tube opens into the uterus; the other end expands into a funnel shape near the ovary. The epithelium that lines the tube is covered with cilia that beat continuously toward the uterus.

Your Ovaries

Ovaries are the ductless gland of the female in which the ova (female reproductive cells) are produced. In vertebrate animals the ovary also secretes the sex hormones estrogen and progesterone, which control development of the sexual organs and the secondary sexual characteristics. The interaction between the gonadotropic from the pituitary gland and the sex hormones from the ovary controls the monthly cycle of ovulation and menstruation.

There are two ovaries in the human, held in place on each side of the uterus by a membrane; each ovary is about the size of an almond. About 500,000 immature eggs are present in the cortex of the ovary at birth. Starting at puberty, eggs mature successively, and one breaks through the ovarian wall about every 28 days in the process known as ovulation, which continues until menopause, or cessation of reproductive functioning in the female. After its release from the ovary, the ovum passes into the oviduct (uterine or fallopian tube) and into the uterus.

Your Pelvic Floor Muscles

The pelvic floor or pelvic diaphragm is composed largely of muscle fibers and connective tissue. It is important in providing support for pelvic organs, e.g. the bladder, lower intestines, the uterus (in females), and in maintenance of continence as part of the urinary and anal sphincters.

The urethral sphincter is at least partially responsible for urinary continence in women but intact vaginal support and levator muscular tone also play an important role in female urinary continence. Lost neural support to either the urinary sphincter or levatorani or lost vaginal support can contribute to an individual woman's urinary incontinence problems.

You Should Know
Age, childbirth, family history, hormones all likely contribute to the development of pelvic organ prolapse.

Unfortunately, damage to the pelvic floor does not only contribute to urinary incontinence but pelvic organ prolapse as well. Pelvic organ prolapse occurs in women when pelvic organs (e.g. the vagina, bladder, rectum, or uterus) protrude into or outside of the vagina. The causes of pelvic organ prolapse are not unlike those that also contribute to urinary incontinence and are likely multifactorial.

Age, childbirth, family history, hormones all likely contribute to the development of pelvic organ prolapse. The common perception that prolapse stems from lost "fascial" support is difficult to support in light of the available evidence.

The vagina is suspended by attachments to the perineum, pelvic sidewall and sacrum via attachments that include collagen, elastin, and smooth muscle. Repair of lost vaginal support may involve surgery.

Your Skin

Skin is a pathway to sensuous pleasure. Everybody part with skin has a chance of being a pleasure zone. Your nerves respond to touching, stroking, massaging, sucking and kissing.

Your Breasts

The breasts are covered by skin; each breast has one nipple surrounded by the areola. The areola is colored from pink to dark brown, hairless, and has several sebaceous glands. The larger mammary glands within the breast produce milk; they consist of several lobules, and each breast has some 10-20 lactiferous ducts that drain milk from the lobules to the nipple, where each duct has an opening.

Think of silk when you touch yourself.

Chapter 3

The Man's Body

This chapter will help you care for, love and understand the male body.

Yummy is how I refer to the male body. There is so much to see, touch and feel when it comes to a man. If you love men and you want to please your man enough to make him want to please you more, you should know some details about his body. The more informed you are the better your pleasures will be. The more you know about what you can do to make him and yourself feel good, the better your sex life will be.

His Penis

The male organ of copulation and of urinary excretion are formed by three columns of erectile tissue, two arranged laterally on the dorsum and one medianly below; the extremity is formed by an expansion of the corpus spongiosum, covered by a free fold of skin. The human penis is made up of three columns of erectile tissue. The two corpora cavernosa (singular: corpus cavernosum) and one corpus spongiosum

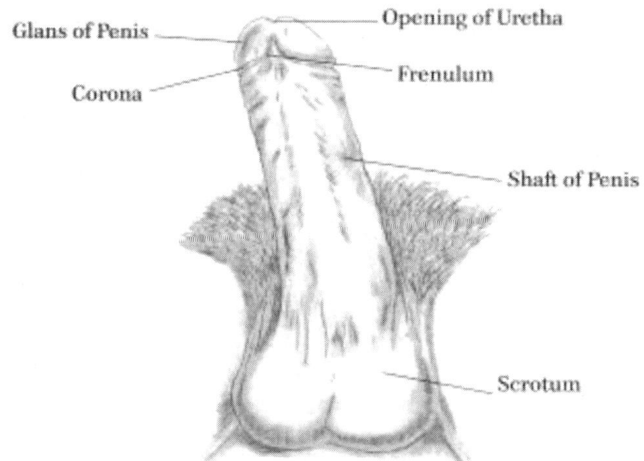

The Penis

The corpus spongiosum lies on the underside (known also as the ventral side) of the penis; the two corpora cavernosa lie next to each other on the upper side dorsal side).

The end of the corpus spongiosum is enlarged and cone-shaped and forms the glans penis. The glans supports the foreskin or prepuce, a loose fold of skin that in adults can retract to expose the glans. The area on the underside of the penis, where the foreskin is attached, is called the frenum or frenulum.

The urethra, which is the last part of the urinary tract, traverses the corpus spongiosum and its opening, known as the meatus, lies on the tip of the glans penis. It is both a passage for urine and for the ejaculation of semen. Sperm is produced in the testes and stored in the attached epididymis. During ejaculation, sperm are propelled up the vas deferens, two ducts that pass over and behind the bladder. Fluids are added by the seminal vesicles and the vas deferens turns into the ejaculatory ducts, which join the urethra inside the prostate gland. The prostate and the bulb urethral add further secretions. The semen is expelled through the penis.

Raphe is the visible ridge between the lateral halves of the penis, found on the ventral or under side of the penis, running from the meatus (opening of the urethra) across the scrotum to the perineum (area between scrotum and anus).

His Erection

Erection is the stiffening and rising of the penis, which occurs in the sexually aroused male, though it can also happen in non-sexual situations. The primary physiological mechanism that brings about erection is the autonomic dilation of arteries supplying blood to the penis, which allows more blood to fill the three spongy erectile tissue chambers in the penis, causing it to lengthen and stiffen. The now engorged erectile tissue presses against and constricts the veins that carry blood away from the penis. More blood enters the penis than leaves until equilibrium is reached (equal volume of blood flowing into the dilated arteries and out of the constricted veins). A constant erectile size is achieved at equilibrium.

You Should Know

During ejaculation, sperm are propelled up the vas deferens, two ducts that pass over and behind thc bladder.

Erection facilitates sexual intercourse though it is not essential for some other sexual activities. Although many erect penises point upwards (see illustration), it is common and normal for the erect penis to point nearly vertically upwards or nearly vertically downwards, depending on the tension of the suspensory ligament that holds it in position. Stiffness of erectile angle also varies.

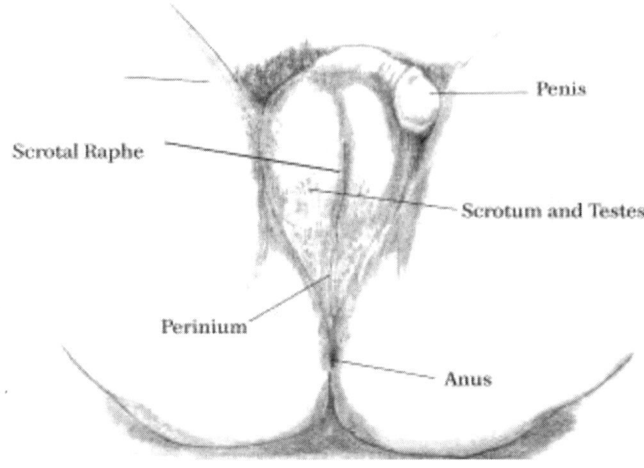

The Perineum

His Perineum

The perineum corresponds to the outlet of the pelvis. Its deep boundaries are - in front, the pubic arch and the arcuate ligament of the pubis; behind, the tip of the coccyx; and on either side the inferior rami of the pubis and ischium, and the sacrotuberous ligament. The space is somewhat lozenge-shaped and is limited on the surface of the body by the scrotum (in males) or the vulva (in females) in front, by the buttocks behind and laterally by the medial side of the thigh.

A line drawn transversely across in front of the ischial tuberosities divides the space into two portions. The posterior contains the termination of the anal canal and is known as the anal region. The anterior contains the external urogenital organs, and is termed the urogenital region. Try gently stroking or massaging this area. It creates pleasurable sensations for your partner.

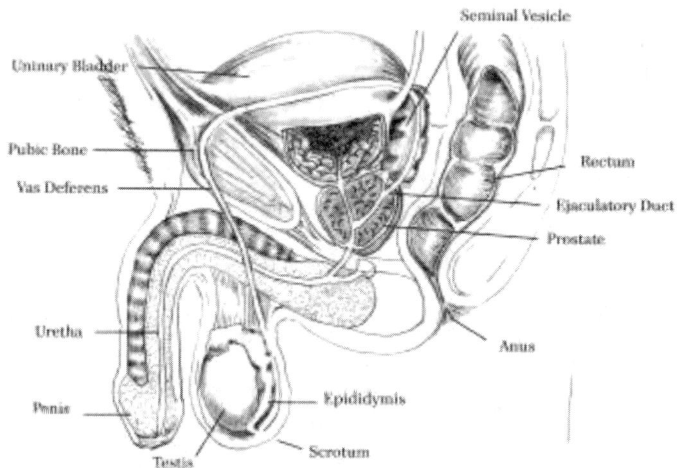

MALE INTERNAL ANATOMY

His Testes / Testicles

The male gonads, testes, or testicles, begin their development high in the abdominal cavity, near the kidneys. During the last two months before birth, or shortly after birth, they descend through the inguinal canal into the scrotum, a pouch that extends below the abdomen, posterior to the penis. Although this location of the testes, outside the abdominal cavity, may seem to make them vulnerable to injury, it provides a temperature about 3° C below normal body temperature. This lower temperature is necessary for the production of viable sperm.

His Testicle Structure

Each testis is an oval structure about 5 cm long and 3 cm in diameter. A tough, white fibrous connective tissue capsule, the tunica albuginea, surrounds each testis and extends inward to form septa that partition the organ into lobules. There are about 250 lobules in each testis. Each lobule contains 1 to 4 highly coiled seminiferous tubules that converge to form a single straight tubule, which leads into the rete testis. Short efferent ducts exit the testes. Interstitial cells (cells of Leydig), which produce male sex hormones, are located between the seminiferous tubules within a lobule.

His Scrotum

The scrotum is an external bag of skin and muscle containing the testicles. It is an extension of the abdomen, and is located between the penis and the anus. The female homologue during fetal development is the labia majora.

The function of the scrotum appears to be to keep the testicles at a temperature slightly lower than that of the rest of the body. For the human, a temperature around 34.4 degrees Celsius (94 degrees Fahrenheit) appears to be ideal; 36.7 degrees Celsius (98 degree Fahrenheit) may be damaging to sperm count. The temperature is controlled by making the scrotum tighter or looser, hence moving the testicles closer to the abdomen when it is cold, and conversely away when hot, through the cremasteric reflex, the gradual tightening and loosening of the cremaster muscle in the abdomen and the dartos fascia (muscular tissue under the skin) in the scrotum.

The scrotum consists of skin and subcutaneous tissue. A vertical septum, or partition, of subcutaneous tissue in the center divides it into two parts, each containing one testis. Smooth muscle fibers, called the dartos muscle, in the subcutaneous tissue contract to give the

You Should Know

The temperature is controlled by making the scrotum tighter or looser, hence moving the testicles closer to the abdomen when it is cold, and conversely away when hot, scrotum its wrinkled appearance.

When these fibers are relaxed, the scrotum is smooth. Another muscle, the cremaster muscle, consists of skeletal muscle fibers and controls the position of the scrotum and testes. When it is cold or a man is sexually aroused, this muscle contracts to pull the testes closer to the body for warmth.

His Prostate

The prostate is an exocrine gland of the male mammalian reproductive system. Its main function is to secrete and store a clear, slightly basic fluid that constitutes up to one-third of the volume of semen. The prostate differs considerably between species anatomically, chemically, and physiologically.

A healthy prostate is slightly larger than a walnut. It surrounds the urethra just below the urinary. It is located in front of the rectum and can be felt during a rectal exam.

His Urethra

The male urethra has two functions: to carry urine from the bladder during urination and to carry semen during ejaculation. Within the prostate, the urethra coming from the bladder is called the prostatic urethra and merges with the two ejaculatory ducts. Semen is composed of sperm and seminal fluid of the seminal fluid is produced by the prostate gland, the rest is produced by the two seminal vesicles. The prostate also contains some smooth muscle that helps to expel semen during ejaculation.

Prostatic secretions are generally composed of simple sugars, and are often slightly basic. In human prostatic secretions, the protein content is less than 1% and includes proteolytic enzymes, acid phosphatase, and prostate-specific antigen. Its secretions contain zinc and citric acid.

To work properly, the prostate needs male hormones (androgens). Male hormones are responsible for male sex characteristics. The main male hormone is testosterone, which is produced mainly by the testicles.

Some male hormones are produced in small amounts by the adrenal glands. Prostate glands are found only in males; Skene's glands in females are homologous to the prostate gland in males.

His Breasts

The male breasts are essentially the nipple and the surrounding areola. Men don't have the fat and glands that a woman have - the tissue that gives a woman her cup size -

but like ours his nipples can be very sensitive and become more sensitive when he becomes aroused. A few men can experience orgasm when aroused by their breast.

What Happens During Erection

Erection happens during arousal - one of the phases of the sexual response cycle. A number of changes in the body happen during this phase. In both men and women, the heart begins to beat faster and blood pressure rises. The muscles in the body grow tense, and the nipples may get hard. People may have what's called a "sex flush" - they redden around the chest and neck.

> **Heated Pleasures**
> The penis and the clitoris are very similar. They're both made of spongy erectile tissue and are full of sensitive nerve endings.

Increased blood flowing to the genitals will cause a guy's penis to become erect and guys will notice their testicles drawing closer to their body as the scrotum thickens. In girls, breasts enlarge, the vagina lubricates, and the clitoris begins to swell.

The penis and the clitoris are very similar. They're both made of spongy erectile tissue and are full of sensitive nerve endings. The penis extends out from the body for several inches. The clitoris extends into the body for several inches. Like men, women get erections, but they're not as noticeable.

His Ejaculation and Orgasm

Ejaculation is the process of ejecting semen from the penis, and is usually accompanied by orgasm as a result of sexual stimulation. It may also occur spontaneously during sleep (called a nocturnal emission), due to stimulating of the prostate or, rarely, due to prostatic disease.

Ejaculation is a reflex, which usually cannot be stopped once it has started, without painful cramping. It has two phases: emission and ejaculation proper. During emission, the two ducts known as vas deferens contract to propel sperm from the epididymis (where it was stored) up to the ampullae at the top end of the vas deferens. The beginning of emission is typically experienced as a "point of no return." The sperm then passes through the ejaculatory ducts and is mixed with fluids from the seminal vesicle, the prostate, and the bulb urethral glands

You Should Know
When a man ejaculates before he wants to it is called premature ejaculation.

to form the semen or ejaculate. During ejaculation proper, the semen is ejected through the urethra with rhythmical contractions.

The force and amount of ejaculate vary widely from male to male. A normal ejaculation may contain anywhere from 2 to 15 milliliters (from half a teaspoon to a tablespoon), although 2 to 6 ml is typical. Ejaculate volume is affected by the amount of time that has passed since the previous ejaculation (i.e. the duration of ejaculatory abstinence). Larger ejaculate volumes are seen with greater durations of abstinence. Also, the duration of the stimulation leading up to the ejaculation can affect the volume. Abnormally low volume is known as hypospermia.

You Should Know

When a man ejaculates before he wants to it is called premature ejaculation. If a man is unable to ejaculate in a timely manner after prolonged sexual stimulation, in spite of his desire to do so, it is called impotence.

The number of sperm in an ejaculation varies widely, depending on many factors, including the recentness of last ejaculation, the average warmth of the testicles, the degree and length of time of sexual excitement prior to ejaculation, the age, testosterone level, and general fertility of the subject, and the total volume of seminal fluid. An unusually low sperm count, not the same as low semen volume, is known as azooapermia.

Most men experience a lag time of some half-hour or so between the ability to ejaculate consecutively. During this refractory period it is difficult or impossible to attain an erection, because the sympathetic nervous system counteracts the effects of the parasympathetic nervous system.

There are wide variations in how long sexual intercourse can last before ejaculation occurs. Studies have shown that most men can only avoid ejaculation during active thrusting for five minutes or less. A minority can ejaculate more or less at will, and delay ejaculation for an hour or longer during sexual intercourse.

At the conclusion of sexual intercourse, most men ejaculate while inside their partner. However, some prefer to withdraw their penis from their partner's body, and ejaculate elsewhere, such as upon their partner's face or chest. This is referred to as coitus interruptus. Ejaculation can also occur during oral sex where the man's partner orally stimulates his penis. Ejaculation can occur in the partner's mouth or he can withdraw from the mouth and ejaculate on the face or other parts of the body. This type of ejaculation can be just as enjoyable as ejaculating inside the mouth, vagina or anus.

When a man ejaculates before he wants to it is called premature ejaculation. If a man is unable to ejaculate in a timely manner after prolonged sexual stimulation, in spite of his desire to do so, it is called impotence.

Whether you are after a quickie or an extended sensual session, vibrators are the ideal sex toys to get your motor revving

Part 2

Improve Your Personal Profile

Improving Your Feminine Hygiene

This chapter will help enhance and improve and upgrade your feminine hygiene.

For really hot sex, nothing works like me-time moments. Prior to sex you can sit in a very warm bath or, if available soak in a Jacuzzi. The increased stimulation from the jets will enhance the effects of the warm water.

If you don't have time for a bath take a warm, moist washcloth and place it over your vulva for a few minutes. If you have a hot water bottle, discover its other uses. Fill it with warm water and sit on it or lie down and rest your vulva and love button on it. Want to share your heat with him? Wrap a clean thick, warm, moist, hand towel around his penis before a hand or blowjob. It's great and he'll love you for suggesting it!

Bathing to Stimulate

Any bath can be used as sensual stimulation toward other fulfilling moments. Your mind, body and love life will benefit from these stimulating baths.

What you'll need: Steamed water, scents and ability to touch.

The most important element of a sensuous bathing experience is the ability to indulge and time to do it. It's been the same since people flocked to public steam baths in ancient Sparta. Bathing helps women care for their bodies. The rituals of bath treatments help unify mind, body and spirit for overall well-being.

Today bathing therapy increasingly addresses our more active and inquisitive lifestyles. Bathing is so popular because it restores the body, balances life, revives the mind and energizes the spirit.

Bathing to Moisturize

Body treatments are offered everywhere, from chair massages in grocery stores to full-day pampering at luxury spas. You should do a moisturizer treatment each night before falling asleep. Start by telling everyone that you would like some privacy and relaxation, then go to your room and start your moisture therapy.

What you'll need: Music, moisturizer, scented candle, bathtub, and a fluffy bath towel.

- ❖ Run a warm bath and add a spritz of your favorite bath oil, cologne, or fragrance. While the tub is filling your body down with a favorite before-bath moisturizer and read your Heated Pleasures book.
- ❖ Play your favorite music selection.
- ❖ Light a small scented candle, turn the lights off and ease into your freshly filled tub of water. Allow the water to envelope your awaiting body.
- ❖ Relax completely; physically and mentally. Let the lit candle dance in your mind as it flickers you into an intensely mellow mood.
- ❖ Guide your mood toward relaxation. Enhance your senses as you think of nothing but relaxation and sensual pleasures.

- ❖ Allow your quiet surroundings to swallow you as the scents entice you. Let the mood romance your desires as you humble your soul to the pleasures.
- ❖ Now, pull a hand full of water toward you and feel the water as it trickles down your chest, between your breast and across your neck.
- ❖ Now unwind and let your senses lock in. Ummmm that should feel good.
- ❖ Close your eyes now and listen to the music playing softly as you gather your senses and adore the peacefulness that surrounds you. Discover the serenity as the ripples of water disappear. Get lost in your thoughts and when you begin to feel drowsy, remove your new self from your tub. Pat yourself dry with a fluffy towel, lightly moisturize again.
- ❖ Ease into bed and drift off to sleep. Sweet dreams.

Bathing to Enjoy Your Body

In this phase you will learn how to enjoy your own body. Each person's body is unique, and no matter what kind of body you have you are special. Enjoy yourself as you discover you. Have pride in your body. You will love experiencing what makes you feel pampered.

What you'll need: bath towel, scented candles, lotion, oil or moisturizer.

- After a soothing bath dry off very slowly. With every stroke of your towel blot yourself gently.
- Slowly massage your body with your favorite lotion, oil or moisturizer - try not to miss any areas.
- Applying by candlelight is very soothing and romantic. Begin a friendship with your body. Know where every bump and mole is on your body. Get to know your body!
- Once you've rubbed on lotion, pull your bed covers back and ease into your bed while naked.
- Sensuously pampered is how you should feel. Think only good thoughts about the skin you are in.
- Enjoy the body you have been blessed with. In a short while fall asleep. Sweet dreams.
- Don't forget to blow out the candles.

Scents, Fragrances and Arousal

Aromas lift the female sexual arousal, but men might be surprised at the scrumptious scents that light a woman's fire. The road to romance apparently isn't doused with he-man cologne. Baby powder works better, says Alan Hirsch, a neurologist and psychiatrist at the Smell and Taste

Research Foundation. Hirsch did a similar study on male sexual arousal and his report confirms that both sexes find some of the same fragrances exciting.

Odors that excite women are usually fresh smelling or nostalgic reminders of childhood - perhaps eating candy in movie theaters, sniffing pies at family gatherings or powdering babies. "It may also bring back memories about safety and security, that could possibly make women feel comfortable and more sexual," Hirsch says.

Watch Out

If you notice an unusual smell or discharge that you can't seem to get rid of, rather than trying to douche it away consult with your family doctor or gynecologist.

Cherry might be a turnoff because it's mentally tied to medicine and cough drops taken during illness. The barbecue odor is a mystery, he adds, "but avoiding the barbecue isn't a bad idea if you're interested in feminine arousal." To say the least odors are associated with either a happy or sad memory. Think about it? Do you recognize the fragrances that turn you on and can you also identify the scents, odors or fragrances that turn you off?

Your Best Feminine Hygiene

Okay, okay … I know I mentioned basic hygiene in my last book, but I received so many letters and emails about how great the information was that I thought I should expand on the subject in this book. Come on you know we need it.

Mature women understand that hygiene is important in all sensuous relationships. Before any woman can whole-heartedly indulge in sensual activity she should consider the importance of her personal hygiene. A woman should be very conscious and selective about how and when she cleans her vagina, her love button and her anus. Each has its own special odor and fragrance and naturally some will have smells that are more alluring than others.

> **You Should Know**
> Odors that excite women are usually fresh smelling or nostalgic reminders of childhood - perhaps eating candy in movie theaters, sniffing pies at family gatherings or powdering babies.

Common Causes of Body Odors

Every woman's body odor is uniquely different. No two smell the same. Just as fingerprints are different, so are body odors. There are common factors associated with body odors so get in tune with your body to find out why you possess any bothersome odors. Some common reasons for feminine odors are:

- Diet and eating habits
- Medications
- Exercise programs
- Rest factor
- Body oils and perfumes
- Lotions and powders
- Water source
- Soap products
- Skin type
- Body condition
- Body functions
- Masturbation habits
- Masturbation fluids
- Vagina secretions
- Menstrual cycle
- Urine residue
- Frequency of sex
- Physical activity
- Female maintenance

Cleaning Your Vagina

Watch Out
The normal vagina will not have a continuous bad odor. An odor exists when an infection is present.

Douching is not necessary to keep your vagina clean. The normal, healthy vagina naturally cleans itself, but you must help it. If you feel it's necessary to douche after your period, you can do so with little worry of developing problems. Women who douche too frequently can destroy the colonies of beneficial bacteria that normally inhabit the vagina, leaving it vulnerable to organisms that cause Vaginitis (inflammation of the vagina).

Some women douche too much because they smell unpleasant odors or experience excessive discharges. The normal vagina will not have a continuous bad odor. An odor exists when an infection is present. Unhealthy odors in the vaginal region means unhealthy vagina.

Good, personal hygiene makes sex more attractive, but you don't need to douche in preparation for sex. Simply wash the external vagina area carefully. Using your gentle soapy hands to wash the outside of the vagina is a favorite of most women.

Heated Pleasures
Good, personal hygiene makes sex more attractive, but you don't need to douche in preparation for sex.

Apply a dash of perfume or fragrance on your inner thighs or slightly above your panty line to add sensual allure. You will appreciate it and your lover will love it.

Use perfumes that are light and pleasant, not too spicy or strong. You don't want your lover to love your smell and hate your taste.

Cleaning Your Clitoris (Love Button)

The clitoris is hardly ever mentioned when we talk about cleaning the sex organs, but it needs proper cleaning too. Located at the head of the vagina, covered by fluffy skin under the labia the clitoris stands to be dealt with in more ways than one.

Heatology
The clitoris is often called the love button due to its sensitive nature in helping women achieve orgasms

It is often called the love button due to its sensitive nature in helping women achieve orgasms. To clean the clitoris as you pull the skin of the labia back, gently take a cotton swab and with circular motions swab gently any mucous build up that is embedded there. Don't try to clean it too well because the natural secretions of this orifice are healthy. They help the clitoris work smoothly. Just don't allow it to build up.

You would only want to cleanse the clitoris after lovemaking or your monthly period has ended. Sometimes the fluids from sex and period trash will hide inside the skin folds of your love button causing nasty odors that are rarely detected and never cleaned. Bacteria and unwanted odors are difficult to detect because women never look for them there, but your partner will be able to smell any signs of foul odor as soon as he gets near. The main thing to remember is you must keep your body and your clit clean and fresh.

Cleaning Your Anus

The anus should be cleaned just as any other part of your body. Wiping with tissue after a bowel movement is not enough to say that it is thoroughly cleaned. Time and care should be given to cleaning it too.

Women have personal accessories that are included within their douche packets that can be used to clean the anus, but men are left to dig, pull, and wipe endlessly only to share their skid marks with the rest of the wash. One of the best ways suggested by women to clean the anus is to wipe from front to back several times after a bowel movement. Cup the tissue and wipe again, even if you think you've cleaned all residues, wipe again for practical reasons. You'll use more tissue than normal, but it's worth it to feel clean. Use baby wipes if needed.

Women wipe their anus more often than men. The fact is men stand while urinating, women sit, therefore women wiped fifty percent more than men.

Women are taught as children to wipe their vagina sections after each use on the toilet. We are taught and trained to wipe from the front toward the back, which leads me to believe that we actually wipe our anus with almost every toilet use. Each woman that I interviewed said that almost every time that they used the toilet they wiped their anus whether intentionally or not. It was primarily a habitual reflex. Physical evidence proves that men are susceptible to producing long-time streaks in their underwear far more than women.

Biggest Complaint about Women

The biggest complaint I receive from men about a woman who has a vaginal odor is that it smells like onions or it taste like urine.' This leads me to believe that women need to not only clean better; they need to wipe their vaginal area better after urination.

"When I'm good, I'm very good,
but when I'm bad, I'm better."
- Mae West

Chapter 5

Improving Your Appearance

This chapter will help you correct any bad areas and create a new and healthy attitude about your appearance.

You are a product to be promoted and you should make sure you're packaged in the most positive way. It's beneficial to keep your personal appearance up to part. You don't have to be a beauty Queen, but you should at least have a pleasing personal appearance.

> **Ms. Real Suggests**
> Don't buy clothes because they're practical. They tend to look cheap. Unless it jumps off the rack try not to buy it.

You'll never get into a man's heart or head unless you're pleasantly attractive and interesting to him. Even if you're not trying to please a man you should at least be trying to improve yourself. Don't fret; all women have areas that need work or improvement.

If you find a need to improve certain areas begin as soon as possible working to create a new and healthy attitude about your appearance and your personality.

Become Fashion Consciousness

Evaluate yourself and recognize your faulty areas. Pay close attention to areas that you think need extra work or attention. If you think these areas need extra work, then, they probably do.

Collecting fashion magazines, articles and pictures will help you coordinate and suggest ideas for your existing wardrobe. By devoting some time and effort to your appearance on a regular basis, you'll be able to find flattering clothes that compliment your finer points. Seeing an improved YOU take concentrated effort.

Watch Out

Sometimes the fluids from sex and period trash will hide inside the skin folds of your love button causing nasty odors that are rarely detected and never cleaned.

Another way to enhance your appearance or flatter your figure is to go to department stores, boutiques, or even discount stores with a friend and try on new kinds of clothing that you always wondered what you would look like in. Get away from your figure faults. Work with your good points. Be fashion conscious, dress for success, but don't let fashion enslave you.

Be a trendsetter. When everyone is wearing baggy pants and loose blouses, be the one to wear slightly tight pants and a skimpy blouse. You'll turn heads, especially men's heads. Most men are attracted to the colors that women wear. In a survey of one hundred men, seventy percent chose blue as their favorite color, so try to wear plenty of blue.

When trying on clothes, look in the mirror at all angles, sitting, standing, squatting, and bending. Observe strengths and weaknesses as you walk. Ask yourself about your presentation.

Look At Your Angles

When trying on clothes, look in the mirror at all angles, sitting, standing, squatting, and bending. Observe strengths and weaknesses as you walk. Ask yourself about your presentation.

- Does the clothing lie smooth or slide up.
- Is clothing maintenance easy or difficult?
- Does your skirt hike up in the back or front?
- How clean do you look?
- Is your skin smooth and beautiful?
- Do your teeth have stains and discolorations?
- Is your hair clean, fresh and manageable looking?
- Are your ears and nose free from unsightly hair?
- Are your eyebrows evenly shaped?
- Is your makeup even and beautiful?
- Are your hands rough and harsh looking?
- Are your nails chipped and in need of a manicure?
- Are your shoes scuffed or scarred, run over or dirty?
- Do your clothes appear dingy, rumpled or faded?
- Are you wearing clothes that fit too tight or are they obviously too big or too small?

Don't be guilty of these things. If you are, start working to improve today. Be aware of your weaknesses; men certainly will.

Presentation Is Essential

Wear Your Best Underwear

Never, ever be caught with dirty underwear, or underwear held together by safety pins. Wearing bras held together by safety pins are one of the worst things a woman can do. Invest in new ones and throw the old ones away. In the past clean underwear was encouraged by our parents in case you were in an accident and had to go to the hospital. You took a bath whether you thought you needed it or not, and bathing fulfilled the main requirement of cleanliness.

Ms. Real Suggests

Throw away torn or faded dresses or blouses. Use them as cleaning rags instead. Wear crisp and clean clothing that will impress instead of distress.

Remember that very brief, thin underwear looks good on both men and women. The more sensuous the undies, the more inviting they are. Since women and sex have replaced American's favorite pastime, personal care and grooming has become a national symbol of wholesomeness. With television commercials, radio, movies, reality TV and talk show hosts advertising flavored edible underwear, our society can't help but think basic hygiene. You should think that way too.

Work On Your Neatness

Even if you are a little on the wild side, punk rock type or the mild, meek and mannered type person, you should still be neat, clean, and attractive in your appearance. No runs in your hosiery, no holes in your socks, no faded fake earrings, no running mascara, no smudges in your make-up, no smeared-uneven lip stick, no tacky eyebrows, no lumpy eyelashes, no scuffed handbags, no missing buttons, no broken zippers, no threads dangling and never wear day-old make-up. Freshen up and remove old make-up from your skin on a daily basis. Touch up new make-up as needed.

Check your clothing from top to bottom to make sure you are put together in the best way possible.

Shoes Should Compliment Feet

When wearing shoes, flats can be worn in your true size, but heels should be at least 1/2 size larger for comfort. This method also eliminates corns and calluses, which are not a pretty sight on a woman. Shoes on a woman should display a sense of purity and cleanliness. While donning shoes that you wear a lot, consider choosing a pair made of leather or woven fabric. These materials breathe and are usually more comfortable than shoes made of synthetic materials.

Ms. Real Suggests

If you decide to wear polish remember to wear nail polish that compliments your natural skin tone.

Wear shoes that compliment your feet. A friend of yours might be able to wear sling backs because of the size and shape of her foot, but you might not be able to. Make sure your shoe wardrobe includes a pair of shoes in a neutral color that goes well with a wide range of clothing colors. Be selective, and true to yourself, as well as complimentary.

When selecting or wearing shoes make sure they are:

- Clean and shining.
- Neat and fitting.
- Never too tight
- Never too small.
- Polished and even.
- Kept free of any scuffmarks.

Wear Heels That Are Seductive

Women have their own interpretation of how to seductively wear heels. They think of heels as their stature or pedestals and they wear them as a sensual statement. High heels entice some men because of the sexuality they reveal. Heel appeal gives a woman's legs curve, elegance and sexiness.

> **Ms. Real Suggests**
> Women with long legs can create dramatic effects when donning a pair of high heels.

Women with long legs can create dramatic effects when donning a pair of high heels. Women with short legs can give added height to the frame of her body. Your heels can be as selective or as seductive as you chose.

Focus on Your Hands and Nails

Take time to make sure your game is on when it comes to your hands. As far as the hands are concerned the minor things can quickly become major. When you extend your hand make sure it is a hand that others will want to hold. Hands are the finishing touch of a welcoming touch.

Beautiful nails are a plus. Clean, neat and smooth textured nails help you feel good about yourself. Attractive nails speak to the time and attention you pay to yourself. Keep your fingernails and toenails well-manicured and polished, even if it's only a clear coat of polish. There will also be times there is no need for polish. Be sure to make it a habit to clean under your nails. Trim unwanted cuticles or apply cuticle cream to soften your look. Wearing the same color as your best friend may not be the best choice for you.

> **Ms. Real Suggests**
> Invest in a good haircut and hairstyle that compliments the beautiful features of the face.

Colors that look good on her may not compliment you. Remain an individual by wearing what looks good on you.

- ❖ When nails chip excessively, it may be caused by the use of nail polish remover. Leave your nails unpainted for a few days to see if the condition improves.
- ❖ When you're preparing anything with lemon and vegetable juices, which contain acids that are hard on your fingernails, rinse your hands under cool running water.
- ❖ Break the habit of nail biting or cuticle chewing. Carry a tube of cuticle cream with you. Whenever you want to nibble, put the cream on your cuticles.

You'll promote healthy nails and break yourself of a bad habit.

- Prevent polish from thickening, store in the refrigerator.
- To rescue nail polish that has become hardened or gummy, place the bottle into a pan of boiling water for a few seconds to get the polish flowing smoothly again.
- A light color nail polish gives hands the illusion of being longer and more graceful. Dark polish shortens fingers.
- Use an emery board. File nails in one direction.
- To prevent nail polish bottle tops from sticking rub the inside of the cap and the neck of the bottle with a thin layer of petroleum jelly before closing.

Invest in Your Hair

Invest in a good haircut and hairstyle that compliments the beautiful features of the face. Every hairstyle is not presentable or intended to be worn by every face. Be different, yet complimentary. The basic cut is the key to an attractive hairstyle. If the cut is not right, the style will not last; and it will not flatter your face, nor will it look fresh and neat on a daily basis.

If the hair looks too greasy, dull, or messy; the beautiful designer clothing, perfectly applied make-up, and fine jewelry are all wasted. Fortunately, no one needs an expensive professional hair salon or expensive hair products to have hair that looks professionally cared for and styled. With the right techniques for shampooing, drying, and styling, hair can be one of the woman's most attractive features.

Heated Pleasures

For men the removal of the pubic hair can make the male identity seem more vulnerable and much larger, which is a real turn-on for women.

The most obvious and effective way women can let a guy know they're interested in him is if she tussles her hair or strokes it continuously in his presence.

If a woman who sits in front of a man is constantly stroking and braiding her hair, and she's been doing it for several days (but never did it before), she's trying to tell him something. Women utilize the art of touch with great effectiveness.

Unwanted Hair

Under the arms and legs should be sheared of any hair. Try not to wear that mustache that keeps peeking out. Get electrolysis if needed. As far as the rest of your body hair, it's up to you whether you trim or shave it.

Don't get carried away with trying to remove any hair other than the underarms and legs, or obvious pubic hairs. Trying to shave the hair surrounding your navel or hair on your nipples is not what we call unwanted hair. When you shave hair from these places it comes back in triplicate. Whatever hair you decide to remove be consistent and stay aware of unsightly hair.

Women tend to become very relaxed in such things when they are involved in a long-term relationship. This is being personally inconsiderate. The abrasive stubble can ruin a once beautiful situation.

Groom Your Genital Hair Area

Pubic hair can be trimmed to help keep unwanted odors to a minimum. Be sure to trim or shave any long hairs that peek out from your panties and bikini's. It's unattractive and barbaric to present yourself with hairs hanging out of your underwear. Many men and women find that if the genital region of their lover

> **Heatology**
> Removal of the pubic hair can make the male identity seem more vulnerable and much larger.

is shaven it's extremely erotic. For men the removal of the pubic hair can make the male identity seem more vulnerable and much larger, which is a real turn-on for women. For those of you, who are interested in shaving, talk to each other about making it a fun activity that can be shared. Here are a few suggestions for women who choose to shave their pubic regions:

- ❖ If you have long pubic hairs, trim it with clippers or scissors before using a razor to shave in close. Electric clippers are best for this.
- ❖ Take a very long, warm bath beforehand.
- ❖ Before applying shaving cream, rinse the area with cool water.
- ❖ Apply shaving cream a few minutes before shaving to soften hairs. Consider using shaving cream with additional conditioners or aloe.
- ❖ Use a sharp blade. Use two new blades if you are shaving a large area.
- ❖ When shaving, stroke an area no more than twice to reduce skin irritation. On the first stroke, go "with the grain" to remove most of the hair, then go "against the grain" for a smooth, close shave. If "going against" tends to irritate you, then skip that and use both strokes "with the grain."

- Clean the area afterwards with soap and water to reduce the risk of infection. Give the area a second cleansing using cotton balls and aloe.
- Some people find a daily application of baby powder or talcum powder especially helpful after shaving to keep the area dry and irritation-free.
- Practice clean hygiene after shaving, washing the area at least once a day to reduce sweat and oil build-up.
- Go as long as possible between shavings to reduce skin irritation.

Shampoo Your Hair Regularly

If you'd rather shampoo your own hair check with your local pharmacist or hairstylist on which product or brand is best for your type of hair. After shampooing, rinse your hair with cool water to seal in the moisture in the hair shafts.

- To distribute the natural oils in your hair, bend over and brush your scalp and hair from back to front until the scalp tingles; then massage your scalp with your fingertips.
- If you have dandruff, use a good dandruff shampoo. Try the following treatment every two weeks:

Section your hair and rub your scalp with a cotton pad saturated with plain rubbing alcohol. Let the alcohol dry, then brush your hair and rinse thoroughly with warm water, but don't shampoo.

- ❖ To cut down on static electricity, slightly dampen your hairbrush before brushing hair. Avoid using a brush on wet hair, because it is subject to breakage.
- ❖ To get a fuller look to your hairstyle, bend over so that your hair falls forward and blow the underneath layers dry first.
- ❖ To perk up curly or permed hair between shampoos, lightly mist your hair with fresh water and push the curls into place with your fingers.
- ❖ Dull, lifeless hair can be a sign of a poor diet. Try cutting down on cholesterol and fats.
- ❖ For color: Wait at least 48 hours after coloring hair before you shampoo it again. Every time you wet hair you open the cuticle, so give hair time to seal in the color.
- ❖ Hair sprays, mousses, gels, and other styling aids build up over time, despite shampooing and rinsing. If you find this happening, buy a clarifier, which removes product build-up without stripping essential oils. Make your own, mix one (1) part vinegar with twenty (20) parts water.

Your Eyes Speak Volume

Even though silent, a woman's eyes speak volume. A woman loves using her eyes to communicate her feelings. She can use them to send seductive looks or the classic "glancing away and then looking back to see if he's still watching" technique that all women employ. A hybrid of this is when she looks over her shoulder, smiles and then walks away.

A woman should look at a man's eye movements when she's talking to him. If there's a break in eye contact - she should look at his lips or chest and slowly work her way back to his eyes...it lets him know that she's interested. Your eyes are the windows to the soul. They tell the world who you are.

To add allure and ravish eyes try the following:

- ❖ Apply foundation over the lid area. This helps everything else adhere.
- ❖ Pluck your eyebrows from underneath, and then fill in the eye shadow that's a shade lighter than your natural color. Some women draw on the shape they want before they pluck or after they pluck.
- ❖ Use mascara on your lashes. Then, if you need more depth or thickness, paste one or two rows of false lashes on top.

- ❖ Warm a spoon with a lighter and then curl real or fake lashes over the spoon to bead and blend. (Professional model's secret)
- ❖ Gently pull your skin around your eyes outward as you sweep back liquid liner across your upper lid line.
- ❖ Define the bottom of your eyes with brown eye pencil, both underneath and inside them.
- ❖ Dot concealer one tone lighter than your skin over dark circles that usually surround the eyes. Smooth in to blend.
- ❖ Use two shades of eyebrow pencil to make brow color look more natural.
- ❖ Use your eyes as a flirtatious vehicle to send signs, signals, and gestures in positive ways.
- ❖ Placing sliced raw potatoes over and under eye bags for ten minutes can help to aide your assets. The chemical composition draws the excess water from the skin that causes puffiness.
- ❖ Hawaiian trick for thicker lashes; apply a tiny bit of castor oil with fingers before bed. This encourages new growth.
- ❖ Plucking is a must! Try icing before you pluck to ease pain.

- Some women have been known to use an ordinary number two (2) pencil to fill in brows. I wouldn't recommend it since lead is dangerous.
- Revive tired eyes by covering with cucumbers, or kiwi slices (leave on for ten minutes)
- Do try subtle colored contacts for a change in eye color.
- Invest in good make-up brushes for foolproof make-up application.
- To make the whites of your eyes appear whiter, line your lower lashes with a deep-blue color stick.
- To bring out deep-set eyes, apply a light, frosted shadow on both your lids and brow bone, use a darker shade in the eyelid crease.
- Avoid matching the color of your eye shadow to the exact shade of your eyes. Some colors cancel each other making eyes look drab.
- Protect eyelashes with a thin coat of waterproof mascara when outdoors.
- For thick looking lashes, apply mascara and let it set for a few minutes. Then add a little more mascara to the tips. If you use an eyelash curler, curl lashes before you add mascara to the tips.
- Applying fresh mascara over the old makes lashes brittle. Use mascara remover before going to bed.

- When your mascara begins to dry out, before throwing it away run hot water over the tube to soften the remaining mascara.
- Limit the use of eye drops during summer.
- Small eyes can be made to look larger by applying eye shadow under your lower lashes starting at the center of the eye and blending to the outer corner. Sweep the color along the brow bone out to the side of your eye.

The spirit behind your eyes is only one of the many keys to unlocking your sensuality. Using your eyes as a creative and seductive tool can produce some of the most pleasurable moments in your life and your relationship.

Keep Your Skin Clean and Healthy

No matter what the color of the complexion, a woman should keep her skin clean, healthy and smooth. Someone other than you is celebrating your complexion, so revel in it by keeping it wholesome. Exfoliate your skin at least twice a month to keep it clean and healthy looking. There are wonderful over the counter exfoliating products available in local stores.

No matter what the shade or flavor of your skin as long as you take proper care for it, you'll get desirable attention. Taking care of your skin allows its finer properties to shine through.

Your skin is bell weather to your overall health. If you're not healthy, it will reflect in your complexion, but that doesn't mean you should neglect your skin if you're feeling fine. Here are some easy ways to rid your skin of minor problems:

- ❖ Don't play with or pick pimples. Put notes on mirrors to remind you.
- ❖ Try not to touch or lean your cheek on the cradle of the phone. Particles of food or secretions from the face or mouth may be there.
- ❖ Drink water to flush out impurities, never sleep with make-up. If you hate to sleep with a naked face, dust lightly with pressed powder and blush.
- ❖ Get at least eight hours of sleep per night.
- ❖ Use oil-free powder during exercise so that your pores won't clog. Clean your face with astringent after working out.
- ❖ To diffuse stress, take vitamin C.
- ❖ Avoid laundry detergents with sodium laurylsulfite (pimple-producing ingredient).

- ❖ Take ibuprofen when cysts pimples appear. It reduces the inflammation.
- ❖ To calm facial redness, take ice breaks twice a day for two minutes. Place cold towels or towels with crushed ice gently against the face for several minutes each morning. You'll feel revitalized as well as fresh and perky.
- ❖ Switch to low dose or triphasol birth control pills.
- ❖ Read all cosmetic labels. Avoid products containing isopropyl myristrate, isopropyl palmitate, stearic acid, decylo-leate, mineral oil, lanolin and fragrance.
- ❖ Avoid getting hair styling products on your forehead.
- ❖ Use make-up that camouflages. Apply oil-free foundation with cover cream; with a tiny make-up brush dab away imperfections. Pat lightly with translucent powder to set.
- ❖ A surprising blemish fighter is good SEX.
- ❖ Sun does not dry zits. It damages follicles, making the break out worse. Use sun blocks that contain titanium dioxide or oil-free ones.
- ❖ To prevent irritations do not apply fragrances or colognes to your face.
- ❖ Apply sun block on hot summer days.

- Always wear a moisturized sunscreen when outdoors, winter and summer. The sun's rays can burn you even if the air feels cool, and sunlight reflected off water or the whiteness of snow can be particularly powerful.
- No matter what your skin type; use a protective lotion and try not to expose your skin to direct sun for more than fifteen minutes. Use sunscreen on your face and the back of your hands, because these are constantly exposed to the sun's rays.
- Go without makeup and allow skin to breathe.
- Use a humidifier to lessen drying effects of indoor air on your skin.
- Take baths in the evening to avoid exposing your skin to the outdoor air.
- Darker skin can get skin cancer; don't exempt yourself from sun block because of your race.

Pamper Your Lips Daily

Lips comes in all sizes, shapes, colors and textures… full, thin, pouty, voluptuous, streamlined, you name it.

- To keep lips going all day, pencil lips with a soft colored lip pencil. Apply lipstick and then blot. For fuller looking lips, line lips and then blend the edges with a sponge applicator. Cover with light glaze of gloss or petroleum jelly.

- ❖ To keep lipstick off teeth, pucker lips into an extreme "O". Cover your finger with tissue, and pole it into your mouth and slowly twist out of your mouth, removing excess color.
- ❖ To achieve a pouty, sexy mouth, emphasize your top lip by dabbing just a touch of gloss in the center.
- ❖ Highlight your lips with a very light eye shadow that coordinates with your lip color tones. Place it in the center of your upper and lower lips.
- ❖ To balance unevenly shaped lips, use a lighter colored lipstick on the smaller-sized lip.
- ❖ To keep lipstick in place while dining, keep lips off utensils. Let lower teeth and tongue to do the work.
- ❖ Rub a washcloth over lips before applying lipstick to smooth lips.

Embrace Your Full Lips

You are lucky if you've been blessed with large lips. Women everywhere are trying to replicate with collagen, but large lips can take over your face if you're not careful.

- ❖ You really don't need lip liner, but if you like the look, soften edge with your finger or a Q-tip.

- ❖ Don't wear any lip color that is too glossy or shiny. Full lips began to look more like a butt than lips.
- ❖ Wear lip colors that accentuate your fullness by wearing clothing that coordinates with your lipsticks, lip glosses or lip liners.

Compliment Your Thin Lips

Draw slightly beyond the lip with a neutral-colored lip pencil, and then apply lipstick. Your lipstick will "catch" onto the liner.

- ❖ Apply white shadow on center of lips over lipstick and spread slightly.
- ❖ Don't wear very dark shades of lipstick. It makes lips look small and dirty.
- ❖ Always protect your lips with a thin coating of colorless lip balm whenever you aren't wearing lip-gloss or lip color.
- ❖ For a long-lasting lipstick, apply a generous coat, and then let it set for about two minutes. Blot with a tissue, puff on some powder, and then apply another generous coat of lipstick. Wait again and blot.
- ❖ Choose warm, tawny lip colors for office light.
- ❖ To make full lips appear slimmer, draw a line inside your lip line and fill with a darker shade of color.

- To make thin lips appear fuller, draw a lip line outside the natural lip line and fill with a lighter shade of lipstick.
- If upper and lower lips are uneven, apply make-up over your lips, and then fashion a new lip line with a pencil a shade darker than your lip color.

You Never Know Whose Looking

People don't see the color of a woman's skin; they see the condition of it. Is yours satiny smooth, blemish free, and healthy looking? Does it look as if it's been kissed by the glimmer of the sun? Does it have a beautiful glow? Is it rich with vitality and alive? It is skin you would want to touch even though you reserve the impulse for a more appropriate time? My friend, that kind of skin is worth the time and effort.

Master Your Foundation and Blush

- In the winter, use oil-based, rather than water-based, make-up to protect skin against dry, cold air.
- In the summer switch, switch to a water based foundation to help moisturize your skin, but use

waterproof make-up for lips, eyes, and lashes to prevent running and smearing.

- ❖ To apply foundation evenly, use a damp sponge, allow color to blend and give natural coverage.
- ❖ Emphasize facial contours; select a foundation that's a shade lighter.
- ❖ Use a large make-up brush to dust translucent powder lightly over your face after you've applied make-up then further set the make-up with a light spray of mineral or ordinary water.

Project Overall Good Health

A healthy smile projects youth and good grooming. It can be so beautiful that you'll continue to look at it over and over again! You want to kiss it. A beautiful smile showcases white-smooth teeth that fill up the area within the lips.

The lips frame a great smile like great masterpiece of art has frames. Sexual attraction causes the lips to fill with blood, enlarge and turn red. Perhaps this is why red or hot pink is preferred colors of lipstick.

You Should Know
A neck can be a tender place to put lips upon.

You Should Know
A woman's neck portrays elegance grace, power, beauty and prowess when working it from side to side.

Enlarged lips are less obvious as we get older because as teeth wear down the lips thin. As a result there's less lip. Older worn teeth are often the same length but a youthful sexy smile displays longer central incisors, slightly shorter laterals and smooth unworn cusped. It takes the lines from the face, enlarges the lips and shows more teeth when smiling.

A beautiful sexy smile showcases the upper front teeth and hardly any of the lowers. Revealing too much gum is considered unattractive, but a fantastic smile is white teeth and beautiful gums.

Use Your Arms as Sexual Tools

We adore great looking arms. Men notice them because they denote strength and firmness. They don't need to be muscular, but nicely toned arms are appealing to men. A woman's arms are made for embracing and holding onto the one she loves. Reaching with outstretched arms that are fit and tone are sexy on any woman.

A Beautiful Neck Is Sexy

A woman can use any part of her body to speak to a man, but jokes are made daily about a woman having a neck roll of excess skin. When a woman has a neck that's smooth and sleek she is rewarded with flattery. A taunt good-looking neck reflects pride humility and sexiness.

A neck can send messages of I need a kiss, a rub, or a gentle stroke from someone who cares. A neck can be a tender place to put lips upon. Perfume them and train them to tease the opposite sex. A woman's neck portrays elegance, grace, power, and beauty.

> **You Should Know**
> Your feet are your indication of how much attention you pay to your overall grooming experience.

Beautiful Legs Can Woo

Men tend to observe how a woman positions her legs. It's hard to understand the exact scientific mechanics of how women flirt with their legs, but legs are highly visible and useful for turning men on. That's not by accident.

It doesn't matter whether a woman's legs are long, short, skinny, or thick - it's every man's dream to caress them. Wear a dress, skirt or shorts that compliments your legs and then go ahead and strut your stuff with grace and elegance.

You Should Know
It doesn't matter whether a woman's legs are long, short, skinny, or thick - it's every man's dream to caress them

Beautiful Feet Are Sweet

We all know at least one man who loves a woman's legs, but to find a man who loves feet is quite unique. Men may not touch feet as often as we like, but they sure do notice them.

Are your feet clean and neatly manicured, or are they hard callused and looking like you just participated in a barefooted marathon? Your feet are your indication of how much attention you pay to your overall grooming experience. Do you take the time to care for all parts of you? How you take care of yourself says a lot about you. Give honor to all parts of you, especially your feet.

Admire Your Own Body Parts

It's obvious that men cater to a woman's breasts, hips, butt, legs, arms, necks, and so on. Perhaps you got it from your gene pool…like mama like daughter. This is another area where style, size, and shape are purely subjective. Boobs and more boobs. The phenomenon can't be shaken.

The truth is; women love breasts just as much as men. The right bra on beautiful breast can make a man's tongue drop to the floor. Bras with cotton straps are perfect for accentuating large boobs and they keep you holding steady.

You Should Know
Apply perfume and cologne on your skin, rather than your clothes.

Visit the lingerie department of your favorite store and ask a fitter to size you properly so that your breast won't sag or hang. , or you won't get fitted in a bra too small, too tight or too large.

Improve Your Posture Position

If you're interested in a man, you might have a very perky posture when he's around. Your back will be arched and chest will be slightly pushed forward. Try to close the distance between you and the man you're interested in.

When you are leaning into the man or standing closer than normal with a relaxed stance, you're making yourself approachable. However, if you stand upright with arms crossed, you're not interested.

Wear Complimentary Fragrances

Unless you (or your man) have allergic reactions to perfumes, colognes, or fragrances, please wear it. Cheap imitations are simply that, "cheap imitations." When a woman is complimented or asked the name of the perfume she is wearing it should be taken as a well-deserved compliment. If you are asked more than several times a day, it is usually a very good indication that you've hit on a good fragrance, one that compliments your body chemistry. Ask yourself these fragrance questions

- Do you wear fragrance for yourself or other people?
- How often do you wear fragrances?
- How does wearing fragrance make you feel?
- How many different fragrances do you own?
- When was the last time you purchased a new fragrance?

Get the Most from Fragrances

To get the most from your fragrance, perfumes should be worn on all pulse spots of your body. Apply perfume and cologne on your skin, rather than your clothes. Chemicals in fragrances may weaken fabric or change the color.

- Dab lightly, Colognes may clash with other smells.
- Choose fragrance that compliments your natural body odor.
- Don't mix too many smells like deodorant, lotions powders and perfumes. All on the same body can be quite repulsive. Many companies make lotions, body oils, perfumes, soaps and bath gels of the same scents to help women in choosing. You can also find odorless deodorants.

Where to Apply Your Fragrances

Apply your fragrance onto your body several times a day.

- Ankles
- Palms
- Back of your knees
- Bend of your elbows
- Between your thighs
- Behind the ears
- Base of the throat
- Bosom
- Inside your wrists

Fragrance is seductive, and it really gets a woman noticed, but a quick spritz is not the only way to go. To make a definite and lasting impression, here are more simple techniques:

- ❖ Twirl! Spray eau de toilette in the air, and then spin in the mist. The misty molecules of your spray should settle all over your awaiting body, hair, and clothing ... yummy.
- ❖ Ultimate Allure. Lightly scent a cotton ball or a hankie and stuff it in your bra, pocket or glove.
- ❖ Re-scent! Just as you would touch up your lipstick, touch up your fragrance. This combats fade out and olfactory overload because your nose doesn't register odor once you've used it.
- ❖ Can't afford the real thing! Less expensive bath oils and moisturizing erosions are potent and REALLY last! Dab as you would perfume.
- ❖ Check out new Eau De Perfumes. They fall between toilet water and perfume in strength, but are much less expensive.
- ❖ Use matching bath and body products to layer fragrances.
- ❖ Multi-floral and oriental scents stay vital the longest and are arousing.

- ❖ Avoid scent buying just prior to menstruation, when your sense of smell is weakest. (The birth control pill is said to also alter odor-detecting ability)
- ❖ Hair is a fabulous perfume vehicle. Mix a few drops with conditioner then run it through your hair.
- ❖ The best time to apply fragrances is after you shower; your open pores will soak up the aroma.
- ❖ Dab petroleum on pulse points, and then apply perfume to these areas.
- ❖ Apply perfume and cologne before putting on your jewelry. The alcohol and oils in your favorite scent can cause a cloudy film on both real gold and costume jewelry.
- ❖ Don't stick to one fragrance all year long. Temperatures affect the intensity of fragrance. Use heavy scents and oils in winter but lighter fragrances in smaller quantities during the summer.

Use Your Sexual Sensibilities

A woman is equipped with sensuous tools, but to achieve great levels of sexuality she should learn how to use these tools. There are things a woman should know and understand about what it takes to become turned on? Have you ever walked past a stranger who was wearing a fabulous scent and thought "How can I get to know him better?" Have you ever listened to a favorite song and it reminded you of someone close to your heart?

Before Reading Any Further

- Consult your gynecologist before trying any suggestions in this book.
- Read and discuss this chapter before attempting any of the suggestions.
- If fragrance causes a bad reaction or abrasions appear in that this area it will most likely make your life a living hell (temporarily).
- If irritations come from shaving, why not avoid shaving, or try hypoallergenic shaving creams.
- If you have sensitive skin you may wish to avoid shaving. Consider closely trimming your hair instead. It provides many of the benefits of shaving without all the risks!
- Letting hair grow out after shaving the pubic area is a bothersome task. The sharp hairs combined with the sensitive skin will make you realize just how much movement happens in that area on an average day. Chaffing is nearly unavoidable.

A Sensual Note:

You should talk with your lover about arranging to shave each other. This can be a very erotic and sensual activity. Be sure to communicate clearly and proceed very slowly. Find out what he likes, what feels good, and what doesn't feel good. If you take time and learn how to do this, he will love you all the more for it. Happy shaving!

You Should Know
Sexual sensitivity can free your mind if you use your five senses along with your God gifted femininity.

"If anything is sacred, the human body is sacred."
— Walt Whitman

Chapter 6

Improving Your Sexual Radiance

This chapter will help you find your inner sex Goddess.

You've seen her, a woman whose face and body would never grace the cover of a fashion magazine, yet all eyes follow her when she enters the room. You notice her because her walk attracts you and she exudes confidence, and radiates positive energy. Everything about her says, "I'm hot. I'm desirable, I'm sexy - and I know it." She's the woman who feels comfortable in her own skin and her actions show that she's confident with her sexuality. We all know that this kind of

Heated Pleasures
If you want to become an expert lover you should practice the fine art of mental foreplay.

self-confidence is great for any woman's ego. Everyone who meets and greets her wants to be around her.

Men confess that they admire a woman's confidence. When a woman is confident in herself she almost always appears to be sexier to men. When a woman has inner confidence and displays that she is sure of herself she has an inner beauty that shines outward.

Become Sexually Confident

The best way for you to become sexually confident is to truly believe you are deserving of female pleasures. Embrace your sexuality by embracing your inner vixen. All it takes is an attitude change. Instead of wondering if you are sexy, know that you are. Here's seventeen ways to help you become sexually confident.

1. Indulge in self-pleasuring.

Don't be afraid. It helps you understand how your body feels when you explore self-love. It also helps you understand what you like and how you like it. No one else has to know.

2. Know your body.

Know it better than any man ever could. You should not allow a man to touch your body before you are familiar with your own body. You should know what you like and dislike when touched.

3. Dress sexy as often as you can.

Don't wait for a special occasion. Dress up, just because. Get rid of dingy, torn, beat up and faded clothing. Dress up because it makes you feel good.

4. Invest in sexy underwear.

Visit a lingerie store and buy the sexiest underwear that will fit. Once you put it on, notice how sexy you feel. Wear sexy underwear under your everyday clothing for no reason at it. Wear it just because.

5. Bring your sexy back!

Radiate with sexiness. When you know you're sexy, you feel sexy. If you feel sexy you'll radiate with sexiness. Remember the great saying "You are what you feel." It's true. Sometimes a woman might not feel sexy, but the moment she begins to think and believe she is, people around her will begin to think that she is. It's amazing how much your sexiness begins to blossom when you feel it. As your sexy mood increases the slightest touch from your lover becomes electric. The way you look at him will send waves of sensuality. It's all-mental.

6. Possess sexual confidence.

The most positive thing you can do for your self-esteem is learn what to do and how to act. You should learn to present yourself in a way that improves your confidence level. The most beautiful woman becomes more graceful and charming when she radiates with self-esteem. Women who communicate with confidence often display sassy feminine assets in a positive way and are more appealing to men. You're magnetic because your self-confidence is a very attractive asset. He'll want to get to know you better.

7. Give him affectionate attention.

A woman who takes pride in making her lover feel good in bed knows that in order for her to get his attention she has to find his libido. Focus your attention completely on him. Taking a few tips from the female pros isn't a bad idea either. Don't waste valuable time worrying about things that don't matter while in bed. Focus your attention on his face, ears, skin, arms, legs, chest, and the rest of him. Get so involved in him that he feels like he's the only person in the world. He should feel like you've been mesmerized by his presence.

8. Do sexy things to him

You should notice all of the places he touches you and the way he does it, and then later reverse the touching so that he enjoys it just as much as you do. If he strokes you between the thighs and it gives you chills - you should do the same to him later. If he likes to suck on your fingers you should do the same to him. A man enjoys a woman who does joyous things to him. Alternate love making skills by doing some things he likes now and other things he likes the next time you make love to him.

9. Avoid negative people and situations.

Replace them with positive and empowering messages. Any negative messages you've received in the past should be replaced with encouraging messages. If he says hurtful things, get rid of him and move on to a positive person.

10. Adopt a positive attitude about life.

Life is too short to let the good pass you by. Open your heart and your mind to new experiences.

11. **Begin your day with "I love me because ______."**

It makes you feel better during the day and for the rest of the day.

12. **Indulge in your own nakedness.**

When you get out of the tub, don't be so quick to put clothes on. Walk around naked for at least fifteen minutes. Enjoy what you see and appreciate your body.

13. **Write your own story with you as the main character.**

14. **Initiate sex tonight.**

Be open to making the first move. Go ahead what have you got to lose?

15. **Study sex manuals**

They will help you become more open and accepting of your lovers love.

Create a romantic atmosphere in your home.
Buy sensuous candles, sexy clothing, and plush bed covers and indulge in stimulating foods.

Chapter 7

Improving Your Mental Foreplay

This chapter will help tune up your imagination so that it is the sexiest of all.

Since your brain is the most erotic part of your body, how and what you think - sets the tone for your sensuous moments. What encourages you to feel and act sexy when you're with your lover are those delicious thoughts of being romantic, touching, feeling, tasting and of course making sensuous love?

Now for a moment, let's think about what turns you on. What does it take to get you sexually motivated and excited and what sexually satisfies you? Does kissing your man turn you on? Does rubbing certain parts of his body against yours excite you? Do the thoughts of sensuous penetration move your mind into a sexual zone? What does he do that makes you squirm by thinking of it?

Can you imagine wonderful things that bring you to great levels of sensual excitement? Use them to help you get in the mood and you're half way there. A man can get turned on just by thinking about how you looked the last time he saw you. He'll adore you for being turned on by thoughts of him. That's enough to get him really excited. Your imagination is the sexiest turn on of all. Give your lover something to think about that will make him sensuously hard in all the right places. Here are twelve ways to combine sex and imagination so that you and your lover will reap sensuous rewards.

1. Tell your lover about the big and small things he does that turns you on and say it like you mean it.
2. Share erotic pictures with him. Men love pictures that have woman doing erotic things together. You can find these in men's magazines. To open up the lines of communication simply say you have something you want to show him and present him with several erotic magazines. He'll live it.

3. Share sensuously erotic pictures of you with him. If you don't have any… get busy and take some sexy photos.
4. Read him paragraphs from either book: Sexual Healing, Heated Pleasures or Will the Real Women Please Stand Up. Find the most erotic chapters and read with the goal of turning him on.
5. Greet him at the door dressed in the typical maid costume: a tiny cap, very high heels, a small black apron, sexy hosiery.
6. Make a tape of you and your lover's sounds during a sexual act. Turn the lights down low and get really turned on at the thought of being together. Listen to the tape afterwards and if you need to redo it; happily redo it.
7. Place a tape recorder beneath your bed. Let it run while the two of you are making love, and say nothing to him about it. Try your best to forget that it's there and then later play it back to him. You'll be surprised at the things you said and the sounds you made while in the heat of passion. The sounds of erotic love making from the two of you will probably have you back in bed making love all over again.
8. Write him a sensuous poem and slip it into his wallet or jacket pocket. He'll be warmly surprised.

9. While together in a restaurant, waiting in line, or visiting friends look into his eyes, whisper to him what you're going to do to him when you get him alone. Be very specific, then smile sensuously and change the subject.
10. Buy sexy clothing to wear for him. Model it for him.
11. Buy a piece of sexy underwear that has a hole cut in the crotch area and be sure to put his protruding piece of beef inside the hole while you're wearing it. He'll love you for it.
12. Send him a different piece of lingerie in the mail. Enclose a note that tells him what you're going to do with it later.

Because you are deserving of pleasure; pleasure is best when it is embraced

Improving Your Conversations

This chapter will help you say what you need to say in the sexiest and most sensuous ways.

Conversations consist of not only what you say, but also how you say it. The more accomplished your conversation, the more you make use of voice tone, facial expressions and variation of gestures for emphasis, thought, wit, and empathy for expertise.

Conversations that involve sensuous talk can be very delicious. What a wonderful rush that travels up and down a woman's spine when her lover is saying the things she likes to hear. Her brain and body takes what he says and imagines what the words will be like when turned into

Heated Pleasures
Exposure to sex talk can be rewarding and quite an experience if it's with someone you love and adore.

actions. Women are turned on by verbal fantasy. Sensuous conversation is not simply an exclamation of moans, groans, and squeals until finally-ejaculation. Erotic turn on's can be interpreted in several different ways.

The best turn-on's are in the ears of the receiver. It creates and describes one of the most potent means for changing direct and sensuous into an inviting sexual adventure.

Noise can be associated with sex whether the sex is good, bad, pleasurable or painful. Most women still feel inhibited or even foolish when being verbal during lovemaking because of its unfeminine like characteristics. Women sometimes don't want men to recognize the fact that they are enjoying themselves.

If a woman wants sounds to be a natural part of her sexual pleasure she should verbally express it. As a woman becomes more aroused, her heart rate and breathing speeds up. As she begins to reach orgasm it speeds up three to four times faster than normal. No sensuous woman can keep still when all this excitement is going on.

Embellish Your Sounds of Ecstasy

Many men are genuinely turned on by a woman's sounds of ecstasy. It makes him feel like the king of her night, but there are still some men who feel noise is a turn off or distracting. Exposure to sex talk can be rewarding and quite an experience if it's with someone you love and adore. The biggest complaint is that sex talk makes women feel cheap and dirty. Then there are other women who love sex talk and everything about it.

> **Heated Pleasures**
> Use your speech organs to produce provocative sounds when speaking with your lover.

The best advice I can give about sex talk is it depends on the openness of the woman. Some like it and some don't. Some women are so into it that they script out what they want their lovers to say to them.

Relax and Loosen Up

Relaxing and going with the flow might initially seem crude and disgusting, but you'll shortly find yourself being turned on by sex talk in a sensuous way. As he says one thing, mentally reverse it to your positive thoughts. For example if he says, "Suck me baby," then you'll say to him "I love the way you turn me on." Then, one night when you're making love, get immersed in the sensuous thought of it all and let your private thoughts become a matter of verbal arousal between the two of you. After doing this a few times you won't be embarrassed to verbalize your feelings.

If you still find that sex talk is not for you, then seductively verbalize your feelings by saying simple things like, "Ummmm, I like that" or "Ummmm I needed that." It will give you the practice you need without talking dirty. As you make love, practice verbalizing your desires and feelings, so that you can communicate with your lover.

> **Ms. Real Suggests**
> If you still find that sex talk is not for you, then seductively verbalize your feelings by saying simple things like, "Ummmm, I like that" or "Ummmm I needed that."

Another great way to start verbalizing is to tell your lover what you want, how you want it and whether or not it feels good during your lovemaking. Saying things that make him feel good or making sexual requests while making love is a great way to let your guard down and start verbalizing. He'll love you for it.

Work on Smoothing Your Voice

Nothing is more erosive to a man while making love than a woman who has an irritating voice. No man wants to hear a scratchy voice when he's holding you while in the heat of passion. You can practice improving your voice by listening to it on a tape recorder. You should not sound as you have laryngitis. That can be very nonsexy and unromantic. Don't spend all your time and money being beautiful and when he hears your voice, he's completely turned off. Voice improvement techniques are:

> **Heated Pleasures**
> Some women use baby talk when communicating intimately with their lover. Anna Nicole Smith was famous for using baby talk when she wanted to receive affection.

- ❖ Take a deep breath and hold for approximately five to eight seconds before you answer the phone. Release your breath slowly as you speak. This adds to the sensuality of your voice. Continue practicing this technique while holding your breath until it's natural, fluent and pleasant.
- ❖ Soften your tone by lowering your voice each time you speak. Women who have loud and boisterous voices are a turn off.

❖ Practice on your pronunciation and correct word usage. To have a beautiful speaking voice and good pronunciation are double threats to other women.

A good point to remember about voice quality is to think, act and talk sensuously. If you believe in your sensuality, you will become the sensuous person you've always wanted to be. Practicing each time you speak. Your voice should not be abrasive or harsh. Use words that compel you to make sexy sounds.

Words that encourage provocative sounds are words that begin with the letter "S". I've listed a few: suck, sucked, sucking, sex, sexy, sensuous, sensual, sequence, seduction, seep, semaphore. To find more sensuous "S" words, look in the index of this book. Reciting "S" words build your sensuous vocabulary. Don't use any 'Sh' words. They aren't sexy. Use your speech organs to produce provocative sounds when speaking with your lover. If you are willing to put forth the effort a sweet, soft, sexy voice will lure any willing man in your direction. Look at it this way, men want to be needed and

Ms. Real Suggests

Turn your lover on with phone sex you should at least sound like a person who is genuinely interested in the phone conversation.

men need to be wanted. It's up to you as a woman to make your man feel he's needed, just as it is his responsibility to make you feel needed. Imagine what could be accomplished when you say the right things in the right way in the correct tone.

Heated Pleasures

Giving good phone sex is necessary to keep the relationship steamy. Use it to make a man feel good and build his ego.

Express Yourself in Your Way

It isn't what you say so much as how you say it. The flavor of your language is part of your personality and sex appeal. Some women use baby talk when communicating intimately with their lover. Anna Nicole Smith was famous for using baby talk when she wanted to receive affection. Some women use foreign language and some moan and groan passionately. You don't have to do it all at once; you can work your way into it gradually. So go on and slowly express yourself.

How do you express yourself in your everyday situations? Once you figure that out, you can better understand how you can express yourself sexually. Are you funny, witty, straight to the point, or clever? Do you jump from one subject to the next? When you have pinpointed the type of talk you emanate you can use that same formula to translate your sexual needs and desires.

Practice Telephone Savvy

Phone sex is a particularly wonderful way to spin out your most brilliant fantasies. No one can see you, so you can feel safe and not quite as silly as if you were face to face with your lover. It's almost like being alone, but reminding yourself of your deepest fantasies.

Giving good phone sex is necessary to keep the relationship steamy. Use it to make a man feel good and build his ego. Being savvy on the phone keeps many men interested. Seduce your lover by calling him and saying erotic things. Assure him you miss him and then tell him why he won't regret your time together.

Even the telephone companies have ventured into the phone sex business. Many newspapers and magazine have advertisements that feature sexy women with large breasts or male hunks with large male identities (penises) encouraging you to phone in for a dollar or two per minute. They make you believe you are the caller they've been longing to hear. Some want you to masturbate as they listen and others want to meet women or men.

Some other obvious reasons for phone sex are:

1. There's no need to dress for the occasions
2. Threats of unsafe sex are not present.
3. Phone sex is non-threatening to the listener because face-to-face rejection doesn't exist.
4. There's always someone to talk to.
5. People calling for phone sex can use their imagination without embarrassment or belittlement.
6. Experiencing phone sex can teach you many aspects of sex that you've never thought about before. Exaggeration is natural on the telephone.

There are professional phone sex lines, but this section will deal with your personal phone as a means of phone sex with your lover.

Your Attitude Is Important

A woman's overall attitude is very important. Turn your lover on with phone sex you should at least sound like a person who is genuinely interested in the phone conversation. Be as verbal as you possibly can. As you talk to him use adjectives that describe your favorite sexual encounter. If you haven't had the pleasure of a sexual encounter but want one describe yourself and what you would like to do to him. Your description should help your man create an image in his mind.

Use Your Sexiest Sounding Voice

Practice by using a hushed-low sexy voice. Making sounds of pleasure that will give vivid images to your partner. Making love over the phone usually lasts longer than it does in real life. Don't fall into the trap of using the phone as a way to avoid intimacy or to avoid a real relationship. Phone sex is just for entertainment and is not a replacement for kissing, cuddling or a real beating heart. Here are some things you can do to help pull your best and sexiest voice from within.

- Practice your sexiest voice with your cassette.
- Call a phone sex line and learn the do's and don'ts of phone sex. This will help you to learn what works.
- Remain mentally seductive by having a gentle introduction, slow build up and soft resolution.
- Create a pet name that you only use in the dark.
- Choose his favorite song as your background music. Make sure it's seductive and relates to the two of you.
- Choose a long-playing song that makes you feel romantic.

- Choose a comfortable, uninterrupted environment.
- Turn the ringer off on your phone.
- Try not to sound rehearsed.
- Use his name or the nickname you gave him.
- Tell him about any sexy thoughts you've had about the two of you.
- Choose sexy clothing. Take them off before taping and go naked. Taking them off heightens your romantic mood.
- While masturbating tell him what you're doing.
- Be as honest as possible. Intensify... no faking.
- Rest for at least an hour after you complete your tape, then listen to it and if you decide to mail it to him, send an erotic note to him. One-day mail services are quite nice.
- Put it in his lunch box or slip it in his car audiocassette.

Breathe when you talk, and your voice will sound sexier.

Part 3

Enhance Your Sensuality

Chapter 9

Enhancing Your Touch

This chapter will help you communicate better by touching sensuously and attentively.

We've heard so much about the power of touch has been taken for granted. Physical touch is so powerful it can sway the opinion of the opposite sex and it can change his appearance.

All of us - young and old, single or in a relationship - need to be touched. The act of touching communicates more than words. Physical contact is a prerequisite both for a healthy individual, and for a fulfilling, mature, loving relationship.

Our bodies require touch: it relieves stress and it makes us happier and healthier. In our fast-paced lives we often forget the importance of giving and receiving affection through physical touch. We deprive ourselves of this very basic need and we often deprive our loved ones. I can't emphasize enough how important touch is in any loving relationship. We strive to diet, to quit smoking, to drink in moderation, and to exercise, in order to promote a healthy body.

> **You Should Know**
>
> Touching promotes a healthy mind, body, and soul. Touching calms us down, it relieves our stress, and it allows us to demonstrate our love for one another.

Touching is the most vital gift that you can give and receive.

Touching promotes a healthy mind, body, and soul. Touching calms us down, it relieves our stress, and it allows us to demonstrate our love for one another. If you have young children, and you arrive home, when they're excited to see you they'll want physical contact from you. They want a hug, a cuddle, and a kiss. It makes them feel loved and cared for, and gives them the security that they need from you. After a long, stressful day a hug and cuddle from your child, partner, or even a friend, is the best medicine you can give yourself.

Sexual Touching

The most basic form of sexual pleasure begins with your touch. You begin by becoming familiar with your own pleasures, wants and needs. Do you know where you want to be touched? Do you know how you like to be touched? I hope so, because knowing what you like is the key to achieving your very own sexual satisfaction. I suggest women take the time to physically get in touch with their bodies and their sexuality. I recommend that women also get in tune with their emotional needs and learn what they like when their lovers touch them and when touching themselves.

Ms. Real Suggests
I recommend that women also get in tune with their emotional needs

Singles Need Touching Too

You may be single at this time, but being single doesn't mean that you won't need touching and physical closeness in your daily life, especially if you have recently ended a relationship. You may be missing the hugs, kisses, embraces and hand holding that you once had.

Your life and the world do not stop because you're not in a loving relationship - neither does your need for physical closeness and touching. It all starts with you.

The art of touching encompasses non-sexual and sexual touch and it's important to get your daily allowance of touching.

Demonstrating physical closeness with family and friends is one way to elevate your mood, allowing you to feel loved and fulfilled, while giving love to others. This type of touching not only makes them healthier, it does wonders for you.

You Should Know

Demonstrating physical closeness with family and friends is one way to elevate your mood, allowing you to feel loved and fulfilled, while giving love to others.

Receiving a massage, manicure, pedicure, or even a haircut can provide the touching and physical stimulation that you need. If you are in a relationship, both sexual and non-sexual touching is important. During the euphoric stage of a relationship, sexual touch predominates. You can't keep your hands off of each other. When mature love begins, non-sexual touch becomes more important, as touch takes on an additional meaning.

While sexual touch can communicate sexual feelings, non-sexual touch can simply communicate your love, care, and affection for one another.

A Woman's Touch Adds Love

If you are in a loving relationship, make a concerted effort to touch your partner. Don't forget to hug and kiss one another before you leave for work, or when you return home. Take advantage of quiet moments during the day to give affection to one another. Hold hands in a movie, at a restaurant, or while walking down the street. Showering or bathing together promotes touching, and will give you physical closeness with your partner.

> **Heated Pleasures**
> The pleasure of a sensitive touch keeps couples connected from the first time they brush up against each other to the way they move in sync during intimate moments.

A woman's personal touch adds to a man's world and makes her unique in his eyes. Her touch is not just a beautifier; it's a stabilizer to men, children, pets, and ultimately the world at large. We often forget the importance of touching ourselves, our loved ones, our pets, etc.

During intimate moments people noticeably use sensuous touching more frequently. Touching is used to enhance arousal, relay affection, sensitivity and care. The pleasure of a sensitive touch keeps couples connected from the first time they brush up against each other to the way they move in sync during intimate moments. Did you know that orgasms could also be achieved through sensuous touching? When people are touching each other they aren't usually thinking about anything except that moment. They're thinking ... 'This feels soooo good, I want more.'

Sex can become more alluring if touching is incorporated before, during and after sexual acts. Changing positions regularly while touching can improve the sex act. Sex feels different when the male identity is thrusting inside the vagina at different angles and a soothing touch accompanies it.

It also feels great when different parts of the body are being touched at different intervals of sex. Figuring out what turns your lover on when you're touching at different times of the sexual act can be quite exhilarating. For example, if a woman is having sex with the man on top, he can feel her breast on his chest, her nipples rubbing against his skin, or he can feel her butt against his thighs.

Both sexes love touching, but men chose to admire the big picture whereas women love the small intricate moments that touch instills. Women are more in tune with their senses and seek the so-called pleasant surprises in everything they touch, smell, feel, see, hear and taste. They love the idea of doing things that warm their heart. If a man can touch a woman's soul he can transform her mood. Some people refer to it as "a girl thing," but it depends on the woman, the man, the time, the moment and the situation involved.

> **Heated Pleasures**
> Both sexes love touching, but men chose to admire the big picture whereas women love the small intricate moments that touch instills.

Sensuous Ways You Can Touch

There are several pleasurable ways you can become emotionally connected to your lover. First you'll need to take steps to get more in touch with your emotional side. To achieve the rich, satisfying sex you want, need and deserve, take a journey of self-awareness. With such wonderful touching going on you can discover sensuous ways to increase your sexual temperature.

> **Heated Pleasures**
> Sex has a rhythm of its own. Make your own sexual rhythm.

Besides, you and your lover will enjoy a private oasis.

Stimulate him while making love. Once you have learned the magical powers of sensuous touching combine touch with temperatures and sex. Here are several sensuous exercises that will help you enjoy your touching time.

1. Have sex without air conditioning on a warm day and enjoy as the sweat rolls down your body.
2. Have a quickie in a hot tub at its steamiest moment.
3. Try having sex on a cold winter day in the snow.
4. Use ice cubes during sex. Notice the difference.
5. Mix hot and cold temperatures during oral sex.
6. Alternate sexual adventures with hot and cold fluids to give a variety of feelings to your lover.
7. Try gently scratching him, tickling him, running your fingers through his hair or sooth him by stroking his ears.
8. Alternate soft and hard objects with cold and hot touching.
9. Oil your body, and then try rubbing him up and down, side to side and all over with your body.
10. Don't shave and then allow him to feel the true texture of your hair rubbing against his body.
11. Find soft fabrics or textures to rub against your lover's body from time to time. Find out which textures he likes more.

12. Experiment with sensuous touching in locations where you've always wanted to have sex.
13. Imagine having great sex on a cool day and experiencing the breeze sifting over your body.
14. Have sex in the woods with the sounds of autumn while the crackling of leaves on the ground rubs against your body? Have sex in the woods in the wintertime or during hot summer months with nature's scenes, or with the warmth of the sun on your back while you make love?
15. Having sex in the car makes most couples feel sensuous, even though it's a little confining when your body is pressed against the glass windows as the car steams up.
16. Try giving pleasurable body massages without sex.

To give and get the best loving touches you must know who you are, what you want and what you desire. When you know what you want you can accept pleasurable touching into your life. It helps improve your sensuality.

Touching is a do it yourself project.

Chapter 10

Enhancing Your Sexual Rhythm!

This chapter will help you become more sensitive to all the things that make you feel really good.

Although we have tremendous sensual capacity, most of us never come close to realizing our sensual potential. We've been trained to turn ourselves off to much of what surrounds us.

There are times in our lives that you'll have to slow down and feel what we are giving and receiving. During sex we should always try our best to slow down. Sometimes you can move to fast and lose your rhythm. You can lose your balance. Slow down. You need to find your own rhythm. Sex has a rhythm. Open your arms, listen to your heart; close your eyes and get in the right frame of mind. Don't lose your balance. Slow down and feel the feeling. Satisfy your soul and ease your mind. Evolve. Make sexual music. Sex has a rhythm of its own. Make your own sexual rhythm. Find your cure to what ails you. The rhythm of pleasure is the greatest remedy on earth. Let's explore a friend of mine who had lost her sexual edge due to years of emotional neglect from her partner.

You Should Know

We are rewarded for using our common sense, being sensible, having a sense of fair play, and not wasting time with utter nonsense.

My friend Marsha moved to Lewisville after living in Duncanville with an abusive husband and found that she had to desensitize herself to his name-calling and abusive behavior. In order to preserve her sanity she literally restricted her thoughts of what felt well and what was really good in her life. The atmosphere in her home was so bad that she literally placed positive post it notes in every room just to maintain her sanity. Marva had lost her rhythm.

Think for a moment about our ability to turn things off. This skill can be helpful, particularly when dealing with situations that would otherwise be intolerable. A woman may be able to turn off the critical or harmful comments received from an abuser in order to deal with him or shield her from his abusiveness. She can also turn off sexually to a less than desirable partner. However this easy process of turning off or tuning on can become a pattern that is so engrained that it ultimately limits our ability to respond appropriately to new and better situations. Even when the source of anxiety has been removed the patterns are still there. The same woman who shuts out a critical partner may turn into a woman who is not able to feel anymore.

You Should Know

She can also turn off sexually to a less than desirable partner.

The woman who has taught herself to turn off from an uncaring partner may be nonorgasmic even with someone she loves. She has to find her rhythm again. She has to find her balance. She has to find her way. Simply put she has to find her ability to love again.

When it comes to developing our senses as it relates to sexual awareness, we're truly in double jeopardy. We are encouraged to dress in the most provocative and expensive designer clothing, but we're told that we offend others when our clothes are provocative. We are told that masturbation is wrong or sinful, yet if we don't know how to please ourselves we are considered frigid and unaware of what it takes to please our men. "Nice girls don't do that until they are married," has helped numb women to sexual pleasure and sexual feelings. For many women it is an ongoing tug of war. We have become so concerned with preserving our reputation that we fail to experience any real sexual pleasure.

Learn To Tune In

Learning how to get turned on means you are learning how to tune-in sexually. The woman who is oblivious to her sexual feelings will be oblivious to her sexual needs. A sensuously tuned in woman is responsive both inside and outside the bedroom. She has found her rhythm. She lives by rhythm.

Training yourself to become more attentive takes considerable work, so the next few pages are devoted to discussing what feels good so that you can find your own sexual rhythm.

If It Feels Good To You, Do It!

In this section we will review those things that will help you feel good in most every part of your life.

- Kiss good-bye when you leave and upon returning.
- Make like spoons while sleeping. Get as close as you can. Now touch, snuggle and smooch.
- Spend the day running errands together. Stop; have lunch and run more errands. Plan dinner together and then head home for good lovemaking.
- Talk to one another each day about things that happened during the day. Really take the time to listen to one another.
- Say "Thank you" for doing small things that he's supposed to do anyway. Make him feel appreciated.
- Compliment him on how good he looks and smells.
- Touch him, feel him stroke his back and be sure to compliment his body, his attitude on a daily basis.
- Hold hands often. Send messages of happiness by touching for no reason at all.
- Snuggle ever chance you get.
- Practice simple acts of kindness. Clean, shop, dine, grocery shop together, and plan healthy activities with your children together.
- Create passion by doing loving things together.

Get Excited About Sex

- Do five things that will put a smile on your face.
- Keep a sexual journal that puts the spark back in your relationship when things get a little boring.
- Place love notes in numerous places throughout your home and car just for your lover to read.
- Kiss for more than one minute every day.
- Have romantic dates and rediscover passion.
- Enjoy a movie that both of you like.
- Wake him up with loving kisses that create passion.
- Have moments of sensuous talk and moments that make you want to make love. Do this often.

> **Heated Pleasures**
> To achieve satisfying sex you must take a journey of self-awareness.

Develop Your Sensuality

I'll bet if you asked ten women to define the word "sensuality," nine out of ten would say, "sexy." In fact sensuality is a unique dimension in and of itself, and not directly related to sex per se'. Rather, to sense means to experience as it relates to all the senses - smell, taste, touch, sound, and sight. Since sex incorporates the use of our senses, raising your level of sensual awareness and heightening sensitivity will play a major role in making you a responsive lover. When your sensuality is developed you have found your rhythm.

Pay Attention to Your Needs

When it comes to sexual pleasure its best if you pay attention to your physical needs, and emotional needs. Come away from the world's insanity so that you can evolve. Make your own music. That's why great sex can become so good that it brings you to ecstasy and makes you feel closer to your lover.

Good sex can make you throw up your hands, kick up your feet and shout with joy. Sex can be so good that it brings you to tears. Sometimes all you have to do is take the first step.

Women are so eager to please their lovers and so caught up in making them feel good that she forgets how important it is to find her own personal pleasure. She forgets that she really

Ms. Real Suggests
To keep your breath kissably fresh brush at least twice a day, floss daily see your dentist regularly, drink lots of water and eat more raw fruits and vegetables.

does like making love and sharing feelings of love. Before you can begin to discover what feels good physically, you need to take steps to get in touch with your emotional side. Here are some exercises that will help you find your way.

1. Indulge In Self-Pleasuring

Let's begin by doing something very simple. Go to a secluded spot of your choice...it would be your special place, your lounge, or your bed. This will improve your memory skills.

- *What you'll need: Assorted sized and different shaped hard objects of your choice.*

Close your eyes and let your body relax. Have a close friend or lover bring the different sized and shaped objects to your secluded place. Examples are: frozen links, cucumbers, carrots, bottles, soaps, and different shaped sponges or whatever makes you feel comfortable. Familiarize these objects. Recall their size, shape, length, width and texture. Think of each and compare their differences. What are your likes and dislikes about these objects. You'll be amazed about how good your memory is.

For a week, practice on your memory skills to increase your awareness of shapes, sizes and textures. This also improves your ability to touch your partner in sensitive and more caring ways. Another good thing you can do is change out the items each day and discovers how they come to life in your hands as you touch, feel, and caress them. Now, close your eyes and bring out your sensitive side with each touch. Get mentally lost in how each object feels. This helps you become better at visualizing things by touch, texture and size.

2. Awaken Your Senses

In this exercise you'll use your mind to arouse your sexual appetite. You'll begin to feel more sensually awakened too. If you practiced exercise one as suggested, you should be able to move into this phase with ease.

What you'll need: Your favorite lotion.

To help improve your senses, use the following exercises as a way to find mental pleasure in the smallest thing you do. These exercises are designed to help you coast into the pleasure center of your brain. Imagine …

- Slowly moisturize every part of your body that you can reach while blindfolded. Imagine the eroticism and you'll soon feel the pleasure of it.
- Massage your scalp or shampoo it in the shower with your eyes closed.

- Take a bath with your partner. Wrestle naked and continue the fun after stepping out of the tub.
- Put on some mellow music and dance slowly Control of each movement.
- Take a shower in a darkened room with a small tea light candle. Enjoy the sensuality of your body and feel the presence of you in your own world.
- Read Heated Pleasures - as erotically as you can.
- Kiss your lover passionately every time you kiss.
- Give full hugs every time you embrace your lover.

3. Show Your Appreciation

Appreciating your partner makes you feel good about your relationship. Appreciation can take many forms, from a phone call or compliment to a gift of flowers or a love note. What about dancing to his favorite music while in the nude and wearing a pair of three-inch heels. Or why not try preparing his favorite meal while he watches you move about in the nude. Do something every day that you and your partner will appreciate. I takes from you is a little effort and a creative imagination. Now is that asking too much from you?

4. Get Away Every Now and Again!

Whether it's for a few hours, a day, or a weekend you need to create a little for yourself. The best way to do this is to get away from everything and everybody. Plan a special mini-retreat alone. Be bold and creative. Make this one of the most peaceful times you plan. If you, decide to take your lover plan it as a spicy romantic date. Change your looks, your setting and do different activities than the norm. Make sure everything is positive and upbeat. Promise yourself you won't argue or bring up any problems. This is a time of planned rejuvenation, escape and coming together. Get lost in each other and shut the outside world and its problems out for a while. Sometimes it's nice to get lost.

5. Have Some Fun

Romance and sex are fun!!! Why do you think they call it "Fore-Play"? Duh! Do something wild together. Visit an amusement park, arcade or carnival without the kids! Play charades, strip poker or trivial pursuits. Go ballroom dancing or serenade each other under moonlight. Go for a canoe ride. Romance is another word for "Adult Play." Loosen up, be creative, have the kind of fun and passion you had when you first started dating? Do it again and again!

6. Fulfill Your Fantasies

Don't be embarrassed. We all have fantasies. Find out what turns your lover on and fulfill his desires. Arrange that weekend away. Greet him/her at the door in a new (sexy) outfit or in no outfit at all. Rent a costume. (Be a nurse, policeman, fireman, doctor, Indian chief, or whatever you desire.) Design the evening around your romantic fantasy. Make it the best fantasy time you've ever had.

7. Go Ordinary to Extraordinary

Transform everyday events into mini-celebrations. Eat dinner by candlelight. Enjoy breakfast or dinner in bed. Take a shower together using special soap. Give him a six-pack of his favorite beer for fixing the fence or doing the grocery shopping. Then share.

8. Be Prepared For Pleasure

Always have on hand: champagne, candles, romantic music, massage oil, some of his favorite foods, great lingerie, small gifts, romantic cards, tickets to a special event and take-out menus for when you'd rather "get cooking" than cook dinner.

9. Cultivate a Romantic Psyche

Romance is not only a state of mind it's an attitude. Romance is the art (not science) of expressing your love. It starts by thinking of you as a couple first and second as individuals. It's not just what you do, but how you do it that counts. Little heated gestures and sexy words are the glue that holds couples together. Romance is not logical or predictable. Loosen up, get creative and have some fun. Bring the heat back into your relationship by cultivating your romantic psyche.

10. Take A Break from the Kids

Send them to somebody you trust for a short while. Do it for you and your lover. Pay the babysitter to take them out for the afternoon. If all else fails: send them to bed early or place them in front of their favorite video with plenty of popcorn. Hang a do not disturb sign on your bedroom door and pop your own corn.

When it's right you'll know it and when it feels good you'll want to do it again.

Enhancing Your Kisses

This chapter will help you become a better kisser.

When was the last time you and your partner had a wonderful soul searching kiss that peaked passion, romantic interludes and a desire to get lost into one another? Was it the kind of kiss that you didn't want to end? Was it the deep soul searching kiss that let you know this man loves you and wants you badly? Or was it the kind of kiss that made you run to the nearest bathroom and rinse your mouth out?

Sadly, many times the kiss is the first sign of true intimacy. Women really enjoy kissing and if more men paid attention to the kiss they could pass first base. Many women consider romantic kissing foreplay. It should be good, stimulating, pleasant and fresh. A kiss should reach other parts of the woman's psyche... her brain, her senses and most of all it should reach deep down in her soul.

Kissing is one of the most intimate acts of affection a man and woman can share. Yet, for most couples it is the first act of affection and intimacy that's lost when they get in a long-term relationship. If your sex life is missing stimulation you can reinstate passion while kissing.

Is Your Breath Ready for Kissing

Bad breath will ruin a kiss faster than you can drop a dime. Bad breath occurs when your mouth becomes dry and stale, usually first thing in the morning or after eaten certain foods. Alcohol, certain vegetables, smoking and strong coffee may also make your breathe stink.

On days you're planning to see your lover avoid food like cheese, garlic, onion, tuna, anchovies, salami and sausages. They release odors for hours due to the oils in them. Discretely lick the back of your hand, move it in front of your nose, and take a whiff. If your breath fails the sniff test, drink some water or suck on a mint or breathe freshener to make your kiss more appealing.

Get Your Lips Ready for Kissing

Your lips have many nerve endings and are covered by a thin layer of skin. The softer and moister you keep your lips, the more responsive they are to stimulation. To get the most from your lips do the following:

- Wash your lips daily with a clean, moist washcloth to clean and exfoliate.
- Apply lip balm as needed, especially during the winter months when your lips tend to get chapped.
- During hotter months use a lip balm with sunscreen.
- Avoid licking lips frequently. They will dry out.
- Always remove lipstick before going to bed.
- Use long-lasting lipsticks in moderation. They tend to dry lips out.

Relax Your Mouth

The second step to becoming a good kisser is to keep your jaw and lips relaxed. Stiff, stingy lips make your partner feel like he's kissing

You Should Know

Face it, sometimes you'll have to teach him how you liked to be kissed and vice-versa. Playing this kissing game is a great learning experience for couples.

a vice. To prepare for great kissing do the following:

Gather some of your favorite breath mints or breathe freshener. Go get your partner and share your freshener. Prepare to play some kissing games that will also help you become more sensuous as you become better at kissing. Practice this little exercise: part your lips slightly and brush them gently against your partner's lips. Focus on the physical sensations as the nerve endings in your lips are stimulated. Are you getting excited?

Heated Pleasures

Sensuous kissing is like a sexy dance with your tongues - where couples play and chase, lead and follow and dance back and forth with one another's playful ins and outs.

Take his lower lip into your mouth as he takes your upper lip into his mouth and suck on it gently. Then switch. Take his upper lip and offer him your lower one. Do this several times, each time getting better and better at doing it. Smile at one another as you practice. Make this fun and sensuous practice time. Don't study the technique too much, simply relax and go with the flow.

After a while, slowly open your lips a bit more and extend the tip of your tongue toward his mouth and trace your partner's lip from corner to corner. Now begin relaxed mouth movements; using your tongue to sensuously play with your partner's tongue. The initial contact with your tongue can be quite arousing. Continue to touch and explore each other's tongue moving your tongues up and down, side to side, in and out, and in circular motions. Sensuous kissing is like a sexy dance with your tongues - where couples play and chase, lead and follow and dance back and forth with one another's playful ins and outs.

Watch Out

There is nothing worse than kissing a man who can't kiss.

Keep playing and now extend your tongue a little farther and explore his mouth with your tongue along his teeth, gums, and the roof of his mouth. Revel in the various textures, the stiffness of his lips, the slightly rough texture of his tongue, and the smoothness of his teeth. After a while retreat and let him explore yours.

Use your hands and fingers while kissing; rub his face, trace his mouth, massage his shoulders, rub his back hold his face, run your fingers through his hair. Wrap your arms around him and squeeze his butt. Sensuously moan and groan while kissing. He'll know how much you enjoy kissing him.

There is nothing worse than kissing a man who can't kiss. His tongue barely enters your mouth, he barely touches your lips, and when it does it darts in as fast as a snake and back out just as fast.

Slow romantic interesting tongue action is more romantic and enticing. Face it, sometimes you'll have to teach him how you liked to be kissed and vice versa. Playing this kissing game is a great learning experience for the both of you.

Incorporate Erotic Kissing

Because his body is one huge pleasure zone filled with wonderful nerve endings; any part of the body will respond to licks, sucks, nips, gentle biting and slight tugging. Start by planting soft, gentle kisses on his forehead, cheeks, eyelids, earlobes and neck leaving his lips for last. This will make him eager to pull your mouth into his, but don't let him - not yet. You're the one in gentle control during these heated moments. Sensuously kiss your way down his chest, nipples, stomach, and navel areas. Keep kissing him - going toward his pelvic area, but move slightly outward toward his hips. Slowly massage this area with your moist tongue; then moving to his inner thighs making sure not to touch his yearning penis area. This will tease him and set his soul on fire. He'll try to get you to kiss his penis, but resist it; no matter how bad you want to. Now, slowly move a little lower toward his knees and stay there a little while, this area gives him goose bumps and he'll squirm and wiggle with excitement. Then move a little lower toward his shin and onward to the top of his feet and toward his toes. Kiss every part very slowly with lingering kisses at least twice. He'll melt like butter.

Next, start moving upward to his lips, taking your time to get there. Kiss any part of the front of his body that you have missed. Take control of his body as you slowly use your hands to persuade him to roll over. While he's turning continue to kiss all the parts of his body that you desire; his shoulders, back, spine, hips, buttocks, thighs, lower legs, calves, heels and feet. Plant kisses everywhere you can think of. Plant kisses in the least likely places. Get creative and surprise him.

Heated Pleasures

Licking in and around the ear is a great turn on for most men, just as long as you don't make loud slurpy noises.

While covering his entire body with kisses, lavish his body with licks. Licking in and around the ear is a great turn on for most men, just as long as you don't make loud slurpy noises. Lick your way down his spine, lingering on sensitive spots where his buttocks and spine meet. Lick across his skin as if he's a lollipop. Notice his reaction. Pull his nipple into your mouth and kiss his nipple and around his areola.

Oral Kiss All Over

It's very natural for couples to move from kissing the mouth to other pleasurable parts of the body. The neck and throat are very sensitive areas when it receives kissing, as are the breast and nipples. It's pleasurable for both men and women to give and receive kisses so try to do it often.

"A sex symbol becomes a thing.
I hate being a thing.
-Marilyn Monroe

Chapter 12

Celebrating 'Us' Time

This chapter will help you incorporate an atmosphere that will keep the homes fires burning with sensuous lover's night in party.

Get together with your partner for soothing relaxing massages, beauty treatments, great conversation and good times by hosting a lovers night in party. It's easy to turn a normal evening with your lover into a fantastic intimate party of pampering.

Imagine that it's about midnight on a Friday, and lavender aromatherapy scents fill the air. The evening is going great. Wonderful selections of chilled wine, champagne, sparkling water, cold drinks, fresh vegetables, cheese, sliced fruit assorted meats and meats are spread out

Ms. Real Suggests
Give a spa gift of an aromatherapy candle, bath salts, neroli mist, foot balm or something sexier. It's up to you!

next to the bed. The sounds of soothing instrumental music fill the air. You and your lover are feeling good. With eyes closed, head cushioned, feet being massaged, all the while a joyous smile is planted on your face. Or maybe he's stretched out on a massage table - lying in a semi-dark private room, enjoying a firm pair of hands working methodically over all parts of his stressed body.

You could choose to experience soothing mud pack facials wrapped in fluffy white bathrobes while stretched out on a lounger with cucumbers on your eyes. The headphones are playing wonderful music while hot paraffin wax moisturizer soothes your hands and feet.

"Ummmm," "This is simply divine." You feel so good you let out a moan saying "God knows I needed this." Welcome to the latest embodiment of Lover's Time In celebrations. By day, couples lead busy lives. So to relieve stress they gather their pampering supplies, put on soft music, change clothes and let massage therapists and other professionals work their magic.

"It's a lot more intimate than a health spa," says Marva, the flight instructor. "And your time is not limited. It's very stimulating to get together with your partner for pampering, happy times, or relationships, goals.

> **Heated Pleasures**
> You will be surprised at how much you can learn about sex just by listening to someone else's fantasy.

Have you ever shared sexual fantasies with your lover? This is a great time to do it. Why not open up to your lover about some of your fantasies during this time. Talking to each other during pampering moments naturally heals and educate. Sharing intimate secrets can enhance the pleasure. To create a lover's night in all you have to do is invite your lover over for some good ole fashion pampering then work your magic on him. It's important the environment be filled with trust, positive thoughts and feelings in which all discussions are nonjudgmental and supportive.

Fantasy Time

Write down four or five of your sexual fantasies on index cards before meeting. When he arrives his fantasies are placed in a large bowl with yours. After meeting and greeting, socializing, eating and sipping on your favorite drink it's time to read the fantasies. Take turns pulling a fantasy from the bowl and reading it to one another. Be ready for laughs and rejuvenation. You'll be surprised at how much you can learn about sex by listening to someone else's fantasy. By the end of the fantasy time neither of you will be able hold back your sensuous thoughts. You'll be anxious to get your hands on one another.

Passion Time

Invite a local adult-store or Passion Party representative to give a presentation on erotic toys. The sales associate will display erotic toys, explain how they work, and offer them for sale. This can be a great learning experience. Passion Parties are designed to inform and educate women through tasteful in-home presentations. You have an opportunity to experience sensual products designed to enhance your relationships.

Field Trip Time

Take a field trip with your lover to a local adult store to explore, sample, learn and purchase. Take advantage of the wealth of knowledge available through the sales associates. They are eager to help you.

Dinner Time

Invite your lover over and have him write down his favorite recipes on several index cards. Place the cards in a bowl. When the two of you are ready, take turns making dinner over several different dates. You can take turns selecting a different recipe to cook each week. Each of you is responsible for selecting one or two of the recipes and making sure they are fulfilled within the next few weeks.

Massage Time

Throw a sensual massage party for your lover. Unwind, relax and distress with the aid of a massage. Give your lover a range of complimentary massages. Choose from the following types of massages.

Indian head massage	Aromatherapy Body massage
Hot stone massage	Indonesian massage
Ayurvedic therapy	Hopi ear candles
Holistic facial	Holistic pedicure reflexology
Cupping	Reiki
Tibetan head massage	Thai seated massage
Korean hand massage	Algae body wraps
Ayurvedic leg/foot ritual	

You Should Know

A massage helps relax you and your lover and can be accompanied by beauty treatments or other complimentary therapies.

It's up to you to choose the type of pampering treatments that you will appreciate. A massage helps relax you and your lover and can be accompanied by beauty treatments or other complimentary therapies.

Many spas bring every element of the massage to you, with a custom menu of pampering. You can enjoy luxurious treatments in the comfort and convenience of your home with the same sensory details that you experience in a spa - aromatherapy, relaxing music, candles, robes and slippers.

Look at everything as though you were seeing it either for the first or last time.

Chapter 13

Bringing the Heat to Your Bedroom

This chapter will help you enhance your bedroom environment.

W**alk** into your bedroom and run your hand across your bedspread and pillows. Do they feel soft and inviting? Are they warm or sensuous? Now look around the room. Is the atmosphere of your bedroom sensual?

Even little things such as the feel and texture of sheets can have a big effect on how inviting your bedroom is. Because you will spend nearly one-third of your life asleep

> **Watch Out**
> Bringing work and unnecessary items into the bedroom will associate your bedroom with negative emotions – stress, work and clutter, etc. This is referred to as negative anchoring.

your bedroom should be a place where you can go to renew at the beginning and relax at the end of each day.

Make your bed cozy by using cool cotton sheets during spring and autumn. Use crisp linen sheets in summer for a peaceful sleep. Cuddly flannel sheets and fluffy down comforters create a cozy refuge in the wintertime. Lay plush carpeting and wear comfortable slippers to coddle your bare feet.

A woman's bedroom should be her temple of comfort, relaxation and intimacy. It should not be cluttered with items that have nothing to do with sleep or intimacy. Your bed should have a sensuously yummy feel so that you can cuddle, make love or drift peacefully off to sleep.

Remove any dirty piles of laundry and put away the exercise gear. Hide the home computer too. Bringing work and unnecessary items into the bedroom will associate your bedroom with negative emotions – stress, work and clutter, etc. This is referred to as negative anchoring.

Remove negative memories and associations from your bedroom and you'll find that your bedroom will become a place where you can embrace and revitalize. Your bedroom is an expression of who you are. Compliment it with furnishings and beautiful items that show cleanliness, coziness, care and concern. Everything placed in the bedroom whispers hints of what kind of personality you have and what kind of woman you really are.

Is your bedroom decorated in a way that nothing about you shows in your environment? Is your personal flavor depicted in your surroundings? Take a look around and see what your bedroom says about you. Is it?

- Cluttered
- Junky
- Dirty
- Messy
- Cold
- Drafty
- Insensitive
- Warm
- Inviting
- Conservative
- Imaginative
- Sensitive

Do others see you as a person that's …?

- Caring
- Family oriented
- Faithful
- Neat
- Junky
- Messy
- Uncaring
- Religious
- Romantic
- Pet lover

Is scenery important to you? Are you cold or hot natured? Are you romantic or conventional? Are you a pack rat? Are you unclean? Do you feel healthy? Are you romantic? Are you sensuous? Are you true to yourself?

Starting today try to set goals that will help your bedroom stay pure and true. You should know what your bedroom says about you and become more tuned in to its overall presentation.

Replace the brightly lit lamps with flickering candles. Replace the dirty linens with fresh and clean items and replace old, tattered and torn rugs with rich carpet. Change old outdated curtains or blinds with sheer, or lined to update window treatments.

> **Heated Pleasures**
>
> Your bedroom should denote sensuality more than sex. Decide whether or not you want to be sensuous or sexy, or both.

Place a collection of your favorite scents where the computer once was. Place sensuous or brightly colored magazines around the room. Potpourri, flowers and bright colored candles help add beautiful touches here and there. Add a few inexpensive things or your lover's favorite colors just to make him feel at home and welcome when he's in your environment. If the relationship doesn't work you can easily change it.

Over time, you and your lover will begin to associate good times, good smells, good things and sensuality with your bedroom environment.

If the sensuous cues are powerful enough and the bedroom is free of negative anchors, you and your lover will experience an automatic and positive "sexy trance" upon entering your bedroom.

Even if you live in a small apartment or a home with limited space, you don't have to go crazy trying to make it the perfect room for intimacy. Be practical and do what you can. Once your sensuality plan is in order you'll begin to see and feel the quality of your love and lovemaking. Your bedroom should denote sensuality more than sex. Decide whether or not you want to be sensuous or sexy, or both.

Ms. Real Suggests

Replace the brightly lit lamps with flickering candles. Replace the dirty linens with fresh and clean items and replace old, tattered and torn rugs with rich carpet.

First and Last Impressions

Give your bedroom sensual serenity. Turn it into a private sanctuary by adding details and treatments that are personal and chic. Bedrooms are meant for sleeping, reading, reflecting, romancing, intimacy, recharging your battery, and escaping from the cares of the day.

The quality of sleeping you receive every day in your bedroom is very important for your happiness, health and productivity. To create your perfect bedroom, think about what you like to do in your bedroom and define a style that's appropriate.

Consider your bedroom as a sacred retreat. It's very important that your connection with every object in your bedroom elicits a positive, nurturing response. Remember to thrive for sensual instead of sexy.

> **Ms. Real Suggests**
>
> The art in your bedroom makes a strong impact on your psyche so why not make it a positive one. Include sensual, serene or romantic images that calm and inspire you.

A cozy, bedroom atmosphere invites rest and rejuvenation of your body, mind and spirit. The comfort and safety you feel in the world is directly connected to how safe and comfortable you feel in your home - bedrooms should be included.

Here is the place to plunge on fabrics that are sensual. Include chenille, flannel, silk, cotton, satin, or velvet. The view from your bed is very important; put a beautiful frame, a piece of art, or a vase of flowers that inspire and makes you dream. The art in your bedroom makes a strong impact on your psyche so why not make it a positive one. Include sensual, serene or romantic images that calm and inspire you. If you want to honor your five senses, focus on creating truly sensual environments.

Your Bedroom Environment

Before retiring at night, consider writing in your journal, reading, or reflecting on your day, rather than watching television. If you have a television in your bedroom, store it in an armoire or cabinet when you're enjoying intimate moments with your partner. Your bedroom environment can strengthen and nourish an intimate relationship. Placing importance on your bedroom environment can help you connect better with your lover.

> **Ms. Real Suggests**
> Placing importance on your bedroom environment can help you connect better with your lover.

Your bedroom should make a pleasing impression. The more active or hectic a couples lifestyle, the more crucial it is that they have a private and appealing bedroom sanctuary in which to, rejuvenate and replenish intimacy. Couples can nurture and enhance intimacy by thoughtfully creating a bedroom of allure, romance and celebration.

What is Your Bedroom Style?

Define the style of bedroom you want. Comfort is the prevailing language of all well designed bedrooms. How it is translated and interpreted depends upon the individual. To some, soothing, soft and serene is comforting. To others, clean lines are most relaxing, while still others find plush, opulence the most blissful. Bedrooms are as individual as you are. To create yours, simply "follow your dreams" and use your personal likes to bring it to life. Plan your bedroom design with private times in mind, beginning with the purpose of the bedroom.

There are several important factors you should consider. Let's discuss them.

Creating a Relaxed Bedroom

What are some of the most enjoyable ways to soothe your senses of sight, hearing, smell, touch, and taste? Make a list of what engages and delights each sense, then add to it as you think of new ideas. If you share a bedroom, ask your partner what he or she is sensually nurtured by, and incorporate those ideas as well. You should be struck with happiness each time the beautiful qualities of your bedroom come to mind.

Close your eyes and imagine the most comforting bedroom you can think of. Imagine a pile of fluffy pillows, a lofty down comforter, and stream of natural light warming the room. Soft colors and patterns, blond wood floors, white sheer draperies swaying in the breeze, if you think about that, the relaxed-style bedroom is for you.

The relaxed-style bedroom is made for sunny afternoon naps and leisure weekend mornings spent reading in bed. It is soft, nurturing and peaceful. The relaxed bedroom is perfectly suited for a beachfront cottage or a cabin in the woods.

You Should Know

The relaxed bedroom is a celebration of simple and honest detail.

The relaxed bedroom is a celebration of simple and honest detail. All your senses are nurtured with the freshness and calmness of the room. Every element must be chosen for its ability to bring visual and emotional serenity to the space. The floors should be soft underfoot with polished wood, scattered rugs, or natural sisal. The walls padded in sun-washed colors, may be covered with painted paneling, floral or striped papers, or satin-finished paint.

You Should Know
Your bedroom can be a temporary escape from your daily routine as it transports you to some tropical island.

Cool and tranquil, blue and white are classic color companions in a relaxed bedroom. A splash of bright sunny yellow or spring green brings warmth to the space and adds cheer.

This kind of bed can be grand and impressive or low and understated. In either case, it is the linens that cover it that set the tone for the room. Buy quilted cotton, soft linen, and warm woolen blankets mixed and matched with downy pillows and cushy bolsters.

Creating an Exotic Bedroom

If you want an exotic bedroom, all it takes are a venturesome spirit, a discerning eye, and imaginative details. Your bedroom can be a temporary escape from your daily routine as it transports you to some tropical island. Choose a statement piece; a unique bed, distinctive piece of artwork or sculpture, or perhaps an exotic rug or fabric. You may choose a plantation style canopy bed, and then stylize it with bamboo flooring, grass-cloth wall coverings, and a large breezy ceiling fan. Use materials and colors from cool seaside hues and bleached driftwood to spicy Mediterranean colors and chiseled stone.

You Should Know
The relaxed bedroom is a celebration of simple and honest detail. All your senses are nurtured with the freshness and calmness of the room.

Choose the accents and accessories, potted palms, tribal textiles, animal prints, and one-of-a-kind-lamps. Today the products and designs from around the world are more accessible, so creating an exotic bedroom is easy. All you need is a sense of adventure. For example, African drums create unique nightstands and accent tables. Asian temple doors make wonderful room separators and headboards. Beaded shawls and embroidered textiles fabricate fascinating pillows, draperies, and table runners. Tribal rugs make head-turning blankets.

Many cultures use unique carvings and woodwork to put their own signature of style on distinctive furnishings. Incorporating these pieces into your décor instantly imparts the flavor of the land from which it came.

Creating a Passion Boudoir

Today's homemakers often plan for sex and decorate creating evocative, enticing bedrooms. Here are a few suggestions for creating a Passion Boudoir: Flattering colors contribute to personal beauty and are erotically appealing. Choose seductive colors like rouge red, lipstick reds, creamy peaches, and subtle pinks. Make sure the colors enhance your natural beauty. Be daring and use bold colors on the walls.

Luscious fabrics will set the stage for sensuousness. Use silky, velvet, and chenille textures in combination with fluff textures. Use fabrics that remind you of a favorite-shared memory. Exotic patterns, such as animal prints or floral prints can conjure images of faraway journeys.

> **Heated Pleasures**
>
> The comfort and safety you feel in the world is directly connected to how safe and comfortable you feel in your home - bedrooms should be included.

Placing mirrors in unusual places, such as the tops of dressers or side tables, reflect dancing candlelight. Tropical plants and trees, uplift with special lights, also cast exciting shadows.

An intimate bistro table, set with two chairs, invites private conversations. Dressing tables, furnished with feminine accessories and intimate objects, add mystery and romance to a room.

The presence of a bed tray suggests the possibility of the ultimate pleasure: breakfast in bed, while soft lighting, candles, essential oils in a diffuser, and gentle oscillating fans effectively complete the décor in a Passion Boudoir.

Creating a Bedroom Sanctuary

Perhaps you'd rather turn your bedroom into a personal retreat where you can escape and unwind from a busy day. Surround yourself with photos of friends, family, and places you love, as well as your favorite artwork and meaningful mementos. Under-furnished private sanctuaries can also give you the space to contemplate and daydream.

> **You Should Know**
> Make sure the colors enhance your natural beauty. Be daring and use bold colors on the walls.

Good colors for private sanctuaries include dark Forest Greens, deep Chocolates, Mochas, Navy or Cobalt Blues. Darker colors create a womb-like feeling and aid deep sleep. A small refrigerator will help you enjoy time in the bedroom. Room-darkening window coverings also encourage deep sleep and aid in the restoration of your soul.

Creating a Bedroom Pleasure Zone

Here are things you can do to make your bedroom a pleasure zone that you and your lover will enjoy.

- Paint the walls a warm inviting color.
- Purchase nightstands and lamps if you don't have any.
- Place a few erotic photos, books and sensuous statuettes in strategic locations.
- Place several exotic plants in your bedroom. Use some of the petals from the flowers to tickle him from time to time.
- Bring a fur rug or huge soft and fluffy throw into your bedroom. Include fabrics that will invite touching, feeling and comfort. Fabrics that feel like smooth silk, soft cotton, silky satin, rich velvet, overstuffed pillows, cozy comforters, and fluffy bedspreads are most inviting. These fabrics make him want to touch your skin as well.
- Play soft and sensuous music. Compromise with the music you like and play a little of his and a little of yours. Be sure to play his favorite tunes. Once you get the music started find a reason to leave the room for a short while. This allows him to become relaxed while listening to his favorite

music. Upon your return be sure you focus on him and not the music.

- Scatter pleasant scents around the room. Fresh and clean are considered the best smells, but other scents will enhance his pleasure zone. Placing scents that he likes around the room will remind him of you when he smells those scents again.
- Keep chilled wine or his favorite drink on hand. It's great for sipping before, during and after intimate moments.
- Have a picnic in bed. Include his favorite finger foods and be sure to have plenty of fresh fruits and vegetables for him. The things he likes in bed should be a part of your "List of things to bring." Don't forget the napkins.
- Place soothing colored lights in various outlets. Red, or pink lights are great! To help things get heated dance sensuously while dimmed lights shadow the background.
- Candles are great illuminators for soft lighting. Scented candles are even better. The flickering of the candlelight can help lovemaking become more exciting.

- Make sure the bed linens are clean, fresh and a pleasure to lie upon. Lots of pillows and soft, plush blankets are highly recommended.
- Place a props and supplies box beside your bed. (See the Chapter on Hope Chests) Keep your sex toys, games, condoms, body oils, scents, clean towels, tissues, erotic literature and other sexual props here.
- Battery operated boyfriends (aka vibrators) silk scarves, beads, stockings, breath mints, will help keep you in bed.
- Find out what colors he likes and have touches of his favorite colors on hand. If he's crazy about jazz be sure to have it. If he likes peanut butter, have some for him. Whatever he likes - be sure to have it. Stock up, let the passion flow and work on becoming the sensuous lover you can be.
- Let him see you wearing your most sensuous clothing without underwear so that all day he'll think of you.
- Keep an assortment of ribbed and studded condoms. Light a candle and tell your lover he can do anything he likes to you - while candles are lit.

- Live in the sexual moment. Keep your mind, body and spirit where you are - with the person you're with.

A woman's bedroom should be her temple of comfort, relaxation and intimacy.

Part 4

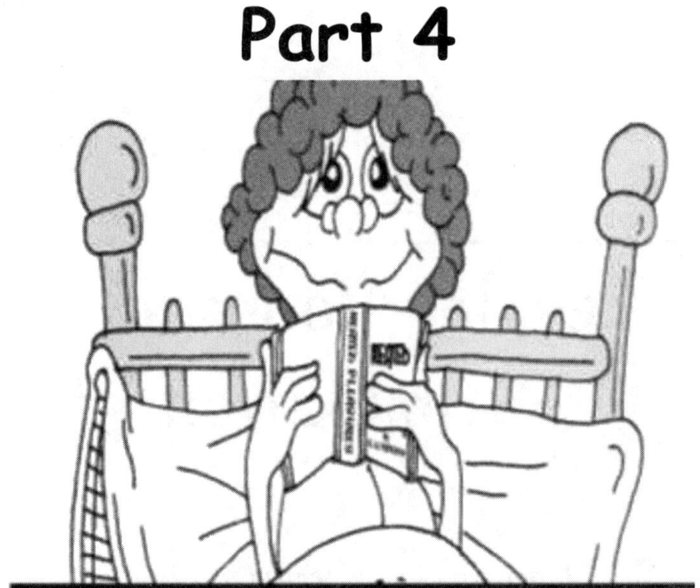

Incorporate Stimulating Pleasures

Chapter 14

Giving Yourself Stimulation

When you really need to get in the mood the first and most important thing you need to do is get yourself in the mood. Every woman's level of sexuality varies in how they like to relax and get themselves ready. Some are in the zone just by lying on the bed and reading an erotic story. You may want to take a shower or a bath and rub on some moisturizing cream or light a few candles. You may even like some relaxing background music to get you in the mood. If you are planning on using a sex toy make sure you have it close at hand. Whatever it is that makes you feel good and puts you in the mood then that's what you should do.

Make sure you have privacy; you don't want to be interrupted halfway to ecstasy. Always make sure you won't be disturbed, put your phone on silent and close the door. Now you're in the mood, comfortable, relaxed and feeling a little frisky let's move to the next step.

Self-stimulation for Beginners

Ms. Real Suggests
Get to know your toys on a personal level.

If you're a beginner, lie on your back with your legs straight and bend your knees to expose more of your love button and vulva. Do what feels good, whether you're placing a vibrator directly on your love button or alongside of it. If your vibrator is shaped like a male identity you may enjoy penetration. When you're pleasuring yourself you don't have feel pressure to have an orgasm, simply concentrate on what feels good to you.

Before we can experience sensuality, touch and pleasure with a lover, it is important to explore her body, to pleasure it, and to appreciate it.

Yes ladies - you can't always blame your lover for your failure to launch. Take a good look at your sensual world, your relationship with yourself, your sensuality and erotic sensibilities.

You and Your Vibrator

Once you've selected a vibrator, you should get to know it more intimately. Initially, I suggest you experiment with your new toy alone - so you can figure out what works best for you before you share it with your partner. Find a quiet, private place and carve out some 'get-to-know-your-vibrator-time.' Take your time and enjoy your self-pleasuring without being disturbed. To increase your pleasure and prevent friction burns, use some water-based lubricant to moisten your vagina and vulva as well as the vibrator. For the most pleasure, keep the lubricant at room temperature or a little warmer. If you have a battery-operated vibrator, you can warm the end of it in warm water.

Begin by asking yourself a few questions:

- Have you experienced female self-pleasuring?
- Are you aware of sensual sensations of your body?

- Are you aware of the emotional feelings associated with your body? Your sexuality? Sexual power?
- Do you know what words, actions, and touches give you more pleasure?
- Do you know what things relax you, your mind and body? Is it food, music, candles, the feelings of silk on your soft skin?

Well when you have answered these questions, explored yourself, always keep in mind that you are a powerful sexual goddess and you deserve to be treated with respect, love, appreciation, pleasure and admiration - by yourself as well as your lover.

Nurture with Self-Pleasuring Tips

1. Set the mood, create the scene. From the answers to the questions, prepare your most ideal environment, i.e. one which helps you to relax, enhance your senses and sensuality.
2. Think music, lighting, fragrance, cushions, oils, toys, clothing - or lack of!
3. Relax mind, body and soul. Have a slow luxurious soak, or give yourself a massage.

4. Slowly begin touching yourself (leaving the genitals until the end). Stroke, caress, and admire your body, your hands, legs, stomach. Some women feel uncomfortable admiring themselves and their bodies. If any such feels come up just note them and let them go. Don't stop and analyze, just continue touching and pleasuring your body, and make sure your last thought or feeling is a positive one.
5. Feel the energy begin to flow around the body. Feel your skin start to tingle, your breathing deepen.
6. Now start to stroke and caress your breasts, touching them slowly in admiration. Stroke your nipples, feel the skin on the breasts tingle and the energy flow around them.
7. After at least 20minutes of body sensual touching, you can proceed to the intimate areas. Lightly caress your yoni (the tantric word for Vagina which means sacred space), clit, lips. And any area you wish to explore!
8. If you experience waves of intense pleasure and emotion simply note them, breathe slowly and deeply and let these feelings go. Always end on a positive thought and feeling. Continue with your female self-pleasuring.

9. Explore your inner erotic beauty by inserting a finger slowly into your **yoni** - just to within an inch or two initially. Note the physical and sensual sensations - the heat, moisture, and textures. Insert another finger if you're comfortable. Explore your yoni, g-spot, vary your touch, and drape a lovely silk scarf over the area. Tease your clitoris, starting at the base of the clit and moving towards the head.
10. (If indulging in intimate massage - make sure you use organic, cold-presses virgin oils such as almond, olive and sesame. Do not use essential oils in any form - on or near the genitals).
11. Allow the powerful erotic and sensual sensations to build and flow in waves throughout the body. Bring yourself close to climax, then slow down breathe deeply and start again. Do this a number of times to allow you to be in a state of arousal and pleasure for good amount of time.
12. Enjoy the sensations until you can't take it anymore. Claim and enjoy your female sexual power - the greatest power on the planet!
13. If touching yourself feels good and the way you plan to go about it causes no risk of injury, then you should seriously go for it.

14. Self-pleasure or masturbation is a great way to have some solo fun or just release a little tension. Masturbating will also relight your inner flame if your sex drive is somewhat lacking. The more sex we have the more our body wants/needs, so masturbating 2 or 3 times a week can rapidly have you wanting more sex more often.
15. So, if you'd like to know a little more about self-pleasure and bringing yourself to climax let's get started.
16. Masturbation is a great way to find what turns you on and what kinds of physical touching and fantasies make you most likely to reach the big 'O'.

Stimulating Your Clitoris

Now is where the fun begins. Women are very lucky to have this little gem called a clitoris. The clitoris purpose for a woman is to bring sexual pleasure. Don't waste your sexuality by never discovering how to benefit yourself with your clitoris. It is there for your enjoyment only, so start making the most of it. The clitoris when aroused grows a little bigger in size. This is the female version of the penis, so you can stroke it and play with it in much the same way. It's yours, don't be afraid to play. Slowly begin to gently rub your fingers over your clitoris. For some ladies rubbing directly may be too sensitive. Try rubbing around the area instead for a more indirect contact. You will learn to know how and where to touch yourself for the best feeling the more you play. Your body will respond to your senses. It will know exactly what feels good and what doesn't.

When you began to get excited you might want to bring your vibrator or sex toy in on the fun. Your vibrator is great for more exciting stimulation. Gently pass the head of the vibrator around the clitoral area. Don't place it directly on the clitoris yet. Stimulate with your vibrator around the area of the clitoris and slowly move it toward and then on your clit as you get the desire to become more excited. If your clit is too sensitive simply turn down the speed of the vibration. You can also use a piece of fabric to put between you and the toy to lessen the effect. There are many vibrators to choose from, you may want to try different toys on different days with different speeds and vibrations. Always use a lubricant when using sex toys to ensure you don't cause yourself any harm.

Ms. Real Suggests

Be careful not to shoot strong streams of water into your vagina as this could cause trapped air (which isn't pleasant).

The removable shower head is also very sensually stimulating. If you can regulate the flow of water find a setting that gives you a steady stream of water building up to a strong jet and move it around letting the H2O stimulate your senses. Be careful not to shoot strong streams of water into your vagina as this could cause trapped air (which isn't pleasant).

Heated Pleasures

When it comes to pleasuring your body will say a lot more than your words. When you like what you're getting your body will respond in positive ways.

Some women enjoy a pillow between their legs to rest against. Squeeze your thighs around a nice soft pillow or cushion or any other soft object you prefer. Start to gently rock your pelvis up and down causing the fabric to gently stimulate your clitoris. This is a nice feeling as you are not touching yourself so it feels like someone else. Imagine rubbing yourself against and squeezing on your ideal man's thigh for example.

There are so many ways you can stimulate this tiny little pleasure spot so find one that suits you. With all the above methods its best if you start off massaging your clitoris slowly then gradually build up how intensely you touch it as you are reaching your climax. Then as you climax, ease off as it will be incredibly sensitive to touch. Sometimes it's almost unbearable to touch the clitoris once orgasm has been reached. Sometimes on other occasions you will be able to ride the orgasm into a second wave of ecstasy, these orgasms are the best.

Stimulating Your Vagina

Sometimes you want nothing more than good penetrative sex. In this case you need to call in the trusty dildo. A dildo is a non-vibrating sex toy that will happily replace your fella's penis. They are also plentiful on the market and come in an abundance of shapes and sizes. With the dildo thrusting inside you, you still have a free hand to stimulate your clitoris. This gives you the best of both worlds. It takes a little more effort but is a lot of fun. You can always use your fingers if you don't like the idea of a dildo. With great stimulation, hopefully the vagina becomes well lubricated. If a long time is spent here even the juiciest woman can start to dry out, so it never hurts to have a nice vaginal lubricant handy. K-Y Jelly is

> **Ms. Real Suggests**
> I strongly recommend plenty of foreplay before allowing a man to dive into your feminine area. At least half an hour or longer is fine

recommended highly and it can be found at any pharmacy, but there are lots of alternatives. Don't use Vaseline or baby oil. Vaseline is too thick and baby oil is too thin.

Stimulating Your Breasts

Squeezing and flicking the nipples can also add to the enjoyment of all of the above. Your nipples will shrink and harden when aroused; sometimes just running a fingertip gently around the nipple can cause all kinds of wonderful sensations.

There is no wrong or right way to masturbate so don't dismay. You can be dressed or undressed, sitting up or lying down, whatever feels good for you is the right way. Get to know your body, every nook and crevice could be holding some sensual delight, if you don't explore you won't find out.

Your breasts are an erogenous zone and should never be overlooked.

Chapter 15

Man Stimulating the Woman

This chapter will help you discover fun erotic sexual pleasure.

Your G-Spot!! The G- Spot is the nickname for the Grafenberg spot, one of the most sensuous areas a woman possesses. It's analogous to the prostate in men, which seems to play a more direct role in sex and procreation. A woman's G-spot is a flat area about as big as a nickel, two inches inside the vagina. It's just behind the pubic bone, on the vagina wall that is closest to the belly button. You can reach it with your index finger. It is the gland located behind the pubic bone and around the urethra.

Heated Pleasures

It's very important to have a lover who doesn't mind talking about sex and will gladly give caring instructions before, during and afterwards.

If already aroused, some women find stimulating this area leads to an intense orgasm of different quality than that of a love button orgasm. Stimulation of this spot produces a variety of initial feelings: tickle, slight discomfort, feeling the need to urinate, or a unique yet pleasurable feeling. If the woman is not very aroused she might have difficulty feeling it and the man will have difficulty finding it. The trick is to get the genitals very aroused, and then stimulate the G-spot. The best way to arouse is probably cunnilingus, which is Latin for having a lick, but any technique that provides good stimulation of the love button will do for starters. With additional stroking this area may begin to swell and the sensations may become more pleasurable.

Continued stimulation may produce an intense orgasm. Like the prostate, the G-spot can produce a fluid like semen (but not as much), which may be released on orgasm - it's even known to "squirt" a couple of centimeters.

> **Heated Pleasures**
> Unless the female is coming (having an orgasm), the man will find that the vagina is reasonably form fitting, although some are tighter or looser than others.

I strongly urge and recommend that you incorporate plenty of foreplay before allowing a man to dive into your feminine area. At least half an hour or longer is fine. Once you've achieved a state of interest, allow him to slowly start stimulating your love button (clitoris). Good love takes time. You've got to be really careful, because the love button (clitoris) is very sensitive, and too much stimulation is not really a good thing. Also, different love buttons like different things. Some like very direct stimulation and some prefer one side or the other, and others are so sensitive that they like fondling of the love button hood or the labia. Some like a circular motion, and others like to be lightly flicked back and forth. What's your preference? The best way to find out what your love button likes is to pay attention to what feels good and what doesn't. Start with some gentle experimenting. That's fun too, but don't get impatient if it takes a little while to figure out what works for you. Every woman's body is uniquely different. A man can entertain himself by running his finger around the inside of the vagina, trying to learn more about its shape. If the female is not coming or c consciously causing contractions the man will probably find that the vagina isn't doing anything in particular, just sitting there producing lubricant. If he brings his finger to the front wall of the vagina he'll find it less yielding than the rest, because there is a bone in front of it called the pubic bone, part of the pelvis. If he feels along this unyielding section or just beyond it he'll find a slightly raised area. This is the G-spot. It might not be raised, but it will engorge once a woman becomes excited and starts to come.

Heatology
Masturbation helps you maintain your sexuality when you are not in a partner relationship

He shouldn't poke this spot or do anything with it because it will be distracting. He's got to wait for the female to start to come. Now this might happen in thirty seconds, or it might take an hour. He's has to be patient and keep his rhythm regular and smooth. Unless the female is coming (having an orgasm), the man will find that the vagina is reasonably form fitting, although some are tighter or looser than others.

He'll be able to recognize she is coming when she: 1) tells him, 2) moans a lot, 3) her breathing changes or escalates, 4) her face flushes, and 5) her neck, chest and vagina begins to flutter rhythmically. A man may see and feel all of these things, or none of them. If he misses an orgasm, he shouldn't stop unless he or she wants him to. Women have startling recuperative powers, particularly when they're receiving the right level of attention. Each lover should learn about one another's intimate needs, and desires. They should be willing to keep communication open by adding variety. Here are eight sensual favorites that women agreed they wanted and needed. A man should:

- ### Rub the love button

  The up-and-down motions work better than side-to-side or circular. Vary it from time to time, but up and down on the love button usually works best.

- ### Push your finger in

  When using a finger or two inside of the vagina one of the better motions is to push the finger all the way in, then bend it slightly when pulling it out, so that it slides against the top of the vagina. Not only does this feel great; it gives the man a chance at hitting your G-spot. If he does hit it, he'll recognize he's done it by your reaction. He should work at finding your G-spot and use this knowledge to his advantage. Remember that's the best place to rub when you're getting very close to orgasm.

❖ Be consistent

A man can vary his angle and fingering style during the session, but shouldn't change too often. When the woman is close to orgasm, he shouldn't change unless she tells him to. He can move a little faster and pump his finger a little further into your vagina, but he shouldn't switch when you're near orgasm. It sort of knocks her orgasm back a bit, and that can be frustrating.

❖ Listen

Most importantly, when you're getting closer to orgasm, you'll need the man to do something more. Harder, faster, rougher! You know what you need. It will help your orgasm if your man simply listens to you and does what you say. This is for you, after all.

❖ Focus on more than the genital area

It takes a lot of concentration to get fingered. It makes you feel better and increases your general body sensitivity if he nips at your thighs, rubs your stomach or breast with his free hand. Mostly, it helps you feel like you're more than genitals and that means a lot to any woman's general pleasure. He might even stop from time to time to hug and kiss you. It gives both partners a break and preserves the intimacy.

❖ Touch yourself as he watches, and then ask him to mimic you.

In fact, the first few times, he may want to ask you to finger yourself so that he can watch. He should rub your love button, so that he can take care of one of those aspects. You can have him try more ways that make you feel good in other areas too.

❖ He can make you feel like a person by talking during the act

He can tell you you're pretty. He can ask if what he's doing feels good. He can tell you he wants you to do and what he likes doing to you. That helps keep the intimacy going, making you feel like more than a vagina.

❖ Don't pull his finger out too quick

Unless it's part of hard, fast thrusts his finger should stay in or come out very gradually. Ripping it out all at once can be very uncomfortable or painful. Sliding it very slowly can tease. He should make sure he looks in your eyes and smile when he does this. You'll love him more for it.

Some women like it rougher or faster than others. Some like more vaginal stimulation; others simply want the love button stimulated. It boils down to reading each other's reaction and asking for help. Communication helps both lovers find out what each other want. If both lovers are willing and ready to learn, things will be just fine.

When You Start To Come

Once the man believes that you are coming he should shift his attention from your love button to your G spot. He should keep the same rhythm, but use slightly more gentle pressure. He may want to keep some sort of contact with your love button, but just as his male identity (penis) becomes super-sensitive during orgasm, to the point of discomfort, so can your love button.

As with the love button, he should pay attention to whether you push towards him,

Heated Pleasures

When the vagina begins to contract the lover should go back to the G-spot, keeping the rhythm smooth and continuous. The contractions mean you want more.

draws away from him or he should just try to gauge the amount of pressure he's giving. He probably won't need to vary his speed much, but pay attention to what you say you want. You can help with this by telling him you like the way it feels. If he's smart he'll catch on to your clues. If he's a little slow help him do the things you like.

Now as he goes for your G-spot he'll find that you'll keep coming for longer than he's seen before. He may even experience that most startling of sexual phenomena, a female ejaculation. It's difficult to say whether the fluid comes from the vagina or the urethra. It's quite nice, sort of like salad dressing. It's definitely not urine.. The man should keep aiming for your G-spot. Eventually he will feel your vagina draw away from his finger - it becomes fluffier and the walls get taut, and not form fitting, sort of like a little cave. When this happens it’s time to switch back to the love button. Keep up the same rhythm. When the vagina begins to contract the lover should go back to the G-spot, keeping the rhythm smooth and continuous. The contractions mean you want more.

Heated Pleasures
As with the love button, he should pay attention to whether you push towards him, draws away from him or he should just try to gauge the amount of pressure he's giving.

If he keeps this up for a while (and if your female genitals wants to stop, then stop - this isn't a competition), he'll find that the nature of the vagina contractions changes. This doesn't mean you want to stop; you simply need a change of activity. The cave effect becomes less and less frequent and he can spend more time with the G-spot. Also, the contractions in your vagina become less simple squeezing and fluttering, and more a sort of reverse swallowing - a contraction that starts deep within the vagina and travels to its entrance. It feels like the vagina is trying to push his finger out.

Eventually he feels nothing but these push-out contractions, and he can go on as long as the woman wants to, (it takes time and patience and many tries) and hopefully his tongue and fingers don't wear out. If this goes on for a long time he'll certainly need some extra lubricant. Use it if it's needed. There you have it. Women can have orgasms that last hours and seem to be much better than those that men can have.

Heated Pleasures

If both lovers are willing and ready to learn, things will be just fine.

A Closer Look at Pleasuring

For those who never had a close look at a vulva and are a bit worried, except when aroused, female genitals are usually clearly detectable. The love button likes to hide under its own little hood, the lips stick pretty close to one another, and if the owner of the genitals is standing up and not aroused you won't really see more than some enticing hair and maybe the outer lips.

> **Heatology**
> People whose knowledge of a woman's genitals that derived from Playboy pictorials may be surprised that there's more here than "just a hole".

People whose knowledge of a woman's genitals that derived from Playboy pictorials may be surprised that there's more here than "just a hole". Traditionally, it was thought that all of the sensations available from the female genitals derived from the lips, and the love button. It was thought that the interior of the vagina was practically numb to sexual sensation. But that's not true because the vagina and its counterparts love to be touched.

A Sensual Note:

With the G-spot exercises women will see increased vagina strength and control. When men practice they will see increased ejaculation strength and sexual stamina. Both genders will see greatly increased pleasure and more intense, longer lasting orgasms.

Sex never guarantees he'll like you, love you, commitment to you, or even a phone call.

Chapter 16

Woman Stimulating the Man

This chapter will help familiarize and how to incorporate sexual pleasure in your relationship.

First things are first. Every woman should look at and then examine her man's male identity (penis). I don't mean a short glance; it should not be a hurried, surreptitious examination. You should also take time and talk to him about it. Convince him that some kind of treat is in store for him provided he will allow you to do pleasurable things with his male identity. Make it fun and enjoy playing erotic games with him and his male identity.

We've spent a considerable amount of time studying the female G-spot: How to find it, how to stimulate it and how to turn a woman into putty with a G-spot orgasm. Men are far less familiar with is their own male G-spot. The prostate is, essentially, the male equivalent of a woman's G-spot — but yours is far, easier to find.

Discover His G-spot

The male G-spot isn't all that difficult to find, but it does require a little patience. The most comfortable position for this is while he's lying on his back. Use the bed or perhaps a large sofa. The process will be easiest with his legs elevated, which he can do by leaning his legs against the wall behind the bed or draping them over the back of the sofa. If he's still having difficulty reaching the perineum from this position, you can lift his backside further by sliding a pillow or two under his bum.

Once you've made him as comfortable as possible, start by gently massaging the area surrounding his anus. Most men enjoy having their perineum stimulated, and that can certainly be incorporated into this process. Use your index finger while exploring, and be gentle. As you relax further, lube your finger up and let it gently brush across the surface of your anus. Repeat this move several times, each time increasing the pressure slightly. When he's comfortable enough to let you probe keep things slow and gentle, taking care to tell him to relax your sphincter during the process. Once you've come in contact with the male G-spot, you'll recognize it as a small, chestnut-sized bump situated approximately two inches inward.

Stimulating His G-spot

The first step in stimulating the male G-spot is making oneself comfortable. Bathing beforehand can put a man more at ease with the process, so we recommend starting out with a nice hot shower. If you'd like to take that one step further, enemas are not at all uncommon and you may choose to add this to your regimen. Once you're ready for stimulation, there are a number of methods you can utilize, though we recommend keeping it simple if you're a novice; a finger will be sufficient for beginners. Regardless, you'll want a good supply of lubrication on hand, and you'll want

Heated Pleasures

The love button likes to hide under its own little hood, the lips stick pretty close to one another, and if the owner of the genitals is standing up and not aroused you won't really see more than some enticing hair and maybe the outer lips.

the type specifically created for anal play.
It will take some experimentation to discover what works best for you in terms of stimulation. Return to one of the positions we mentioned earlier (asking him to lie on his back with his legs and backside elevated) and repeat the steps you used to locate the prostate. As you prepare to stimulate his G-spot, keep in mind that some men enjoy gentle thrusting movements, and some prefer intense, constant pressure on the prostate itself or he might prefer a mix of the two or something entirely different.

The key is to give his body the chance to react and respond; take your time, the orgasm is worth it. It's also important to note that he may not find any of these methods pleasurable during the first exploration, and that's perfectly normal; the two of you can always try again in the future.

His Male Identity (Penis)

Are you concerned with your man's penis size? Is it large or small or somewhere in between? No male body part has received greater attention than the size of his male identity. A man's obsession with the size of his male identity is probably a mental vestige of his primitive past, but as far as human sexuality is concerned it's a waste of time.

A large penis doesn't have any effect on a woman's physical enjoyment unless she has a deep-seated psychological attachment to well-endowed men. Therefore size only matters to the woman involved.

What About its Shape?

Is it curved like a boomerang or is it straight like an arrow? Is it short? Is it long? Is it wide or skinny? Does your fist fit around the spongy mass of the shaft? Does your hand completely engulf it? Can you squeeze it all at once?

Being able to appreciate all of this is good, but a woman should not be an organ grinder. She should be gentle, yet firm. If the male identity has an unusual girth, her hand may not completely encircle it. In such cases, she can try both hands to insure she doesn't miss any of his sensitive areas while stroking.

Exploring His (Penis)

A woman should explore every square inch of her man's genital surface area. Be sure to look at the entire male identity. Study it. Learn its areas of special sensitivity and be ready to apply your knowledge to his body with your tongue and lips. Here's how she can get from one point of the penis to the next.

- **Look At It**

  Have him lie flat on his back in a well-lit room. Take his male identity (penis) in your hand and LOOK at it. He will not have the will power to remain soft. What man could stay soft when you are holding it, looking at it and worshipping it?

- **Touch It**

  When you touch his male identity it will become stiff and more sensitive to stimulation by your lips, tongue or hands. The first thing you will note is the size of it, which shouldn't make a lot of difference at this point. Just hold it and respect it for a while. Once you are comfortable with holding it move on to the next phase. Take the time to notice whether or not he's circumcised. You should know this about any penis you play with.

- **Look at the Shaft**

  Next, take a close look at the shaft of the male identity. There is a bulbous part of the organ near the outer end, slightly larger in diameter than the shaft, that's called a head. Technically this is the glans of the male identity (comes from the Latin glans which means acorn.) Look at it closely; it does kind of look like an acorn doesn't it?

❖ Explore the Outside

The outside perimeter of the glans is the corona. This joins the head to the shaft. This is the most sensitive spot on the male identity. It is toward this ridge that you will direct most of your attention when you are giving a blowjob. Follow this ridge around to the underside.

❖ Find His Most Sensitive Spot

Notice the point of juncture where the two ends of this irregular circle come together. If he is not circumcised, this is where the foreskin is attached. This tiny area is easily the most sensitive spot on his entire body, and it is possible to bring him to climax simply by gently tapping the tip of the tongue directly on it. Spend time caressing the glans and those areas immediately surrounding it.

❖ What's Beneath the Glans?

Beneath the glans is the shaft. The shaft does not have many nerve endings and doesn't provide a high degree of stimulation for men when caressed either manually or with the tongue. Many women believe that sucking up and down on the shaft will get a man off. That's not necessarily true!

❖ The Testicles

Beneath the shaft are the testicles (family jewels, or whatever you like to call them, but let's not ignore their significance). The family jewels are extremely sensitive to pain and a woman can add a high degree of pleasure for him by giving his family jewels the right kind of gentle attention.

❖ Where Does Semen Spurt?

Now let's go back to the shaft of the matter. The opening in the tip of the glans is the meatus. Here is where the semen spurts. Be sure to roll your tongue around it, up and down on it and spend valuable time here. It's very sensitive. Flicker and slap your tongue against it from time to time. He'll love it. There is no greater love a woman can show for him than the attention she provides his male identity!

Circumcised vs. Uncircumcised

During the Roman Empire, a man's foreskin; uncircumcised; or draped male identity was important cosmetically to conform to the ideals of beauty. Athletic games required foreskin to cover the glans (head of the penis). Many athletes came from N. Africa and E. Mediterranean, where circumcision was common. Some physicians believed that circumcision was a means to discourage masturbation because it shortened the foreskin.

Circumcision became popular in the United States in the 19th century for the same reason. Today circumcision serves no purpose and it certainly doesn't prevent masturbation though it is suggested and justified as a hygiene measure. A circumcised penis is easier to keep clean.

To clean uncircumcised male identity's a woman would only need to spend a few seconds to get it perfectly tidy. When erect, circumcised and uncircumcised male identities look and feel much the same. Many women have refused an uncircumcised lovers penis because of the extra skin. They feel that the uncircumcised male identity is not very attractive or unclean. They feel that it is unhealthy to participate in sex with an uncircumcised male. This is a myth since most all men are born with an uncircumcised male identity.

Watch Out

Phimosis is an abnormal constriction of the foreskin that prevents it from being drawn back to uncover the glans penis.

Times Have Changed.

When I wrote my first sexuality book; 'Will the Real Women Please Stand Up' (Simon & Schuster), sixty-two percent of the women said that they wouldn't dare perform oral sex on an uncircumcised male identity.

Now, only 25% say they wouldn't. I guess time really does bring about a change. From the first group 46% felt that an uncircumcised male identity was unattractive and nonsexy, and that would keep them from making love to an uncircumcised man.

Today only 22% of women think an uncircumcised penis is unattractive, and does not feel that it would keep them from making love to a man. Of that same group 15% felt that it carried an odor that was not very enticing when making love.

You Should Know

The prostate is the gland that produces most of the seminal fluid that is ejaculated (other than sperm in semen).

Understanding Penile Phimosis

There are men who experience the lack of a full erection due to the prepuce being too tight. This condition is called phimosis. It's an abnormal constriction of the foreskin that prevents it from being drawn back to uncover the glans penis.

Phimosis is painful during urination and sexual intercourse because the foreskin does not willingly slide back and forth during handling. Sometimes medical circumcision is required when the foreskin is too tight due to phimosis causing recurring infections.

Circumcisions among adult men can be very painful and should not be performed purely for cosmetic reasons. Trying to circumcise one's self can result into mutilation and very serious infections. Circumcision is not practiced by all cultures.

As with any indulgence there are advantages and disadvantages of oral satisfaction. It can bring the highest kind of delight to a man or a woman. Be sure you understand both the pros and the cons of sexual indulgence.

Stimulating the Man (in Comparison)

In comparison, the prostate in men is also located behind the pubic bone and around the urethra. The two ejaculatory ducts also end here (bringing sperm from the testis via vas deferens). The prostate can be reached through the anus (as in a doctor performing a prostate exam).

Continued massage type stimulation of the prostate may produce intense orgasms in men. The prostate is the gland that produces most of the seminal fluid that is ejaculated (other than sperm in semen). The prostate could be easily considered the male G-spot. It's that sensitive.

<u>You Should Know</u>
To clean an uncircumcised male identity a woman would only need to spend a few seconds to get it perfectly tidy.

Firm pressure: Especially effective on the underside of the penis, where it is softer. Slow, firm pressure can be very effective and it certainly one to try!

Celebrate and honor indulgence as well as pleasures.

Chapter 17

Stimulating with Pleasurable Hand Treats

This chapter will help you improve your sensual hand techniques.

Sex means more than intercourse. It means exploring all the variations that enhance a woman's sex life and keeps it from getting stale. Then there's the deep satisfying sex with your partner - it's a two way street and making your man feel good will also make you feel good.

Given that hand treats is so much fun and gives both partners so much pleasure, how in the world did we let it get to a point where both women and men fail to recognize its benefits. For many centuries masturbation was seen as something bad. Masturbation was generally forbidden because it could not lead to procreation. In the late 1770's the views shifted to the idea that masturbation or self-touch of the genitals as some people refer to it, was bad for you. It was believed that it could cause disease of the body and even insanity, homosexuality or hairy palms.

Of course, we now know better and understand that self-touch has many benefits. Women have reported that the orgasms they experience with self-touch are more intense. Women who experience masturbation as teenagers are more likely to be orgasmic during sex as adults. Self-touch has become one of the best ways for women to learn their bodies and become more aware of their personal pleasure cycle. Masturbation has been shown to increase sexual self-esteem because women are not afraid to feel good about sex and sexuality.

Watch Out

Most men are afraid to let women handle their male identities. They feel that women aren't skilled enough; their grips are too limp, they lack conviction or exuberance and are afraid to apply the correct amount the pressure.

Heated Pleasures
Any woman can learn to make masturbation very exciting. Masturbation is safe, normal and feels very good.

Any woman can learn to make masturbation very exciting. Masturbation is safe, normal and feels very good. Mutual masturbation can be a thrilling experience, but first, there's a need to explore the basics of manual techniques. Most men are afraid to let women handle their male identities. They feel that women aren't skilled enough; their grips are too limp, they lack conviction or exuberance and are afraid to apply the correct amount of pressure. They pull or tug at inappropriate moments, disrupting the rhythm, or they scratch and don't pay attention to what they are doing. This means that women are in need of more information about the proper methods of hand masturbation.

Self-Pleasuring Hand Jobs

Self-pleasuring is the first way a man learns to bring himself satisfaction. Maybe a hand job was the first thing you ever allowed a man to use on you as you moved into your own sexual exploration. It might have happened early in your life, but this is no teenage thing. A hand job can be an important part adult foreplay. Some women prefer to warm up to bigger and better sexual experiences with the start of a hand job. You will find that incorporating hand techniques into your sexual experiences can bring about great sexual pleasure. This familiar and comfortable technique can bring a man to incredible and intense pleasure, especially if you as a woman take the time to learn some variations on hand techniques. It can create some of the most pleasurable moments for him and you.

Give Him Something He Can Feel

Don't pull, grab, yank or squeeze madly on his crotch. Don't dig inside of his pants and start tugging on his male identity as if you are milking a cow. Ouch, that can hurt! Before you reach for his male identity, take some time to relax him by warming him up with some gentle massaging. You can invest in massage oils that warm his genitals or you can use the reliable and odorless massage oils. Warm it by rubbing it in your hands or place it in a nice dish that makes it easy to reach during the sensual massage.

Your sensuous mission is to relax him before you make love to him. Start your massage away from his genitals, maybe at his feet first, or at his temples or his back. Place a generous amount of warmed oil in the palm of your hands and begin rubbing the muscles along the spine with long, slow strokes.

Start by slowly sliding your hands all over his back. When you get to his spine place your hands just above his buttocks, slide your hands up towards his neck and shoulders and back down again. With each stroke, widen your coverage so that you don't miss a spot. His body should receive equal attention from your smooth flowing hands. Movements should be slow and rhythmic. Pressure should be slow and continuous. Vary your strokes, rubbing upward with one hand while the other travels down making small and large circles with both hands. Stroke outward and away from his spine and toward his waistline and back toward the spine again. Don't apply too much pressure, he shouldn't feel like he's having a physical workout.

Heated Pleasures

Use your body to apply a sensuous massage to his body.

To make him feel better use your body to incorporate sensuous massaging. By this I mean oil your breast, your arms, your thighs and use them as tools to make him feel better. Use your breast to follow the same path as your hands. Use your thighs to straddle his body while you're massaging him. Slide up and down his thighs while straddling him. Use your body to massage his body.

Include his arms and the backs of his legs. Don't forget his buttocks, an often-neglected pleasure zone. These large muscles hold a lot of tension; massaging this area can bring him a great degree of pleasure. Begin with nice long strokes up and down the middle of the buttocks and then back up and down the sides. Vary the speed and direction of your strokes by letting your fingers trickle up and down then the palms of your hands. Take your forefingers and stroke gently between his cheeks making sure you glazed the scrotum with each passing. Do this several times until he's oohing and aaaahing.

Heated Pleasures

Your sensuous mission is to relax him before you make love to him. Start your massage away from his genitals, maybe at his feet, or at his temples or his back.

Now, ask him to reposition by turning over. Assist him as he turns over by gently helping him so you can massage his chest. Your strokes should be similar to those used on his back - long, sensuous sweeping motions. Tease his nipples by slowing glazing over them with each massaging action. If he doesn't like you playing with his breast move just below his breasts and massage his rib cage area.

Sometimes he'll like it here better. Using the tips of your forefingers make gentle and sensuous movement around his areola being careful not to touch his breast if he doesn't like it. If he does want you to play with his breast make tiny circles around it, every now and again be sure to apply little sucks with the front part of your lips. When his nipples are erect, gently glaze over them again with the light touch of the palm of your hand. Continue this kind of massage until you are ready to move on. Don't forget to pay loving attention to his shoulders and his forearms. They are usually tight.

Next, move to his legs, massaging his thighs, under his knees, above his knees, his calves and his feet. When you reach his inner thighs, remain there for a while. Slide your oiled hands along his inner thigh moving toward his sensitive areas and pausing just before you touch his genitals. Now, move back toward his outer thigh and back in toward his genitals and with each stroke you should get closer and closer to his scrotum until you are brushing it. If he's going crazy with excitement you've done exactly what you were supposed to be doing.

Position Your Hands for Success

The best position while giving a hand job is the one that's satisfying and comfortable for both partners. He should be relaxed and comfortable and you should be able to move and massage his entire body with ease. You should be able to switch hand positions without straining to reach other parts of his body. You should be able to move with ease. It takes him a little longer to come while having a massage than it does while climaxing during sexual intercourse, but there are a few positions that can help you along the way. They are:

- ❖ He lies on his back. Straddle his torso with your back to him, facing his penis.
- ❖ He lies on his back with his legs slightly apart. You kneel between his legs while facing him. This puts you a position to use your thumbs to stroke his frenulum easily.
- ❖ He lies on his back. You kneel on either side of his torso or hips. Don't rest your elbows on his. It's painful.
- ❖ He stands. You sit on a bed, chair or desk.
- ❖ You stand behind him and reach around his body to his male identity.
- ❖ Kneel in front of him. Place a pillow under your knees for comfort.
- ❖ You lie on your back with your head on pillows. He straddles your chest, balancing his weight on his knees.

- ❖ You both lie on your side facing one another. Reach down between his legs. He can stimulate your clitoris and you can play with his male identity.
- ❖ You lie behind him. He lies on his side allowing you to grasp his male identity.

Learn Basic Stroking

Begin by getting into your favorite position. A good position is the one where you kneel between his legs. Make sure your hands are well lubricated, then cup them over his genitals, get close to them, but not quite touching. Give him time to feel the warmth and flow of energy from your hands. Now slowly lower your hands until you are lightly toughing him, covering his penis and scrotum. Let your hands pause there for a few minutes before moving on.

> **Heated Pleasures**
> A good position is the one where you kneel between his legs.

Wrap the slightly opened fist of your dominant hand around the shaft of his penis, with your thumb on the underside, along the ridge on the back. Place the thumb and index finger of your other hand at the base of the penis and stabilize it. Begin to gently but firmly slide your fist up and down his shaft. Then you slide all the way down to the base of his penis. As you slide up toward his male identity head use a slightly tighter grip. Now slide all the way down toward the bottom of his male identity. Continue with smooth, steady rhythm; up, down, up, down. Begin slowly and increase speed gradually and as he begins to get harder he'll give you physical signs that he wants more.

Gain More from Your Hand Jobs

As you both get more comfortable with the basic strokes, you might explore some of the following techniques.

- Begin with the basic stroke. When your hand reaches the head of the male identity, twist the palm of your hand completely over the head of the penis as if you are rubbing it and then continue with the downward stroke.
- Begin with the basic stroke. Lubricate your thumb. As you slowly slide your hand up and down his penis move your thumb quickly, up and down in nice circles against the underside of his frenulum (the sensitive tissue on the back of the male identity where the shaft meets the head of it.

- Begin with the basic stroke. When your hand reaches the male identity head twist your hand in one direction and continue down to the base of the penis.
- With your thumb and index finger make the shape of the letter 'O'. Slide the 'O' over the head of the penis and move it up and down the shaft. After a while, lengthen your stroke. Tighten your grip as you near the corona of the head. Slide your fingers up and over the head, and then back down again.
- Start with the letter 'O' movement as stated above, but when you slide your index finger and thumb up to the head; twist your fingers at the base of the penis to stabilize it. Lubricate the palm of your dominant hand and slide it up and down the back of the penis. To add interest, you can slide one hand down his scrotum to his perineum while the other hand slides up along his penis. In his one your hands will move away from one another.
- Wrap your hands around his male identity, with your thumb at the base of his penis and your baby finger resting against the head. Your hand will be upside down. Now slide your hand up and down. This techniques works well if you kneel at his side.

- Cup the head of his male identity in the palm of your hands, with your fingers pointing down toward his scrotum. Grip the sides of his penis and rotate the palm of your hand in one direction and then the other.

Techniques for Using Both Hands

Here are ten great techniques any woman can use to heighten the excitement.

1. Place both well-lubricated fists around his penis, one on top of the other. Move your hands in unison up and down the entire length of his penis. He'll get a sensation similar to thrusting into a tight vagina.
2. Place both hands as above, but as you move them up and down, twist both hands together in one direction and then in the other. Add more interest by twisting one hand in one direction and the other hand in the opposite direction.
3. Lace the fingers of both hands together and encircle his penis. Your thumbs should be free, positioned at the level of the frenulum. Now, keeping your hands still, move just your thumbs

up and down in opposite directions along the frenulum, varying the speed and pressure.

4. Interlock your hands as above, but lace your thumbs together this time. Slide your interlocked hands up and down his male identity.
5. Grasp his male identity head with your right hand and slide it down to the base. When you reach the base, place your left hand on the head and slide it down. Release your right hand and return to the head. Repeat with alternating hands.
6. Grasp the head off his male identity with your right hand and use the same alternating technique as above, except slide only your right hand down to just below the head before you start with the left. Alternate hands for several rapid strokcs. This works best with an erect male identity.
7. This is the opposite of the one above. Place the right hand around the base of his penis and slide it up and over the head. As you reach the head, begin the same upward movement with your left hand. Repeat with alternating hands.
8. Begins just below the head and slides up over the head and back down to an inch or two below it. Repeat for several rapid strokes before returning to the longer strokes described above. This

technique may be used on a flaccid penis, but don't expect it to remain in this state for long.

9. Form the 'O' sign with the thumb and index finger of each hand. Place both the 'O's' around his penis. Now slide on hand up and just over the corona, while moving the other down to the base of the penis. Move both 'O's back and forth. Add more intensity by twisting your hands as they move up and down.
10. Place the palm of your hands on both sides of the penis. Gently rub your hands back and forth, in opposite directions, along the side of the penis as if you are starting a fire.

Enhance Your Hand Jobs

1. The best way to please your man with hand jobs is to watch what he does while pleasing himself. Ask him to help you with learning the moves he likes. Ask him to show you. If he's shy about showing you ask him to place your hand on his male identity the way he likes it. Then have him place his hand on top of yours and move it the way he likes it on his male identity. Have him show you how much pressure he likes and what speeds are best.

2. Show him that you like what you're doing. He needs to know that you're excited about giving him pleasure.
3. Honor his penis. Tell him how much you like his penis, how much you like playing with it, and how much you like holding on to it.
4. Focus your attention on him. Provide unselfish gestures of love by providing him stimulation. Take your time.
5. Communicate effectively. Ask questions about your pleasures and his. Be sure to understand what he likes, wants and needs by communicating that you want to lease him.
6. Begin with nice, even continuous strokes.
7. Provide a great lubricant for hand jobs.
8. Stimulate by using both hands when you massage him.
9. Alternate and vary your hand job movement. Switch from one technique to the other with grace and rhythm.
10. Continue gentle stimulation and watch him for hints of "I want more."

Upgrading Your Hand Techniques

Once you get comfortable with your basic and advance hand moves you can move on to more complicated techniques.

1. Don't stroke or jerk on his male identity. Feel the fullness of it by letting your fingers smoothly run from the family jewels to the top of his male identity.
2. When giving him a hand job swirl around then slide back down to the other half and end back down at his family jewels. The movements should be steady and smooth, without bumping, stalling or nicking him.
3. Tease the more sensitive areas of his male identity. These include: the glans and corona, and the tender parts of the bottom side of his male identity, where the long vein is located. Look at it.
4. Bring the palm of your hands up to the top of the glans and place it there flat out, fingers held together and stiff, thumbs pointed straight out. Spin it around as if remove the lid of a jar. He'll moan and groan with delight. Because his glans is super sensitive this motion will bring him to high levels of pleasure. While you're performing this skill, he

might try to push your hand away, but he'll love it. Even though he'll plead for you to stop, he doesn't mean really it.

5. Slip the hands down to his jewels and ever so gently hold them in your fingers, softly tugging them down away from his shaft. If they are big and bulky, like Grade AA eggs, bounce them up and down a couple of times in the hands .Tell him how heavy they feel and how sexy they are. Caress them gently, but never, ever squeeze them.
6. You might notice that one of his family jewels hangs lower than the other. This is perfectly normal. Once you feel comfortable with the way his family jewels (testicles) feel in your hand, gently roll them up the underside of his shaft. Depending on their size and the amount of room in the scrotum, they might reach half way of his penis. He will like the way this feels. It's pleasurable to him.
7. After letting go of his jewels bring your fingers together in a makeshift goose head formation. Very lightly begin to stroke his erection with your fingers, running them all over his sensitive shaft and family jewels. You may wish to slip the pocket of your goose head handhold over the tip of his male

identity, letting it rest there for a few seconds. This really excites him.

8. About this time, his male identity will probably start to emit its natural lubricant. Pre-seminal fluid is nature's way of moistening the canal of the urethra so that the spermatozoa can swim more easily out of it; it also lubricates the head of the male identity. An uncircumcised male identity gathers up this lubricant within the foreskin and keeps the head very moist and slick. Use the juice to lubricate the shaft. It has a musky smell which can be an aromatic aphrodisiac during prelove sessions.
9. Add a drop of moisturizing lotion to the shaft and gently rub it in. Massage the lotion between the hands before putting it on the male identity because sometimes the cream is cold. Rubbing warms it.
10. Invest in a warming lotion. If he doesn't seem to have a very firm erection, try using a cinnamon-based ointment, which can be found at your local sex novelty store or acquire through a mail catalog. The slight warming sensation often causes the male identity to become rock-hard.

Special Hand Job Exercises

Try any techniques that interest you and your partner. You can perform the following exercises, but these are written with an experienced woman in mind.

❖ Switch Hitter

Use both hands, alternating back and forth in a pattern to offer him the most arousal. He'll notice the difference. Don't get into a routine where the strokes are dull, and noncommittal. Give it to him good. Get him to the point where he's singing your praises.

❖ Double Whammy

Some male identities are so big they require both hands. Use one of your hands to caress and lightly flutter his family jewels, or tighten around the base of his shaft. Move both hands together, up and down, in the typical pumping motion. Imagine holding a baseball bat and vary the directions of your hands, one up, one down at the same time. Two hands are better than one.

❖ The Anvil Stroke

Bring one hand down, letting it stroke the male identity from the top to the bottom. When it hits the bottom, release it. Meanwhile bring the corresponding hand down to the top of the shaft, creating an alternating beating motion, hence the name "anvil stroke." Think of those blacksmith duos that keep up a double beat pounding motion as they beat that rod of iron on a piping-hot anvil.

❖ The Shuttle

Not many people have heard of the "shuttle," but it's one of the best. Take the male identity in both hands, fingers lightly touching the sides of the shaft. In order to visualize the position, think of holding a clarinet. Now flick the male identity back and forth between both hands by holding on to the loose skin of the shaft. Shuttling it back and forth builds up momentum and it will drive him out of his mind.

❖ The Bookends

Place both hands side by side against his shaft like a pair of bookends. Now push hard against his male identity. Lift both hands up and down. Continue in this manner for a while. The constant tugging of the skin around the family jewels and the mons pubis will do the trick

❖ The Flame

Place both hands down on either side with fingers pointing away from the male identity. Roll his male identity between both hands like a stick of wood. This way you'll keep the home fires burning for a long time to come.

❖ The Base Clutch

Tighten the thumb and forefinger around the base of the shaft, pressing down on the family jewels. This will cut off the blood (acting as an impromptu male identity ring) and help steady the shaft. If the skin on it is slick and immutable, stroke the penis with more friction, enhancing the excruciating experience.

❖ The Love Tug

While stroking him, lovingly pull on the wispy strands of pubic hair sprouting from his testicles. Don't pull too hard or fast, but tease them gently.

❖ The Thigh Swatter

Use the hand that is currently unemployed to firmly, but lovingly stroke his inner thighs.

❖ The Best Fist Forward

Place the fist against his perineum (the skin between the butt hole and the balls) while stroking him. He'll probably start opening his legs a little wider, giving more space to press against. This one is guaranteed to drive him wild.

❖ Making Buttermilk

Place the palms of your hands on both sides of his penis. Rub your hands in opposite directions up and down the full length of his penis: as one goes up, the other goes down.

❖ Touch and Go

He gets in doggy style on both his hands and knees. You kneel behind him and reach between his legs. Stroke his scrotum, and then wrap your other hand around his penis. Begin basic up and down strokes. As he becomes aroused, plant kisses on his buttocks and, if you can touch his anus and his scrotum. It will drive him wild.

❖ Head to Head

Find your favorite position that allows you to face him. Begin with the basic stroke. As he become aroused, place your mouth over the head of his male identity with your lips fitting snuggly in the groove beneath the corona. Continue to stroke with your hand, while flicking the tip of the head with your tongue.

❖ Sleeve It

He lies on his back as you begin the basic stroke or one of the variations. While stroking with one hand, reach for a well-lubricated penis sleeve with the other. (See sex toys) Slide the sleeve over his erect penis and move it up and down, using the basic stroke. The sleeve gives him a sensation much like the vagina; he'll love it.

❖ Going Marbles

Place several small marbles in a glass of water. Have him lie on his back as you begin the basic stroke. As he becomes aroused, slip a small marble into your palm and gently stroke his penis. The marble will move smoothly along his penis adding layers of sensations. As you become more comfortable you can add one or two more marbles. Keep your grip light to allow the marbles to move. Don't grip too hard.

❖ The See Saw

Place a latex plastic glove on your dominant hand. Lubricate it well, then hold his penis in your hand and begin the basic up and down or any of the variations.

❖ Water Soak

Run a warm bath for him, adding moisturizing bath oil or baby oil to the water. As he soaks, kneel at the side of the stroke reaching into the water, and begin to massage and stroke his penis. The warm water will increase his blood flow and the water will act as a nice steady lubricant, making your hand movements easier. You can change the sensations a bit by lubricating your hand with a long lasting lubricant that is stable underwater. The lubricant Eros Body glide is great for underwater play. If you want more excitement, slip into the water and let your water soaked body glide against him.

❖ Good Vibrations

Slide a finger vibrator on your middle finger. While stroking his penis cup your other hand gently over his scrotum and press the vibrating finger against his perineum. The vibrations will spread to his G-spot and drive him wild.

❖ Vibrator Slide

Place a hand vibrator over the back of your hand. Lubricate your palm and slide your hand up and down the shaft of his penis. With every two or three up strokes, slide your hand over the head of his penis and then back down his shaft.

❖ The Barrel

He stands while you sit on the bed or a chair. Lubricate both of your hands well with warm oil or silicon-based lubricant. Form a barrel by making two open fists and placing one hand on top of the other. Slide the barrel over his penis and remain still. To add variety, squeeze his penis tight as he pulls back and loosen your hands as he thrusts forward. You can also squeeze and release your fingers rhythmically to create sensations similar to those you can create when you squeeze your PC muscle.

To become the best at pleasing your man I recommend you become a woman who studies her own wants, needs and desires and then incorporate what you like into your own sexual relationship. Explore the outer limits of your own sensuality. Get out of the routine of doing what you've always done and then do something that you've never done before.

Some women like additional stimulation - a finger or two inside the vagina, or perhaps even the anus. Some want the man's hands to reach up and play with her breasts, or want his fingers to hold her labia apart so that his tongue can get at her vulva more directly.

As a woman nears climax, she prefers more direct stimulation. In general, fast, rhythmic stimulation is most effective at causing climax- but the man shouldn't rush to get there. He should always take his time and learn what he can do. Most men who enjoy cunnilingus agree that a clean vagina is a pleasantly acquired taste, so woman should wash first to get rid of any bothersome, unwanted or unnecessary odors.

Get excited about trying new things that will improve intimacy.

Chapter 18

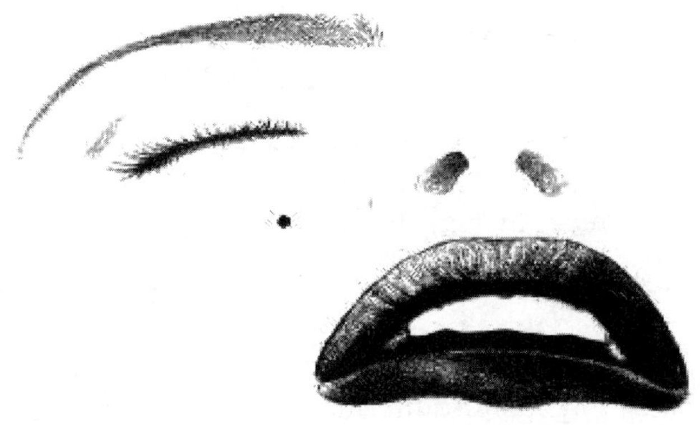

Stimulating with Pleasurable Oral Treats

Performing oral sex takes some courage (at least the first time). At lot of people are afraid they will find the smell and the taste repulsive. A woman may never like the taste of semen, but over time she gets used to it and so does a man who indulges in oral sex with a woman. A woman's sex organs usually taste and smell more intensely than men. That's because of its tight, compact and enclosed structure.

> **You Should Know**
> Getting good cunnilingus is like receiving a precious gift. When performed well it provides most women with intense pleasure.

If the smell of the woman bothers the man, he can use something to cover the taste and smell, like chocolate, a favorite sauce, or jam. Be sure to use something that does not cause rash or irritations. And please do not get any of these flavors inside of the vagina. A dab here or there on the inner thighs are quite nice. He can go back and forth, tasting it from time to time at different intervals.

If the smell of the man isn't enjoyable to the woman she can take a shower with him and participate in cleaning him. That's also fun. Be sure to clean the teeth, gums and breathe before oral sex, and remember the mouth has more germs than a clean male identity or vagina. Hopefully this information will help first timers break down any barriers, which might prevent them from expressing their love and receiving great oral fun from a companion.

The Pleasure of Cunnilingus

Getting good cunnilingus is like receiving a precious gift. When performed well it provides most women with intense pleasure. In fact it's the easiest way for most women to experience an orgasm. If your partner is a little apprehensive about trying cunnilingus it is important to let him know how much you want to experience this form of oral pleasure. Help him by getting rid of any fears he might have about your hygiene, (a common male concern). Suggest showering together prior to sex. If it's lack of experience that causes him concern agree to work with him to help him develop his own unique cunnilingus style. Offer him one of my books or choose one of many sex guides that are devoted to the art of cunnilingus and then read it together. There is no excuse for a man to refuse to provide you with oral pleasure. To fully enjoy the pleasure of cunnilingus, incorporate the following tips:

1. Check your genital attitude

How do you feel about the appearance, smell and taste of your own genitals? You are not alone if your answer is "Not good." Some women are not comfortable with their most intimate parts. We have been conditioned since childhood to think of our genitals as unattractive, smelly or unclean. Having your man get up close and personal to your genitals can make you feel slightly uncomfortable. You might think that he also finds your feminine anatomy unattractive and you might think he is turned off by your taste and smell. You should feel this way because most men find a woman's genitals very attractive and sexually enticing.

2. Get in tune with your own genitals

To get in tune with your own genitals take a closer look at them with a hand-held mirror. Appreciate your genitals color, texture, moisture and complexity. Become familiar with your own unique scent. Place a clean finger in your vagina. Remove it, wave it several inches from your nose and breathe its scent.

Take a deep breath and enjoy how you smell. The natural clean smelling vagina is very powerful and erotic to men. Now take the same finger, place it in your mouth and taste your secretions. The flavor of your vaginal fluids may range from sweet to slightly salty or have no taste at all. The taste may vary throughout the month and be affected by whatever you have eaten, drank or smoked. Smoking, alcohol recreational drugs, medications, vitamins, coffee, and foods like onions; asparagus, garlic and curry may give your genitals a less than pleasant taste. Eating lots of fresh fruits and vegetables and drinking lots of water will help keep your unique vaginal taste favorable and fresh.

3. Learn to receive pleasure

Because so many women are givers, sometimes it is the most difficult thing in the world for us to receive pleasure. In order to reach the heights of sexual pleasure, you must be able to be selfish and concentrate on your own pleasure. Cunnilingus is the perfect opportunity to lie back, forget your worries and be pleasured by your mate. His pleasure is dependent on your pleasure. Few things will make your partner happier than being able to give you the ultimate sexual experience. Men are like that. They want to think that they are the reason for your happiness and pleasure.

Your orgasms should not be the ultimate goal at this point, so please don't worry about how long it will take for you to get one. Relax and concentrate on the pleasure that you are receiving.

4. Choose a good position.

Find a comfortable position that is good for you. You need to be relaxed in order to feel good sensations. The best position is when you lay on your back with your knees bent. He lies between your legs. This position gives his tongue and mouth the best access to the sensitive part of your clitoris and vagina. Increase access to your vagina and buttocks by propping your butt on pillows.

5. Make sure he's comfortable

Be sure to have plenty of pillows available to support his joints and other body parts. Make sure that you move far up enough on the bed or table so that he has enough room to get into a comfortable position. Place fresh water at the bedside just in case he needs to replenish his saliva. Flavored lubricants and gels may add variety and spice to his lovemaking, but may irritate your genitals. Be sure you select non allergic gels, creams etc.

6. Communicate your needs

As with any sexual activity, communication is the key. Don't expect him to know what you want or need. Men assume that the penis and the clitoris want and need the same treatment. When it comes to oral pleasuring, nothing is farther from the truth. The average penis and love button likes to be fondled, kiss and sucked. Use your body language to give him feedback and direction on how to please you. Move and glide your pelvis to direct his tongue to meet your sensitive spots. Move side to side, thrust your pelvis closer to get more attention and farther away if the stimulation is too intense. If you want additional stimulation of your G-spot, perineum, or anus, gently guide his hands to that spot. He will then know what you want and need to be pleasured.

7. Vocalize your pleasure

If you are silent, he might think that you are not interested or bored with his lovemaking. He might think that he's not doing a good enough job. If you display this kind of attitude he will lose interest in making love to you. You have to moan, groan, coo, oooh and aaaah with pleasure to let him know that it feels good to you. Express yourself and he'll want to do it again and again.

8. Give him a hand

Become more of an active participant than a passive participant. He needs to know that you want him just as much as you need to know he wants you. Get involved by pulling your love button hood back, Play with your vagina, nipples, or other erogenous zones that increase arousal. Stroke the back of head, rub his buttocks run your fingers through his hair, massage his arms, talk to him and

Watch Out

A tampon may well hold the flood back, as will a diaphragm, but some men don't like the taste of a menstruating vagina.

let him know you like it and him.

9. Kiss him immediately afterwards.

Let him know that you are comfortable with your juices by kissing him. Taste your own love juices.

10. Show your appreciation.

Let him know how much you enjoyed cunnilingus. Men love to pleasure women. Knowing that he pleased you will make it more likely that he will be eager to do it again and again. Remember, the pursuit of pleasure requires relaxation and feeling good.

Cunnilingus during Menstruation

Some people are particularly turned off at the suggestion of cunnilingus during menstruation. If it is a concern to a man, the woman should wait. A tampon may well hold the flood back, as will a diaphragm, but some men don't like the taste of a menstruating vagina. If the couple is healthy, however, there is no particular danger in menstrual blood, and some women find that orgasms during their periods alleviate cramps. It's purely a matter of personal preference.

Learn to Fellatio

Fellatio is giving a blowjob or sucking a man's male identity. It is the act of applying lips to a man's male identity with the purpose of giving him pleasure. It is one of the pure male pleasures in life. Many women don't appreciate just how much fun it can be because they don't know how to do it correctly or either they have a phobia about it. When it's done wrong the male identity doesn't get hard, the man doesn't have a good time and the woman feels like a sexual failure. The lips and the tongue are the major sources of stimulation for what makes it feel good to the man. Both men and women respond well to direct pressure and continuous rhythm so a steady, strong stroke will be enough to give the proper stimulation.

The best way to give fellatio is still with the lips and tongue, taking only as much as you can without gagging. However, if a couple wants to take it further all they have to do is practice.

It's simple: Take his male identity as far as you can without choking, and then close your eyes and concentrate while taking each quarter inch, telling yourself that you won't choke and that you can take it out at any time. All you have to do is raise off of it just as slowly. Every man’s male identity is different, and each has sensitive spots and preferred ways of being handled. All a woman has to do is pay attention to her lover's needs. The sounds he makes and the feel of his body tensing are the best clues that she's doing it right. Grasp with your hands the parts of the male identity that can't fit into the mouth. Many men like as much stimulation as possible, and the feeling of a wet mouth and a moist hand are enough to send them to an orgasm very quickly.

You Should Know

Don't cheat yourself or your partner out of exploring cunnilingus, not just the basics, but also the finer points. Incorporate subtle moves that feel really great. You won't regret it.

Perfect Your Oral Skills

Here's the good news: It's easy to learn how to be a terrific male identity handler. It doesn't matter the setting you choose. It can be at home, in bed, or parked in the driveway. All that's needed is privacy.

Let's say you're on a couch. We'll assume you played, fondled and warmed each other up. You're with your lover and you know he'd love to receive a good blowjob about now. Slip down between his legs and open his fly. Reach in and touch his male identity. If he's hot for you, he'll already be hard. If he's nervous or uninterested it may still be bent up inside his shorts.

Take hold of his male identity and lean up to his face and kiss him. See if you can feel a response down below. Any movement is a good sign. Now pull it out and see how it stands. If it's stiff and sticking straight up or straight out, you're doing great. If it's wobbly or limp, here's what to do:

- ❖ Pull his testicles (family jewels) out. If his pants are too tight, pull them down. Now hold his testicles (family jewels) in your left hand and his male identity in your right. Squeeze it gently down - toward the bottom of the shaft and get ready to suck it. Run your tongue over your lips to moisturize them and look into his face. He'll want to watch you please him orally. Men love to watch.
- ❖ Open your mouth slightly to tease and excite him and come very close to his male identity. Breathe on him, blow on him with your hot breath. Then stick the tongue out again and reach for him, touch him and tease him with it.
- ❖ Making sure the tongue is very wet, begin at the bottom of his shaft and slowly lick upwards. Turn your head sideways as if to take a bite of him. Slowly and gently place your teeth onto his flesh.

Wet him again using your tongue to help moisten him. A wet male identity looks and sounds a lot sexier than a dry one. Take the left hand and massage his family jewels, perhaps rubbing them ever so lightly with your fingernail bottom. The bottom won't hurt him, but the tips often do.

- Reach behind and underneath his family jewels to touch the sensitive area just before his anus, or run your fingers over his anus very lightly. Since the muscles that cause erection originate here, it will produce a reaction in his male identity.
- After licking his male identity a few times and getting it wet and hard, he'll start squirming with frustration if the serious pleasure doesn't get started. A quick look up at his face will let you know if teasing is too much. Having experience in giving blowjobs is a great education. You'll know when that point has been reached.
- Do an upward swing with your tongue, from the base of his shaft to the rim of his knob. Continue long, moist licks over the top of his male identity. Linger at the hole in the center; stick the tongue into it, if possible, but don't suck the head yet. Save for that later.

- Run the tongue around the rim of his penis making frequent passes on the tender skin directly facing you. This is where most men are the most sensitive. The one thing a good male identity eater has to learn is each man is unique and so is his male identity.
- Squeeze the shaft and see if some clear liquid drips out. If it does, dip your tongue into it and pull away. It will stretch with you and look fantastically erotic to your lover. Closing your eyes helps if she doesn't like the look of slimy things because that's what it will look like.
- Now, make like you love the stuff. Close in on his male identity head like it was chocolate ice cream and take the whole knob into your mouth. Hold it there. Listen to him moan. It will drive him crazy, and that's good.
- Now go down quickly and take as much of his male identity as you can get into your mouth. Don't worry - it won't cause choking. If you bend your neck in just the right way, you can take it clear into your throat.
- Stay there, with the male identity down the mouth, for just a moment. Feel it inside of the mouth. It can

be as luscious as having one in the vagina. It grows on the woman.

- ❖ At this point you can slide back up to the tip of the male identity and flick your tongue against it. Your man will be getting antsy now, wanting you to deep-throat him some more. But you shouldn't let him bully you. If he had his way, it would all be over in two minutes and that's no fun for you.
- ❖ Slide up and down on his male identity as if having intercourse. If he gets too close to coming, stop, or at least slow down. If it's difficult to get all the way down to the bottom of his male identity you can cheat a little by using your right hand to complete the sensation of deep throating him. It will look and feel as if you have the whole thing in your mouth. Slide your fingers and make an O-shape around the shaft. Go up and down with the rhythm of sucking.
- ❖ While mouthing the male identity, you can suck it, which feels quite different. There are deep-sucks and little ones and both feel great. He might have an idea of what he likes, so you should pay attention to his reactions. Taking just the knob in your mouth, you can suck it as if it were a nipple or a straw. This feels good to him and you'll get hot just thinking about it.

- Now, take the whole male identity and suck it all the way up like you would a Popsicle and then go back and do it again, sucking on the way down.
- Any of these moves will feel great the first few times, but after a while, the male identity gets immune to feeling. When you sense this, it's time to move onto the next play. You don't ever want the male identity to go to sleep while you're in charge of it. You want it to be constantly stimulated, but not quite, to the point of orgasm, which is just about where you are now.
- Okay, you have a raging hard-on in your right hand and some tight family jewels in your left. Lean back and take a look at them. Move the right hand all the way to the base of the male identity and squeeze it there. This will cause the shaft to fill and thicken, and by now his knob, will be shining and smooth. You can take the male identity into your mouth and suck if you like. Try various moves until he can't stand anymore and he's ready to have an orgasm.
- Allow his warm, wonderful juices to gush upward and slide your hands around his wet male identity. It will feel slippery and delightful to touch! Run your hands on it, feeling all the way to the top,

smoothing the glistening fluids over his knob. This makes a great image for the woman and the man.

Refine What You Already Know

- There is one further refinement to this basic technique, which will heighten his orgasm. If you place your thumb at the base of his male identity in such a way as to block the tube his semen cannot escape even though he is spasming and going through the reflex action of ejaculating semen.
- If at the same time you can suck on the head of his male identity you can delay his cum for several moments. When you finally allow his semen to spurt - it will last longer and will be more intense for him. Even though the semen is delayed for only a few moments he'll be happy with the intensity.
- You should not be so caught up in pleasing him that you miss out on self-discovery. Find out what works for both you and your lover and make your sucking as

Heatology

Many men like as much stimulation as possible, and the feeling of a wet mouth and a moist hand are enough to send them to an orgasm very quickly.

individual as your signature. After all, you want your man to be able to pick you out in the dark among hundreds slobbering male identity suckers.

Give him head that he'll never forget and you won't be able to get rid of him. One woman in every fifty knows how to give a really good blowjob. The rest act like she's doing the guy a big favor. If the woman doesn't like to give blowjobs or she's hasn't learned to like it she shouldn't give up. Maybe she'll like it more as she grows older as becomes more sexually experienced.

Ms. Real Suggests

Try various positions just to see what works best for you and your lover. It's usually a matter of personal preference.

Men feel that older women are much better at giving blowjobs. As the author of this book, I should warn women; there are a lot of good women who like to give their men good blowjobs. I have met many women who can have full blown orgasms by simply sucking the male identity. Men know if a woman doesn't do it, there is always a woman out there who is willing. Some women just love to do it.

Practice Your Sucking Techniques

The sad fact is that most women do not have the slightest idea of how to suck a male identity properly. Many women seem to think that simply making a circle with their mouth, closing it around a man's male identity, and bobbing their heads up and down until he climaxes. They think this will automatically makes her an expert sucker. Not true my friends!

Take the opportunity to look at and examine his male identity. Now explore each area of the male identity to find the most sensitive parts. Parts are parts, but some parts are more sensitive than others.

Heated Pleasures
Many women seem to think that simply making a circle with their mouth, closing it around a man's male identity, and bobbing their heads up and down until he climaxes.

So, let's discuss some great sucking techniques that are probably the most common male identity sucking technique in the world. In order for a woman to observe the man's reactions and get the most from his responses she can try the following:

- ❖ Take his male identity in the mouth, but not deeply. Slide your moistened tongue lovingly over the head until the lips are closed around the shaft at the point just behind the corona. Don't just open your mouth and close it around his male identity; slide him in. He will enjoy it much more. Encase the shaft of his male identity with your hands. Remember the shaft is relatively insensitive to any kind of stimulation. By enclosing his male identity with your hands you give him the pleasurable sensation of having his male identity encased.
- ❖ Try twisting your head from side to side making sure your moist lips stay in contact with his coronal ridge. While doing this gently move your hands up and down his shaft. Gently suck around the corona as he climaxes so that you can intensify his pleasure and increase the force of his orgasm. As you gain more experience you will be able to tell exactly when his climax is approaching and you will be ready for that initial spurt of satisfaction.
- ❖ While his erect male identity points toward the ceiling, cup his family jewels in one hand and carefully lick along the entire underside of his erect organ. While doing this notice the areas that give him the most pleasure when the tongue is touching

them. He'll usually provide very vivid clues as to which areas are most pleasurable to him.

- Once the areas he likes caressed are discovered concentrate more on those areas. For most men the most sensitive area will be the point where the ring (or corona) of the head and the foreskin are attached, or where it was attached prior to circumcision. By licking and tapping along this area with the tongue he'll arrive at ecstasy. To please him in a hurry try to excite him in this way until he climaxes.
- As he is ready for climax you can note the changes in his male identity. The head of the male identity may swell somewhat larger than it does during the normal course of his erection. He may thrust his hips forward as he wants to send his male identity inside of you. For most men, immediately prior to orgasm there will be a clear drop or two of fluid at the tip of the male identity. When this happens he's ready to have an orgasm.

Where to Use Sucking Techniques

Because of the structure of his male identity, as well as the structure of her mouth, lips, tongue, and teeth a woman can provide a high degree of sensation to her lover and self. Kneel between his legs and approach his male identity from the bottom rather than from the side or the top. Try various positions just to see what works best for you and your lover. It's usually a matter of personal preference.

A woman should place his stiff male identity inside her mouth, but should not tighten her lips around the shaft. Begin a circle motion with the head. The circle should be executed in both clockwise and counterclockwise motions in a slow purposeful manner. The male identity will slide to different places in the mouth as the circle motion is continued. Be careful - teeth are not allowed.

Heated Pleasures

It is not necessary to be a perfect male identity sucker. All you have to do is to find the most sensitive area around the coronal area and focus on it continuously.

A kneeling position will suffice, but it is also effective when he is on his back and her head is directly over his male identity. When the technique is performed correctly there are many hours of unadulterated pleasure.

Get Past the Angle of His Dangle

Don't allow your lover to get carried away at the moment he starts to climax. He will try his best to thrust his penis down your throat if he's inexperienced. You should continue to relax your throat completely while he is thrusting deeply down your throat. It may require practice for you to take your lover completely. If you can't he'll understand that this is not a rejection of him. Don’t give up or feel that you will never master the "deep throat" technique. You need to keep practicing and perfecting. You should not give up or feel that you will never master the "deep throat" technique. You need to keep practicing. If you desire to do it you will ultimately succeed in deep throating. In order to do this, you should get in a position where your head can be turned in such a way that your mouth and throat lie almost in a straight line. The best way to accomplish this is to lie in bed so that your head is near the edge with his body is sprawled across the bed and your head is tipped sharply back. This position will put your mouth and throat nearly in a line and will allow your lover to approach you in such a way that insertion of his male identity can be made so deeply that his pubic hair presses against your lips.

Here are three more past the angle of the dangle tips:

❖ Deep throating

The natural tendency is to gag when a foreign object such as a deeply thrusting male identity is being forced down your throat. You can overcome this by completely relaxing your throat at the moment of insertion. It's equally important that you maintain this relaxation during the entire deep throating.

❖ Practice with him

The man can now place his male identity down your throat and hold it still until he finds the most comfortable way to proceed. He's in full control and must initiate and maintain all the motion. He will relish this moment because it's the first time he can insert his male identity as deeply down your throat as he wants. Because of your position you will not be able to move or offer him any greater stimulation than simply keeping your mouth tightly closed around his throbbing male identity. Try to stimulate the underbelly of his male identity with your tongue. All it takes is continuous practice.

❖ Trust him

When you completely trust a man you're able to relax. This is the only exercise in which you relinquish control of the situation to your lover. Trust him enough to enjoy the pleasure.

Testicles and Lovemaking

Also known as the family jewels, balls or testicles let's turn to another portion of the male anatomy, which should not be ignored. The family jewels, balls, testicles, sacs all describe the same part of the male identity. These are two male owned objects that can enhance the sensual feelings of a man more than any other.

Many people do not think of the jewels (balls) as primary sexual objects. They are extremely sensitive and there must be a certain amount of trust before he allows a woman to have undisputed use of his family jewels (balls)!

A woman should begin to play with the man's jewels gradually increasing or decreasing the intensity as she gauges how he is responding. She should gently caress his male identity with her hand while she is bathing his family jewels with her tongue.

Heated Pleasures

Don't hesitate to explore his body: his earlobes, neck, nipples, family jewels, anus, armpits, fingers, toes, etc.

Because his family jewels are extremely sensitive to pain a man will

Heated Pleasures
A woman should begin to play with the man's jewels gradually increasing or decreasing the intensity as she gauges how he is responding.

lose trust in a woman who does not respect the limits he places on them. She has the same right to place limits on the back of her throat until she is completely ready to receive him in her mouth and he should be able to do the same with his family jewels.

Once a man trust a woman to take his jewels in her mouth, he will be more receptive to letting her wet them with her tongue prior to taking them into her mouth. Wetting the hairs down along the surface of the sac will keep from causing pain to him. The woman will discover an entirely new world of pleasurable sensations for her man when she takes the time to get to know his jewels!

Become Better At What You Do

Because there will be times you'll want to satisfy him in a hurry, you should practice other oral lovemaking skills as well. He will love you all the more if you have more sensuous tricks up your sleeve.

Place your lips around the head of his male identity and twirl them wetly and gently around the coronal ridge at the back of the penile head of his male identity. This skill will help him climax at a quicker rate. This does not require any great male identity sucking skills and it works because this is the area that is most sensitive on the man's.

Watch Out
If the idea of swallowing turns you off, then doing it won't make the experience any more pleasurable.

It is not necessary to be a perfect male identity sucker. All you have to do is to find the most sensitive area around the coronal area and focus on it continuously. It can produce a quick powerful climax. You don't have to bob your head up and down on his male identity to get him off. One other use of this technique is it helps him get hard again after he climaxes so that he'll be rip roaring to go again.

Do It Good Again and Again

Don't be surprised if you find yourself going back for more. After you have satisfied your man you should concentrate on a variety of techniques to get him excited again. Not just to get him hard, but to keep him hard enough to climax again! Sucking alone is not enough to satisfy him. You'll need to combine the techniques you've learned with your own basic sucking techniques to stimulate him for a second and third time. Don't hesitate to explore his body: his earlobes, neck, nipples, family jewels, anus, armpits, fingers, toes, etc. Explore all those erotic areas that were missed while concentrating on his male identity. Remember to include his navel, back of his neck, eyes and any other parts of his body that might tickle him. You can explore a man's body and really get to know what makes him tick. Don't simply focus on his delightful male identity the entire time! This is merely a sign that you're becoming a true male connoisseur.

You Are What You Eat

Macrobiotic nutritionists have actually done research on this statement, and the answer is in: You are what you eat. Common sense dictates that if you taste good, your lover will want to indulge in oral sex more often, so improving your body's taste and smell should be important to you.

In general, nutritionists say that alkaline-based foods such as meats and fish produce a buttery/fish taste. Dairy products, which contain a high bacterial putrefaction level creates the foulest tasting fluids by far.

Everyone I know says that there is one worse than a high dairy content - its asparagus. You can't miss the taste of asparagus-laced semen.) Acidic fruits, sweets, and alcohol give bodily fluids a pleasant, sugary flavor so eat lots of them.

You Should Know

The caloric content of an average ejaculate is approximately 15 calories. Wow, who would have known this?

Chemically processed liquors will cause an extremely acidic taste, however, so if you're going to drink alcohol, drink high-quality, naturally fermented beers.

Secrets of Swallowing Semen

While men fantasize about a woman swallowing his semen, mainly because pornographic movies display it as some kind of hero's badge of honor - some women find the taste or consistency of semen difficult to swallow. It's a tricky situation, because many men feel that if you swallow their semen it’s a sign that you accept them completely. And of course, if you love your partner you won't hurt his feelings by denying him this luxury. If the idea of swallowing turns you off, then doing it won't make the experience any more pleasurable. Fortunately there are is a way to swallow without really swallowing so that you and your partner are happy with the results.

Show enthusiasm and let him know that you are enjoying it. When you notice signs that he's about to come (he begins to pump faster, his breathing gets faster and you begin to feel the initial contractions at the base of his penis) push the back of your tongue up against the roof of your mouth, protecting the back of your throat and the sensitive taste buds. That way when he ejaculates, the fluids will pool in the front of your mouth. While the penis is still in your mouth, slowly allow the semen to flow out of the side of your mouth and onto the back of your hand. Later you can discreetly wipe your hand on the sheets or a waiting towel. He will never know. It'll be your little secret.

Ejaculatory Calories

The question of semen content arises among persons who regularly swallow semen, and who are concerned about calorie intake and nutritional substances.

The average ejaculate contains ascorbic acid, blood-group antigens, calcium, chlorine, cholesterol, choline, citric acid, creatine, deoxyribonucleic acid (DNA), fructose, glutathione, hyaluronidase, inositol, lactic acid, magnesium, nitrogen, phosphorus, potassium, purine, pyrimidine, pyruvic acid, sodium, sorbitol, spermidine, spermine, urea, uric acid, vitamin B12, and zinc. The caloric content of an average ejaculate is approximately 15 calories. Wow, who would have known this?

You Should Know
The biggest obstacle to taking his entire male identity down your throat is the fact that there is a bend of almost ninety degrees behind the tongue leading down into the throat.

Why Men Crave Oral Pleasure

The more a man is disconnected from his feelings, the more he will crave sexual stimulation and release. The intensity of release at every stage of the sexual experience allows him to connect momentarily with his feelings and his heart.

For him sex is the experience of sexual pleasure and love. Although he may not be aware of it, his persistent sexual need is really his soul seeking completeness. As his need to be touched is satisfied his ability to feel is also satisfied. When his feelings are awakened his energy is freed. Through pleasure he can feel joy, love and peace.

Getting Rid of the Gag Reflex

One of the first things a woman encounters when she starts to suck the male identity is the gag reflex. Some men want to force their male identity down her throat as far as they can get it. Particularly at the moment they start to cum!

Consider for a moment that the average length of the oral cavity is three to three and a half inches while the average Caucasian male identity length is five to five and a half inches and the African American male is about six to seven inches in length.

The laws of nature seem to dictate that getting the entire male identity into a woman's mouth is impossible. Fret not! It can be done. The biggest obstacle to taking his entire male identity down your throat is the fact that there is a bend of almost ninety degrees behind the tongue leading down into the throat. So the first thing to do is get the male identity past that angle.

Oral Sex Games

Some women get disappointed with their partner's lack of oral sex knowledge. With some patience and practice everyone can be a fantastic licker, oops I mean oral lover.

Here are some fabulous games that will help you learn how to become a great oral lover.

1. Use cough drops.

The next time you decide to give head to him suck on the cough drop for a few seconds to get the mentholated twist working in your mouth. The heat from your tongue, the warmth of your breath along with the coolness from the cough drop gives him a hot and cold sensation all at once. It will drive him erotically crazy. Flavored cough drops can be used as a sexual stimulator. During oral sex you can lightly blow on the male identity as you suck on it. This will help him keep a very nice and stiff erection. You don't have to suck the entire cough drop. About ten to twelve sucks are efficient. Save the best sucking for his male identity. Continue this thrill until he begs for mercy. Remember to vary your moves.

2. Add your favorite lip-gloss.

Don't let him know that you've added flavor to your vaginal lips because it will take away from the surprise of it all. As he begins to lavish you the added flavor will be an immediate turn on for him. The sweetness of your new taste will drive him wild. It also adds variety to your vagina juices and the flavors that you choose will be complimentary to your sex. Buy two to three different flavors so you can change up every now and then. Additional flavors as suggested by women are: whipped cream, honey, syrup, peaches, chocolate, wine, champagne, beer, fruit juices, powdered sugar, and powdered honey dust. (I recommend Kama Sutra Honey Dust.) This is not to alter the taste or smell, but to add to it. Be careful of anything that you put on or in the vagina area.

3. Treat his male identity like a lollipop.

Make circles around his male identity as you go up and down on it. He'll beg for mercy. Caress his inner thighs, buttocks, anus, tummy and other parts of his body.

4. Lick his testicles gently.

Take them into your mouth. This creates sensational pleasures for him. Move your tongue up and down, side to side and in slow lavishing licks. This is one of the most erotic pleasures and not many women know it.

5. Heat things up with the sprinkle game.

It's sucking at its very best. Sprinkle tiny suction kisses all over his body. Begin from his head and work your way down his entire body, stopping at his toes, then finally coming back up to his male identity. Now slip your tongue over all the areas that you just suction kissed; circling his eyes, ears, and lips. When you get to his nipples circle faster than you did before like a whirlpool. Pull his nipple into your mouth with suction kisses, pulling as much of his entire breast into your mouth as possible. Knead his nipples and gently pull them again. Suck him with pleasure and enjoyment.

6. The Popsicle lick is the most sensuous.

You use your tongue to continuously circle the male identity clockwise. Slide your tongue in and out of your mouth and go counter clockwise. To add more thrills and sensations as you slide his male identity in and out, up and down, go slow then speed up. This has very dramatic effects on a man and it's worth every minute to see the effects of it. An added joy is to really work him over as if you are licking your favorite dessert.

7. Teeth make great props.

Hold your man's male identity sideways, like a buttered piece of corn. Slide your teeth gently up and down his shaft. Giving it a gentle little nip every now and then is a fantastic blowjob.

8. Incorporate fruit.

This is an added treat when accompanied with good oral sex. Bananas, oranges, berries, cherries, and any other luscious fruits can be eaten as an appetizer to oral sex. Rubbing the juices all over his male identity and licking it off will send many sensations all over him.

9. Mint flavored candies.

Mouth washes or breath savers create cool sensations.

10. Shake your head.

Hold his male identity in your mouth and gently shake your head from side to side. This will send little tingles up and down his spine and throughout his male identity.

11. Alternate your mouth and your vagina.

Men love this. This is called stroke dipping. Men tend to desire this one if the women is open to it.

12. Make your lover more comfortable.

Kneel down beside him and take his male identity in the palm of your hand. Run your lips slowly over his male identity. Take your tongue and circle his male identity head so that it simultaneously wets his male identity and your own lips.

Open your mouth and stretch your lips so that they cover the top and bottom rows of your teeth. Covering your teeth will help avoid nicks or cutting his foreskin. Covering your teeth is forms a smooth firm ridge that creates highly sensitive sensations to the male identity.

Now, place the male identity into your mouth down to the base and then come slowly back up.

13. Wet it.

To keep sufficient lubrication for the male identity and to easily slide it in and out of your mouth with ease wet it a few times with your tongue.

14. Vary your speed.

Be aware of your speed and remember to get in tune with his body movements. Study what sensations make him squirm, wiggle or yell out and then concentrate on these sensations. He might like slow, steady, continuous in and out motions or he might prefer strong quick strokes or both. You should know what your man likes. Practice oral sex manipulations on a regular basis and before you know it you'll know.

15. Give him a thrill.

Take his male identity and move it gently between your lips. Hold it with your fingers while pressing its sides with your lips. Gently push it a little farther into your mouth and forcefully suck it in and out as far as it will go. Now press the end of his male identity against the roof of your mouth. Suck it deeply as if you are trying to swallow him. He'll experience ecstasy.

16. As he watches TV or listens to music.

Innocently unzip him and suck away to your heart's content.

17. Complete the eat.

A loving and sexy thing to do is to lavish his penile juices after he's had his orgasm. It's a fantastic topper to sexual encounters.

18. Exercise your tongue.

Want to give the most amazing oral sex ever? Exercise your tongue in front of a mirror twice a day. Point your tongue and push it forward, then flicker it from side to side keeping a smooth and steady rhythm. Try to touch your nose and your chin with smooth and steady motions.

19. Give gentle kisses on his male identity.

Try it in a dark restaurant. Sneaking to do it is fun. Do it under a table. Make sure the table is dressed in a floor length cloth to provide secrecy.

A Note for Women

Fellatio must be performed with enthusiasm. You have to love what you're doing to him, either because you love him or you love sucking his male identity. Loving both is best! Faked orgasms have nothing on lackluster Fellatio. Lackluster Fellatio is one of the worst things a woman can do to a man.

A Note for Men

Don't push it. There's nothing more deadly than having a man push a woman's head down toward his male identity. If she's into it, she'll get around to it, sometimes not until the second time you make love. Whatever the case may be don't force her to do it. If you give her time, she'll learn to like it. If she doesn't enjoy it, perhaps your next lover will.

Every man wants to be completely satisfied. If a woman indulges in sex with a man at least make it pleasurable

Chapter 19

Pleasurable Tune Ups (Aka: Quickies)

In this chapter you will learn how to enjoy a quickie and then make the best of a quickie.

Couples can work as a team to reduce the time it takes to have good sex. Sometimes they don't have a lot of time so they choose to skip foreplay and move right into sexual intercourse. Just about every guy experiences those times when he just wants to take his woman; have his sexual way with her and then get on with the day without having to go through the entire foreplay and after-play process.

Of course, there's nothing wrong with wanting a little quickie sex on occasion; believe it or not, there are plenty of women who enjoy it hard and fast and without all that fluffy stuff. The reality is that you have to know how to go about enjoying quickie sex without making your woman feel like you're about to leave a crisp twenty on the nightstand.

When a woman really trusts the man she loves something deep down inside of her wants to cut loose and completely let go without any restraint or worry of 'nice girls don't do that' kind of thinking. She wants to be free and feel free while making love. She would like to make her partner happy, but she wants to experience happiness too. She would like to be satisfied and she knows the only way she can get that done quickly is with a sexual tune-up. She wants the kind of sex most couples refer to as a quickie.

Heated Pleasures

A quickie may be just what the doctor recommends.

Women affectionately use the term "tune-up" as in Sexual tune-up. It's a grown woman's term.

Every Woman Needs a Tune Up

Did I really say that? You and I both know that all women for whatever reason or another must have a sexual tune-up from time to time. There is nothing more exciting than having a session of slow leisurely sex, but on occasion you just don't have time or energy for the marathon sex, and sometimes even prolonged sex is not what you want. A quickie may be just what the doctor recommends.

You Should Know

You should never do anything that makes you feel uncomfortable, emotionally, physically or intellectually

It's not that you don't want to bump and grind with your man for long periods of time, but sometimes you just want to be sexed. You want it when you want it and you want it as soon as you feel the urge. You don't want to hold back because at that particular time all you need is to get your freak on and you don't want to spend a lot of time doing it.

Sometimes a woman just wants good loving from a good man without all the pre-sex hoopla. Quickies are great for every sexually active couple. The man can follow the woman's lead every once in a while without being told when and how she revels in the freakiness of it all.

When a man knows what to do, how to do it, and when to do it, he then knows what needs to be done to turn a woman on. He knows that she doesn't want to talk about it or direct his actions, she just wants a good screwing to let go of her inhibitions and express herself and she wants it done right.

Enjoy Guilt Free Quickies

Feeling the need to be sexed and acting on it is difficult for many women because they have been groomed since childhood to think differently. Let's take a look at the following scenario:

Ricky always felt a little guilt after having sex with Rosilyn because it was evident that she wasn't satisfied. Ricky felt that foreplay was what she wanted and if he didn't give it to her he felt that he had cheated her. To combat this happening they would always wait until it was bedtime to have sex because it felt right --not rushing it. Rosilyn wanted some quickies though. She would suggest sex right before it was time for the children to come home so she could have a tune-up, but it didn't always work out. He wanted to give foreplay and she only wanted a tune-up. Her quickies made her feel guilt free, but he felt like he was shorting her on sex. They just couldn't get it together. After beating themselves up for a while about their timing problems they decided to negotiate.

Rosilyn told Ricky that she wanted more sexual moments that were spur of the moment. She didn't need foreplay before sex each time. She asked him "What she could do to make him feel better about having more guilt free tune-ups?"

Ricky felt that if Rosilyn only wanted a tune-up (Quickies) the passion in their relationship would die out. Rosilyn felt that if all Ricky wanted were long sexual escapades (Gourmet sex) they would never have time for sex. They compromised about taking turns initiating their special kind of sex and decided to have a romantic get-a-way at least once a month where both of them could indulge in each other's sexual wishes.

Rosilyn loved tune-ups and Ricky preferred Gourmet sex, so they decided to have both. Rosilyn promised Ricky more intimacy, loving attention and pampering and he promised her more pleasurable quickies.

How to Treat a Sexual Tune-Up?

Let's start by answering a few questions. Are your sexual tune-ups a temporary Band-Aid or do the tune-ups make you feel better for longer periods of time? Is it like a fast food that you enjoy when woofing it down or is it the long-term fulfillment of your sexual needs. You should never do anything that makes you feel uncomfortable, emotionally, physically or sexually. Making time for sex begins with a woman's personal journey into her own sexuality and sexual attitude. There are several ways couples can have regular sex.

(1) Fast food sex: Tune-Ups/Quickies
(2) Gourmet sex: longer session with foreplay
(3) More affection with hugs and kisses
(4) Planned sexual get a ways at least once a month.

Stay Committed to the Tune-Up

With a tune-up a couple's anticipation is heightened because they already know they're going have sex. When tune-ups are incorporated into the regular sexual routine the man and the woman both feel free to have the kind of sex they desire. This new found sexual freedom recharges a man's sex life and energizes a woman's. A woman really does want sex, but before she can fulfill her desires she needs to feel the man's emotional support. More than anything else she needs to feel needed.

Sexual tune-ups make the man feel good because there are no restrictions or feelings of rejection. Not being rejected makes the man feel passionately attracted to his partner. Not feeling pressure makes the woman feel more loved, which encourages her to want to have more sex freely and willingly. Because of quickies a woman stops feeling pressured to have sex. She now feels that she's getting the kind of sex she wants and is in return giving him the kind he wants.

Change Your Attitude about Sex

Couples will never reach a higher level of sexual awareness if they don't change their attitudes about sex. Rubbing out ideas of intimacy that come when we we're very young and hushed if sex was spoken takes time. Women tend to think that sex should be done in the dark or kept under wraps. For some that's alluring and to others it's the very reason sex is treated as a suspect rather than pleasure. Some women use sex to cure their ills for the moment: loneliness, boredom, anger and depression.

No act can be quite so intimate as the sexual embrace.

- Havelock Ellis

Chapter 20

Getting Stimulating and Pleasurable Sex

This chapter will help you become a woman who is sincere and eager to please hi as well as yourself.

The popular question is ... When does a woman's sensuality allow her sexuality to take over? It all begins with the woman, but it continues when she's with her man. The most obvious place that sexuality starts is when she looks into his eyes. In order for a woman to capture a man's heart, she's got to first catch his eye. Every woman has this gift! It doesn't matter how young, old, tall, short, thin, wide, dumb, smart, rich, poor, good or

> **Heated Pleasures**
> While a woman continues to evaluate herself under the scrutiny of her own microscopes, men see her quite differently than she sees herself.

bad - everyone serves a divine purpose in this life which includes taking care of yourself. Even if you date on the Internet the relationship begins with your eyes. Let's observe for a moment. What is it that catches your eyes when you first meet a man that you're interested in? Is it his physical aspects? Is it his conversation? Is it plain ole female curiosity? You might think to yourself - Ummmmm, he's not a bad looking guy, but will he wants to meet me? While a woman continues to evaluate herself under the scrutiny of her own microscopes, men see her quite differently than she sees herself.

She sees that he has that 'something' and he sees that she has that 'thing!' Because beauty is in the eye of the beholder … to each of them … it's all good.

You've Got That Thing

Every man has a favorite thing about a woman that he can't resist. It may be her physical aspects, her personality, and her character. It may even be several features that she has, but a woman wants all of her feature to be just right.

That's why she's so hard on herself. She's trying to make sure she has what he wants. She puts in lots of time and effort to be this so-called perfect woman for him, but what she doesn't realize is … she already has what he wants and likes. It's that thing she has; some might say. She catches his eye because it's something about her he likes, even though neither of them knows what it is. They can't quite explain it, but they know it's there. It's inside his head, but he doesn't know how to put it into words yet. It's might be that thing you do, that thing you say while walking, talking, standing, sitting or simply being yourself. It's just that thing! And whatever that thing is, it holds his gaze until she snaps her finger.

Create Your Heated Pleasures

A heated sex life is not just the symptom of a passionate relationship; it's also a major factor in creating pleasure. Pleasure fills most women's hearts with love and can fulfill almost all our emotional needs, but heated sex, loving sex, passionate sex, sensual sex, long sex, short sex, quickie sex, gourmet sex, playful sex, tender sex, rough sex, soft sex, hard sex, romantic sex, goal-oriented sex, erotic sex, simple sex, complicated sex, cool sex, and hot sex are each an important part that keeps passion alive.

Without passion, sex can become routine and boring. By combining heated sex skills with love - a couple can continue to experience great passion and fulfillment. So, instead of becoming less passionate over the years, a woman who sees and touches her lover's naked body can become turned on more than ever. Not only does she become excited by the pleasure of arousal and increasing sexual intensity, she also becomes aware of how much more love, warmth, passion, and sensual affection she can experience and provide for him. This awareness elevates sex to a higher level of passion, excitement and commitment.

> **Heated Pleasures**
> The more a man craves sexual stimulation the more he is removed from his world. Sex allows a man to connect with his feelings and his sensitivities.

When a woman feels passion for a man, he can rejoice in her continued desire to connect with him and provide her lasting pleasure. She is the one who recognizes sex as an opportunity to share her gentleness and love in a way that nurtures him the most. Sex becomes a beautiful expression of her love for him and an opportunity to receive his love.

Sex is fabulous when shared in love. Sex gives love a chance to grow. For a woman to grow in sexual fulfillment, she needs to feel successful in fulfilling her sexual needs. She should not be afraid to try new skills in her bed.

Pleasure Opens a Woman's Heart

A woman's heated pleasure allows her to become more soft and gentle in spirit. The love in her heart is open and she is more willing to accept love from her partner. Her partner's skillful and knowing touch leaves no doubt in her mind that she is important to him. The hunger for love within her soul is fulfilled with her partner's passionate and present attention. An ever-present tension is momentarily released as she surrenders once again to the deepest longings of her feminine being. Her passion to love and be loved is fulfilled.

Pleasure Opens a Man's Soul

A man's heated pleasure helps him release his frustrations and allows him to rekindle his passion and commitment to the relationship. It quickly helps him experience positive results for his efforts.

In an intimate relationship a woman's fulfillment is the ultimate quest of a man. Her warm and moist responses excite and awaken his male being. He feels as though the world is opening up to him. He feels appreciated through her fulfillment. His desire is felt as he returns in his world while still remaining inside of her moistness. He loves the way it feels, smells and how it thrills him. He wants to do it again and again.

When a man touches a woman and feels her softness too, so he begins to feel pleasures that he has longed for. Through touching he can connect with his own kindness while still remaining masculine and focused on taking care of her.

> **You Should Know**
>
> It's hard for men to know what turns a woman on and how to keep her happy in bed because each is expected to already know what the other one wants.

When connecting through sex a man's soul is reawakened and allowing him a chance to understand why it's so important to feel pleasure again. The more a man craves sexual stimulation the more he is removed from his world. Sex allows a man to connect with his feelings and his sensitivities.

Many times after having great sex a man can regroup and regain insight on the beautiful things in life. He's more understanding and kinder in a hard world. He can breathe again and feel inner peace and joy. Sex is good for a man's soul.

Heated Pleasures for Partners

Heated pleasure reminds both the man and the woman of the highest love and heat that first brought them to one another. Heated sex generates the wonderful chemicals in the brain and body that allows the fullest enjoyment of one's partner. It increases the attraction for both partners as it stimulates energy and enthusiasm. It promotes better health practices and makes us appreciate each other for the big and small things. Heated sex helps us makes sex and love a priority in our lives. How couples mate, relate, and communicate has changed a great deal over the years, so has sex skills. To fulfill your partner in bed, fresh skills are required. After a short while in any relationship sex can become boring and routine. Making a few adjustments, women and men can completely overcome this problem.

Improve Your Sex

Sex can always use improvement, but like anything else, it requires new information and the opportunity to practice. Most women are never taught how to have sex, but once they learn how to get turned on or masturbate they are expected to be a sexual expert. Sure she knows where to put it and how to help him have an orgasm, but the art of great sexual fulfillment is a different story all together.

For great sex a woman needs to understand a man's body and what she can do to remain turned on as she pleases him. It's difficult for a woman to know what she needs to get turned on all the time. It's hard for men to know what turns a woman on. And keep her happy in bed because each is expected to already know what the other one wants. She assumes he knows how to make her happy and he assumes that what makes her happy also makes him happy.

You Should Know

If he's smart he'll know he should slow down to make her climb the walls to ecstasy every time they make love.

When a woman isn't satisfied a man thinks it's something wrong with hcr instead of him. He doesn't accept or understand that she needs are tremendously different from his.

Women like Slow, Men Want Fast

When a woman moves slowly during sex, she's trying to tell him that she wants nurturing. She wants her body to be massaged, not beat up. Men won't know what a woman likes unless she shows him. Even when she tells him, he

> **You Should Know**
> Getting to know someone better helps intimacy and love grow and the more sensual the experience the more chance it has to thrive into something positive.

forgets the next time they have sex. He's thinking more of what he wants than what she needs. Even though he knows she likes a slow grind, when he gets excited he speeds up. He thinks she wants it faster because that's what he wants. Women like slow penetration most times. If he's smart he'll know he should slow down to make her climb the walls to ecstasy every time they make love. Over time both lovers discover how to fulfill each other's sexual needs.

Loss of Your Sexual Drive

Being sensuous, alive and vibrant is vital to the success of a woman's inner spirit and her relationship. Women who have lost their sexual desire or sensuous drive grow old before their time. Loss of sexual appetite leads to frustration and the possible loss of a loving man.

When a woman loses the desire to make love or her interest in sex dies, she should start making plans to get in touch with her sensuous side. If she puts out undesirable messages to the man in her life he soon begins to think that he is undesirable, unloved and unwanted.

Many times women who are no longer in a loving and romantic relationship send messages of being a bitch. This is because these women are usually angry and uptight. They need some good loving. When she gets sex she becomes a softer, kinder and gentler person. When she doesn't she appears angry at the world and everyone around her tends to suffer.

21 Ways to Enjoy Your Sex

There are many women who enjoy sex. Some enjoy it some of the time, some enjoy it most of the time; and believe it or not there are some women who enjoy sex all the time. Maybe these women even love the very thought of it to the afterglow. They have more sex than the rest of us, and they thrill their men to the core. Whether they're feeling hot for their lovers or just lukewarm, they'd rather do it than not do it -- they make love, not excuses.

What makes sex great is love. Getting to know someone better helps intimacy and love grow and the more sensual the experience the more chance it has to thrive into something positive.

If you're tired; sex can revive you; if you're stressed, it relaxes; and if you have a headache, instead of falling asleep opt for the orgasm cure.

Here's how you can do it too.

1. Plan and follow through on sex quotas

When you're both juggling a hundred different things, finding time for a little loving can be the last thing on your mind. To ensure it gets penciled in your schedule and takes top billing, assign yourself a weekly sex goal. Every Monday pick a random number and schedule time for sex that amount of times before the weekend. If three days go by with zero action, make up the time fast. Get busy reaching your quota.

2. Crank up your sex drive

Carnal connoisseurs never sit around waiting for the mood to strike -- they make the mood happen. Waiting for sex to happen in the midst of dealing with daily obligations means sex will become a very rare event. Reminisce often about the last time you had great sex - think about his touch, his breath on your skin and, his sweet murmurings in your ear. Focus on sexy moments that will bring about a fired up state of mind. Think of those things that will lead you to the bedroom for some great sex.

3. Take turns giving and receiving

Many times one of the lover's energy won't be tuned in to the same sex channel. This is the time one will have to decide who's going to be the giver and who will be the receiver. The energetic person should be the giver and the one without a lot of energy should be the receiver. The giver ignites the fires and the receiver allows the giver to do the turning on.

There are going to be times when one of you won't have to raise a finger and can relax and enjoy the ride. It's guilt-free because the giver knows the favor will be returned another night. Think of all those times you denied your lover sexual happiness because one of you was too pooped. Now you'll have much happier sexual adventures because both of you are making an effort to keep the home fires burning.

4. Alternate the times you have sex

Your sex life will definitely suffer if the only time you have sex is by a set schedule. Get rid of the ideas that sex should be a nighttime ritual, and you'll soon discover that there are plenty of times you can indulge. Try different times. For instance after work, soon after happy hour, weekend afternoons or midmornings or have sex before leaving for work and satisfaction is guaranteed.

5. Have a titillating soundtrack

Music has a way of altering people's moods in an instant, so it comes as no surprise that the right CD could steer you straight to the bedroom. Play your favorite lovemaking music to pump up the passion.

6. Consider intimacy as a cure-all

Excuses, excuses -- it's so easy to find reasons to put off slipping into bed and making love. You're exhausted. You're stressed. You're annoyed and bickering with your husband over something silly. Stop right there and consider what's sexy. Divas know all too well: that doing the deed can actually alleviate exhaustion, stress and marital tension -- the very things that are supposedly keeping you from having sex in the first place! Sex energizes rather than drain, so find plenty of opportunities to use a little loving for an energy boost. 'Just do it -- you'll be glad you did afterward. Think of sex as a way to connect rather than another thing on a to-do list."

7. Be passionate...all day

Don't reserve your libidinous fervor just for the bedroom. Live sexually happy by adding spice to everyday activities. Wear silk undies. Buy an ice cream cone and eat it really suggestively. Take the most luxurious shower before work with all sorts of wonderful scrubs and creams.

8. Keep him buzzing with intimacy.

Do things in the morning that will keep him lusting after you. "Simple gestures such as stretching while naked or bending over while getting dressed, raising your arms, arching your back and stick your chest out in front of him, does wonders. Calling out to him from the shower to bring a towel gives him sensuous ideas too. Give him hints to rerun in his mind. Sex is usually inevitable that evening."

9. Don't saddle sex with tons of work

Passionately prolific couples have a philosophy: frequent sex, no matter what kind, is an absolute must for a good marriage. So if sex sometimes has to be a quickie -- a.k.a. tune-ups -- so what? It’s still good sex. If the kids are coming home from school in 20 minutes, don't try to light a bunch of candles and dig out your favorite set of love songs. This is when you nab the window of opportunity and jump each other's bones in a hurry. It does wonders for your sex life and relationship.

10. Think about the intimacy of sex

Conventional wisdom and scientific research says that men think about sex more often than women. Rather than censoring their erotic thoughts, some women encourage them. They don't feel guilty about fantasizing, even if fantasies are a bit kinky or have creative casting. And because sex is so often on their minds, it's a lot easier for their bodies to get to "yes."

11. Boost your libido

Indulge in sensuous thinking. One woman might get turned on by looking at a pile of luscious peaches and easily let her mind drift to imagine the fruit as her lovers balls. Another woman might think about her sexy lover and picture parts of him, like his forearm or chest until she is highly aroused. But even the most mundane things can have an erotic appeal. Something as simple as running your hand along the stick shift in a car can be a sensuous experience. It's all in your mind.

12. Put sex on your "things to do list"

Another positive way to get your sexual motor going is to make notes to yourself. Just as you would make a grocery list be sure to add sex as one of your favorite things to do. Because that note is there you'll think about sex more than you usually do. Make your notes interesting and fun. Here's an example of a simple, but sexy note: "Let’s make love on top of the pool table."

13. Take any mood and give it eroticism

Any emotion -- even sadness -- can be the catalyst for passion if you connect with its underlying power in an erotic way. Learn to take whatever mood you're in and turn it to your sensual advantage. Thc positive result is a more passionate relationship.

14. Heal through intimacy and sex

For many women the hardest part about being in a committed relationship is learning to share their emotions -- all of them. It's easy to be happy with someone and more difficult to be sad. Many times when a man is feeling bad or shutting down the communication in a relationship a woman can provide a little pampering and understanding and help him heal through romance. You can find erotic revelations in every emotion. Erotic interludes bring you closer during times when intense involvement might bring a wedge between you and your lover.

15. Indulge in your sensuality

Take pride in the thrill of the feel. Rub silk against your body. Women who love sex delight in all their senses. They breathe deeply of the flowers others merely sniff. They take pride in making love. "Nothing makes a woman feel sexier than self-indulgence. Whether having her legs waxed, buying new make-up, lingerie or a bag of very expensive chocolates to eat on the way home, an indulgence can make you feel pampered and sexy. "No matter how busy you are find time to schedule some indulgence for yourself. No husband, kids, friends, work -- only pampering time for you! Take private time to read a book, hire a sitter or go to a mid-afternoon movie. Occasional time-outs for yourself restore the body and rejuvenate the soul. It allows you time to experience the interesting parts of life. Self-indulgence helps you become more intriguing.

16. Wear sexy, simple, elegant clothing

Invest in camisoles. Wear them often beneath business suits, not to entice your mate, but for yourself. Wearing them will make you feel sensuous and very sexy.

17. Never stop fantasizing

Have you ever heard a women say, "I'm married, not dead," when she's trying to explain how she needs love and affection. Sex-loving women can relate to this statement because they really adore men. They don't stop liking them once they take their marriage vows. They're married, not nuns. Women can respectively indulge in sexual fantasies, whether driving in the car to work, riding in an elevator, waiting in line, or pumping gas; a woman can weave little erotic stories around the men she encounters. Imagine if a construction worker with bulging biceps becomes a secret lover. Fantasize about new sex games with him.

18. Flirt to keep the attraction alive

There's nothing wrong with flirting, but lighthearted flirting with a stranger, a coworker or male friend can also get the juices going. An exchange of smiles, compliments, and flirty gestures with him will also make you feel desirable.

19. Remain body-conscious

Sex-loving women are often not the most beautiful women. They don't always have perfect measurements, but they like their bodies. Exercise in some form is generally a priority, not because they want to be thinner, but because they crave the physicality. They know how to use their bodies to excite men. Exercise makes them feel alive and sexy.

20. Don't be afraid to touch yourself

Women who love sex are comfortable with touching themselves. They aren't afraid to masturbate. It's how they learn about their own bodies; about what they like, and about how they can reach orgasm quickly or slowly (depending on their mood). Since most women don't reach orgasm via intercourse alone, those who feel free to touch themselves during lovemaking control their erotic destiny. They know what they want, and that makes them more confident and relaxed lovers. When a woman knows that she can get up to speed quickly it makes her more willing to follow his lead. Even if she thinks she's not in the mood she can help get herself there with a little masturbation. Why? She knows exactly what makes her feel good?

21. Expect your lover to be a good lover

Sex-loving women have high standards -- for themselves and their lovers. They want to be good lovers, but they also want to get love as good as they give it. They would never fake orgasms because; they know their men want to give them real ones. And if he needs gentle instruction in that regard, she's happy to provide it.

Many women lose interest in sex because their lovers become lousy lovers. Women read sex advice often; men rarely do. Share new ideas with your lover. Help him out.

Sex can get a man, but sex cannot keep a man.

Chapter 21

Pleasurable and Heated Sexual Treats

This chapter will help you become a sensuously mature and give you grown woman sexiness.

It can sometimes become difficult when you want to release your inhibitions and enjoy being a sexually sensuous woman. To achieve intense sensuous pleasures before, during and after sex you should make more sensuous contact with your lover. You will feel more comfortable in your relationship when you are able to loosen up, get rid of sexual hang-ups and express your love.

Mood and privacy are basic concerns, but you should also feel that your environment is safe, romantic and comfortable before you can become completely erotic.

Some women manage to keep their sensuality in full bloom long after their friends have thrown in the towel. You can get in tune with your sensuality and improve your sexuality if you are shown love and sincere appreciation. If you have lost interest in making love and can't seem to get the hots for your lover you are allowing your feminine sensuality to suffer. Maybe you're focused on the bills, family problems or other non-sexual activities. Whatever it is try to refocus and rediscover your sexual self so that you can get turned back on.

Being aware of what it takes to be a sensuous woman is also being in tune with your wants and needs. Here are 159 sensuous suggestions that will definitely help you get the most from your heated moments.

1. Sit close and touch him sensuously as often as possible.
2. Stand next to him and stroke his back, remembering to move your hands slowly and sensuously.
3. When at social gatherings brush your nipples across his body each time you pass him.

4. Pull him closer when kissing him. Don't allow him to be the aggressor every time. He'll love it.
5. Give long, lingering, and playful kisses. Make him feel the pleasure of the kiss by giving lots of tongue kisses.
6. Gliding the hips toward him while kissing him will help you roll onto his male identity sensuously.
7. Play with his nipples each time you kiss him.
8. Do things that you know he likes.
9. Blindfold him and make love to him. Become willing to share sensuous ideas with him.
10. Look him directly in his eyes as you masturbate.
11. Name a new dessert after his male identity.
12. Place your forefinger into your vagina, return to him and as you hug him give him a long sensuous kiss. Now slowly glide your scented finger under his nose.
13. As you stare into his eyes, slowly and seductively suck on an ice cube. Move the ice cube in and out of your mouth with your tongue, then release it from your sensuous lips, lick the rim of your glass slowly and sensuously.
14. Have him massage your love button with his penis.

15. Wear something sexy to bed at least five times a week.
16. Buy a garter belt and wear it with no panties. While he eats dinner open and close your legs so that he can see your hungry vagina.
17. Buy sexy matching bra and panty sets.
18. Buy a vibrator and learn how to use it on yourself and then teach him how to use it on you.
19. Buy sheer stocking instead of support hose.
20. Wear laced bras regularly.
21. Liven up your sensuous thinking by reading sensuous books.
22. Give good phone sex. Don't forget to coo and ahh a lot. Seduce him by making a sensuous call to him for a date.
23. Hire him for an evening of passionate sex. Tell him that you're going to pay him a hundred dollars an hour. He'll think about it all day.
24. Tell him that he turns you on and mean it.
25. Look good when your man gets home from work. He probably sees beautiful women daily, some who probably flirt with him. Don't give him a reason to have an affair.
26. Be a good listener when he talks to you, look him directly in eyes and listen to what he has to say.

27. Think about sex with your lover on a regular basis. The more you think about it, the sexier you'll become.
28. Work to be the best sexual lover he's ever had.
29. See it in your heart to give him his fantasy.
30. Schedule two fantasy dates per month. He's responsible for one and you're responsible for one. Keep all plans secret from each other.
31. Plan an evening around your sexual fantasy. It can be as wild as you want. Make it a date to remember.
32. While giving oral sex take a piece of ice into your mouth. As you slip his male identity into your mouth, rotate the ice cube all around his male identity. Be sure to suck, lick and massage his male identity with your tongue until he begs you to stop. This technique is very beneficial to a limp male identity.
33. Tie your lover to the bed and tease him. Touch him with parts of your sensuous body only. After seductively stripping for him, kiss him all over his body, remembering not to miss a single spot. Alternate soft to firm touches on his body. As he squirms and twitches about, leave him there and get a drink or find something else to do for about

two minutes. These two minutes will feel like twenty to him. Once you get back, start the process over again beginning with light kisses all over his body. It will drive him crazy.

34. Send items of sexy clothing to your lover. These items of clothing can extend for as long as you want. For example, if you want him to receive all items in one week, send everything at once. If you want the time to spread out into two weeks send half this week and half on the following week. This game can be as sensuous and erotic, or as subtle as you want. Clothing should be sensuous and erotic. Once he's received the complete outfit wears it.
35. Skinny dip with your lover regularly.
36. Give oral sex with a mouth full cold water.
37. Suck on a strong mint before performing oral sex.
38. Place your finger and thumb in a ring to your mouth and then use the ring as an outer part of her mouth while you give him oral sex.
39. Help him withdraw from intercourse just before the point of no return, going back to it soon after.
40. Slow down all movement just before he ejaculates. Move all body parts as if you were a belly dancing - very slowly.

41. Provoke a quickie. Strip naked for him while he keeps his clothes on.
42. Leave your panties on during sex or have him tear your panties off to get to your sweet awaiting vagina.
43. Make his male identity hard without touching it. Whisper softly that you want to feel him inside of you, watch how it turns him on.
44. Place his head over your heart and allow him to listen to your heartbeat. Tell him that he helps you live.
45. Let him to pinch your nipples, go from soft to hard. Tell him how hard you like it to be done and make sure he reaches your hard goal.
46. Place lipstick around the head of his male identity and suck it off slowly and gently then give slower and harder suction actions..
47. Place a large rubber sheet on the floor. Coat yourself with massage oil and then have a timed wrestling match. First to achieve two holds can ask the other for any sexual treat they desire. Coating the sheet with oil will add more escalated slippery fun.
48. Send your lover an e-card designed to tantalite and turn on.

49. Hand-deliver any obscene messages. It's deemed illegal to send obscene letters through the mail.
50. The outer third of the vagina is the most sensitive so deep massaging thrusts are essential. A woman can ask her man to stay at the shallow end of the vagina to make sex better. Having him dip the tip of his male identity into her vagina feels great. Here is a few more ways to spice up your sex life by using these sexual basics.
51. Do it in the cupboard under the stairs - seriously. Novelty is an intense aphrodisiac, and any unusual setting with strange sensations, smells and muffled sounds, will make sex feel new, upping the excitement.
52. Sit on top of the washing machine with your legs wrapped around his waist. Washing machine vibrations turns the male identity into a wonderful vibrator. Select the cotton cycle for best results. It's a warm wash so your butt won't get cold, and it has the longest, fastest spin. Feel the vibrations. You'll want more once you try it.
53. Place a pillow under your bottom to create an orgasm optimum 26-degree pelvic tilt, which means maximum contact between his body and

your G-spot. This will help a woman reach orgasm every time.

54. Colors create sexy moods. Red, dark blue and violet are the three most erotic colors. And the least erotic is gray.

55. Sex in the bath is fun, but can be tricky. Try this: fill the bath halfway with water, and then pour plenty of bath gel over each other's bodies. With your man lying down in the bath, lie on top of him and, instead of going for penetrative sex, stimulate each other to climax by rubbing your body's on each other's.

56. Rotate the palms of your hands on areas near his male identity to build excitement.

57. Pull a sexy piece of underwear from your lover's drawer and ask that he wear it beneath his clothing.

58. Plan a dinner out for the evening. Choose sensuous appetizers and a main course. Plan a long meal, but remember to mention lots of suggestive sensuous games and gestures. Make the suspense of what's going to happen later last as long as possible.

59. Good vibrations. Take turns with the Tongue Joy Oral Vibrator. Strapped to your tongue, the

vibrations stimulate nerve endings like you've never felt before.

60. Play Twister in the nude while wet. It removes inhibitions and gets you in positions you wouldn't usually attempt.

61. Don't go solo with your vibrator. Only 25% of women climax through penetrative sex alone, so get your man to pleasure you with a sex toy while he's making love to you.

62. Ask him to talk or hum his favorite tune while he's indulging in oral sex. The vibrations from his voice and the unpredictability of it will make you come quicker.

63. Feed your man cinnamon, cardamom, peppermint and lemon if you're planning to give him oral pleasure. It'll make his semen taste nicer.

64. Convince him to buy you more jewelry by masturbating him with a string of pearls. Use lots of lubrication, and then wrap the pearls around the shaft of his male identity, gently sliding them up and down. They'll add different levels of stimulation to the experience. He'll love buying you jewelry just to see what you'll do next.

65. Remember the mind-blowing sex you had on yesterday was yesterday. Today is a new day so

each lovemaking session should be new and eventful.

66. Don't feel apologetic for your shape, size or physical appearance. Improve it if you have to apologize for it.
67. Be human. The human part of you means more than anything else.
68. Leave a sexually suggestive message on his private voicemail.
69. Don't be judged by others standards. Share intimacy with your lover that might not be normal to others. It's your love life, no one else's.
70. Wake up before he does and make love until he climaxes.
71. Play with him using honey until he climaxes.
72. Ask him to teach you his favorite sex techniques. Let him show you how he likes to do it.
73. Take nude pictures of him playing with his private parts.
74. Let him take pictures of you playing with your vagina.
75. Make up a game called "Find the Cherry," with your own rules and then play it.
76. Bite his butt cheeks gently from time to time during sex.

77. Let him lick you all over until you climax.
78. Greet him at the door wearing heels only.
79. Serve him dinner stark naked, with you as the dessert.
80. Let him trim your pubic hair.
81. Watch him shave his pubic hair.
82. Play with his male identity as he drives you to work.
83. Make passionate love to him before he goes to work.
84. Catch him in the shower and suck him to ecstasy.
85. Put his favorite nude photograph of you into his wallet.
86. Straddle him and make love in the tub.
87. Play with his male identity under the table at restaurants.
88. Buy him a sex toy and ask him to do the most creative thing to you that he can do.
89. Buy a massager or a vibrator and massage his male identity until he begs you to stop.
90. Write him an erotic letter and place it in his briefcase.
91. Buy pornographic magazines and read them on long romantic drives.
92. Buy a vibrator as a gift for your lover.

93. Purchase sexy underwear for him.
94. Take him to a dirty movie and a live strip show.
95. Make up your own strip show for him.
96. Meet him for lunch in your undies and a coat.
97. Have sex in someone else's bedroom.
98. Read him a pornographic story in which he's starring.
99. Give him a massage with oils that are sure to turn him on.
100. Have a full day of naked extravaganza: sex, photos, and more sex.
101. Suck on his private parts gently.
102. Masturbate him as he masturbates you and see who will climax first.
103. Lick every part of his body that you can touch.
104. Masturbate him in the back seat of your car.
105. Give him oral sex in the back seat of your car.
106. Give oral sex in an elevator of a tall building in your city.
107. The next time he doesn't act interested in sex convince him by doing oral things to him.
108. Tie him to the bedposts and have your way with him.
109. Let him tie you up and submit to his fantasies.

110. Go without panties to your next social function and allow him to put his finger into your vagina each chance he gets.
111. Bite his nipples during lovemaking.
112. Spell your name on his male identity with the tip of your tongue and ask him to figure out the direction of each letter as you spell it.
113. Blindfold him and ask him to guess the flavors you put onto your vagina. Use different flavors.
114. Make love in front of a lit fireplace.
115. Make love in a taxi on the way to your destination.
116. Lick the roof of his mouth while kissing.
117. Suck his male identity while he's talking on the telephone,
118. Playfully hold his male identity while he pees, trying to guide it.
119. Give him a vagina massage: slowly rub your wet vagina over his body.
120. Get naked and sit on his face.
121. Lie in the middle of your table and yell, "Dinner is served."
122. Tell him that you love his hard male identity.
123. Kiss him passionately and tell him that you love him.

124. Play strip domino. Every time you score ten points or more, he must remove an item of clothing, your choice.
125. Have him buy a copy of 'Heated Pleasures' and read it together.
126. Emerge his male identity into a glass of bubbly champagne and lick it clean.
127. Challenge him to make mad, passionate love to you for at least six hours in the same night.
128. Let him watch as you slide a microwaved cucumber into your vagina.
129. Let him watch as you slide a dildo into your vagina.
130. Skinny dip in the moonlight with your lover.
131. Send an exotic plant with a sexy note attached.
132. Time each other and see who can make the other climax in the least amount of time.
133. Leave love notes all through your home for him to find.
134. Slip a pair of your favorite panties in his briefcase or lunch box for him to sniff at his leisure.
135. Always smell your best for him. Make it a habit.
136. Keep chilled wine ready before, during and after sex.

137. Strip from head to toe while dancing to his favorite song.
138. Masturbate YOURSELF as he dances for you.
139. Tell him that you love him again.
140. Have a girlfriend take semi-nude pictures of you and give them to him.
141. Suck his toes after the foot massage.
142. Lick his eyelids during lovemaking.
143. Suck his ear lobes often.
144. While waiting in line together, tell him in a low sexy voice what you plan to do to him when you get home.
145. Use your favorite scents on your bed sheets, pillows and bed covers.
146. Have a mold of his male identity made for keepsake.
147. Oil your breasts down with your favorite oils and then give him a breast massage.
148. Suck his bottom lip gently at the end of each kiss.
149. Become a real woman, and remain one during sex.
150. Tell him that you are a real woman and mean it during sex.
151. Treat him like a real man.
152. Love yourself more than you love him.

153. Suck his fingers for no reason at all.
154. Lick his ears and his eyelids for no reason at all.
155. Have him wear a condom, or two, before every sexual encounter.
156. Open your mind to more than what you're already doing with him.
157. Going without panties all day long is a favorite.
158. Go without panties. It's your way of expressing freedom. Whether it was freedom from a marriage, jail, bad habits, etc. Its women celebrating independence and freedom.

Heated Pleasures

A couple can have sensuous moments in every room of the house or experiment with the excitement or fear of getting caught by doing it in a different place each time.

Chapter 22

Stimulating Places, Games, and Fantasies

This chapter helps create pleasure by using games and fantasies on your terms.

What more could add to your sexual amusement? What else can you purchase? Sexy games from sex shops, lingerie stores, catalogs, and the Internet. Or you can create intimate that you can share with your lover. The best games are those that encourage communication, arousal, and pleasure? Erotic games and fun places to explore your eroticism can add another element of fun to your sex life. One of the things most women enjoy about sexual games is the fact you don't have to restrict fun to your bedroom. You don't have to do it face to face you can do it over the phone, or email your sexual thoughts to your lover. You can even text messages or play games alone. Your games can happen immediately before, or after sex.

Below are some fun places to have your sensual moments? Your bedroom is probably the main location, but what other places have you enjoyed sensual moments that make your body pulsate at the thought of them?

Sexual Settings and Locations

If you really think about it, changing sensual settings can add tremendous positive effects to the visual parts of your sexual experiences. Your sexual setting can actually enhance your senses. A couple can have sensuous moments in every room of the house or experiment with the excitement or fear of getting caught by doing it in a different place each time. Maybe even public places, it's up to you; whatever makes you tick. Where would you have sex if you could choose? To help you with this question, here are some fun-to-have-sex-locations that women have told me they enjoy having sex.

1. Under a waterfall.
2. In the bathroom of an airplane somewhere high in the sky.
3. In a best friends bedroom.
4. In a tree house.
5. In a chicken coop on a farm.
6. In the back seat of a taxi.
7. In an empty room next to a room full of people.
8. In the front yard at about midnight.
9. In the backyard under a full moon.
10. In your supervisors office on top of his/her desk.
11. In a locker room at a work out facility.
12. In a limo stuck in traffic.
13. In an empty swimming pool.
14. In a pool filled with watcr.
15. In the ocean at a club med spa.
16. In a parking garage at a Four Diamond Hotel.
17. In the backseat of someone else's car.
18. In the back of a pickup truck.
19. In the seat of an airplane while under a blanket.
20. In the trunk of a car. (Make sure it has a safety latch that opens from the inside.)
21. In the middle of a field of flowers.
22. In an amusement park on a roller coaster high in the air.

23. On a bench in an empty public park.
24. On top of a bar or pool table.
25. On an Amtrak train going nowhere special.
26. On a concrete sidewalk
27. In a neighbors front yard.
28. On top of the Empire State Building.
29. On a hidden staircase.
30. On a cruise boat of course.
31. On top of a printer while your butt is being copied.
32. On top of a washing machine.
33. At the front gate of the City Zoo.
34. At the top of the Eiffel Tower.
35. Beneath a bridge where there's a running creek.
36. Beneath a high-rise bed.
37. Behind an extra-large very expensive painting.
38. Behind an open door.
39. Behind a tall building, in the alleyway.

Go on a romantically sensuous date at least once a month. Each time you go make it a game and find a new place to have fun sex. Fun and out of the way places to have sex should be on every woman's 'Fun to do list.'

Fun and Spicy Sex Games

Here are several erotic games that will spice things up. You can also find these games and others online (see "Resources" in back of book).

- ## 365 Days of Romance:

  Use your sexual hope chest for this one. Fill it with surprising, adventurous, seductive, scratch-and-reveal cards that suggest lovemaking ideas for you and your lover.

- ## 365 Days of Naughty Things to Do:

  These naughty games should be your most erotic and sensuous. Use them with suggestive games, ideas and sex toys that are more naughty than nice.

- ## Sex Suit:

  You need a deck of cards. Couples pick a suit: diamonds, hearts, spades or clubs. Take turns selecting one card from the deck of cards and when the other person pulls your suit ask a sexual question or request a sexual favor. Fun if played in the spirit of sexual exploration.

❖ Sexual Aim:

Draw a circle or a bulls-eye on any part of your body that you want to be the target. Use favored body paint to draw sensuous pieces of art. Give your partner thirty seconds to creatively and sensuously clear the body paint. Each player gets three chances before moving to deeper sex.

❖ Do or dice:

Find some dice or use square wooden blocks found in arts and crafts shops. Write one-word that symbolizes erotic or sexual instructions on each square on the blocks. Examples of playful words can be lick, tickle, stroke, pump, chew, suck, bite, play, penetrate, tickle, etc. You may also use the other side to illustrate sexual pictures such as breasts, penis, vagina, neck, ears, etc. Take turns rolling the dice and follow the instructions.

❖ Find the position:

Get a book that has lots of sexual positions and make several copies of the positions. Fold the pieces of paper and place them in a bowl, box or big bag. Draw a piece of paper from the container on each day and declare it the sexual position of the day. Bring what you have chosen to your bedroom and practice what you see. Enjoy!

- **Keep a sexual calendar:**

On each week, circle a day or days in advance that you would like to declare as your day(s) for good sex. The only rule is you and your partner must follow through on the selected date. It's especially exciting for couples that are very busy or dealing with long-distance relationships.

Sexual Fantasies

Some of the most popular female fantasies are those that are intimate, pleasurable and arouse sexual desire. Warm feelings can come from romance, intimacy, love and moments of laughter. Fantasy allows women to turn moments of great sex into moments of mind-blowing whirlwind sex.

- **Sex with Your Lover**

Imagine doing something more erotic and different than what you normally do with your lover. Shock and surprise him with new and wonderful sex games. Your choices are numerous. Choose to do something very low key or as over the top as possible. Just do it.

❖ Sex with a Stranger

Married women fall in this category more frequently than we would like to know. This does not mean you want to go out and have sex with a total stranger, but I've been told that they do think about how it would be. It doesn't mean that you'll adore your partner less, but it gives you permission to daydream about another man. Men have this same fantasy, so it's normal for your partner to have similar fantasies to yours.

❖ Sex with a Woman

This is the most common fantasy for heterosexual women. Just because you fantasize about another woman does not mean you are into women. If you love yourself and also love other women it's not abnormal to fantasize about having sex with a woman. If you really think you'd like this go ahead and explore it with another willing woman. Giving yourself permission to really enjoy your fantasy helps you find out what you really like or dislike.

❖ Sex with Multiple Lovers

The idea of having sex with more than one person, whether it's male or female is another popular female fantasy. The only reason most women don't act on it is because they are afraid of what people will think.

Remember this fantasy can bring on more headaches than needed. Sexually transmitted diseases are very normal in this kind of relationship. This is not the smartest sexual fantasy.

❖ Sex in a Different Location

Location. You can have sex anywhere you want for as long as you, but please not in front of children. Be sure to make it more romantic, alluring and sexy. Take turns choosing a place to make mad love.

❖ Oral Sex

Women just love it, especially when it's done right! Enough said.

❖ Forced Sex

Better known as "control fantasies." I don't know many people who are into this one, but some women love the idea of being forced to have sex with their lovers. Tearing clothes off, kissing aggressively and wildly falling on the floor can bring heightened pleasure. Forced sex can be absolutely wonderful when it's positive and with the person you love.

❖ Forbidden Sex

Participating in sexual acts that others feel are deviant or forbidden can turn a nice girl into a naughty little thing. Forbidden sex is the safe way to experience something sexual that you know you would never really do. It's considered fantasy sex because you don't have to actually do it.

❖ Domination

Controlling a man is attractive to many women. The feeling of power turns them on, especially power over a man. They like to tell him what to do and when to do it. They like tying him up, placing a leash around his neck, and making him beg for love. This kind of sex turns them on more.

❖ Sex with a Celebrity

Imagine your favorite celebrity who can have any woman in the world, but he wants you and no one else. As he walks up to the stage and accepts his award he thanks you for being his lover and now the whole world knows that you and he belong to one another. What a fantasy!

❖ Romance Novels

When reading a romance novel many women find that this is their chance to enjoy their fantasies. As you read your novel focus on your own fantasy; write it down and then act on it when your lover gets home. Use your own sensuous terms to tell your story. Get detailed; describe your sexual experiences. Describe emotions and physical sensations. Write your own erotic story with you being the star. Remember to give your story a happy ending.

A Final Note

This list is only a few of the ways women can satisfy their sexual fantasies. If you are to set aside other people's judgment, concerns and comments and let your mind go freely you can get rid of all your fears. Fantasy is very important when you're working to enhance your love life.

Use your senses, create your own fantasies and have fun in life and in sex.

Chapter 23

Having the Most Pleasurable Orgasms

This chapter will help you discover ways to have great orgasms

Orgasms are pleasurable and unique experiences for every woman. For a few wonderful seconds she can let go, lose control and enter a different state of consciousness. It's wonderful and heavenly.

Some women who are able to experience orgasms are becoming more and more concerned with achieving multiple orgasms. Not just any orgasm, they want great orgasms. They want mind-blowing, prolonged, multiple

Heated Pleasures
Sex is about pleasing, giving, receiving and sharing intimacy.

orgasms. If it's not perfect the woman feels unfulfilled and disappointment.

Orgasm can be wonderful, but if a woman focuses too hard on getting an orgasm she can lose sight of intimacy and pleasure. Sometime the lack of orgasm is attributed to poor vagina health. Additionally, each orgasm can vary in overall intensity, duration, number of involuntary rhythmic contractions, and so forth. If you're serious about enjoying more sexual pleasure, and want to achieve intense orgasms or magnify the sensations of sex all the time, improving your vagina health can guarantee amazing sex.

Sex is about pleasing, giving, receiving and sharing intimacy. When you take away the pressure to achieve the perfect orgasm, you allow your mind and body to bask in the pleasure of it all.

What Is An Orgasm?

What is an orgasm? Physically, an orgasm is a series of rhythmic contractions of the uterus, lower vagina, and pelvic floor muscles, which lead to a release of sexual tension. Some women have orgasms that are centered in the pelvis, while others may experience mental imagery or auras. Orgasm is the pinnacle of sexual passion. It is that moment of intense pleasure, which results into feeling relaxed and at ease. The female orgasm lasts a few seconds, followed by a feeling of relaxation and pleasure. Continued stimulation may also result in further orgasms.

Orgasm Facts

Experience of an orgasm may vary from one encounter to the next for the same woman and even though every woman can have great orgasms, not every woman does. If you've had either a vaginal orgasm or love button orgasm you'll know it. Nearly all MEN can climax without difficulty, but women just aren't built that way. For a man sexual intercourse alone - that is, penetration of a woman's vagina by a man's male identity may be sufficient to climax. But that's still not enough to make a woman reach orgasm. Coming' isn't all that easy - for a woman!

Types of Orgasms

Basically there are two types of orgasms women experience. They are based on the two different zones of stimulation. The first is a love button orgasm where light touching, massaging or stroking stimulates the love button. The second type of orgasm is a vaginal orgasm. This comes from pressure being applied to the "G" spot, (See Chapter 13 - Your G-Spot) usually by the tip of the man's male identity.

Both of these experiences are very different and women who have experienced both kinds of orgasms know the difference. However; very few women reach orgasm as a result of the male identity (penis) penetrating the vagina. It's more likely to happen through stimulation (touching/rubbing/kissing) of the clitoris - the highly sensitive bump located at the top of the vagina lips.

Factors Responsible for Orgasm

- **Sexual frequency..** In order to reach climax it is important that you have regular sex. The more time that passes between sexual encounters, the harder it is for a woman to become aroused, and less likely for her to have an orgasm.

- **Relaxed and tension free.** For a woman to get the most out of her sexual encounters she must be comfortable with the relationship and the situations she's involved in. Orgasms are impossible in situations where there is tension, or lack of trust. Relax and release.

- **Understanding, caring and attentiveness.** A woman's lover should be a man who knows how to stimulate and arouse and who helps her reach a climax.

Let Him Help You Orgasm

To reach orgasm it is very important that a man co-operate with the woman and understands the woman and her body. She should try not to feel so shy that she can't tell him how to make love to her and what arouses her. Knowing which part of her body will make her climax is helpful to the both of them.

When a woman makes love she should guide the man - helping him to help her reach orgasm. Here are some important things men can do to help the woman become relaxed and at ease.

- Tell her she's marvelous, sexy and beautiful and mean it.
- Stimulate her love button by gently massaging it.
- Be sure to touch/kiss/stroke in succession, this will help her reach wonderful orgasms.

- Women adore oral sex and some claim that they cannot come unless a man 'goes down' on them.
- Caress her breasts and give attention to her sensitive spots. Few women climax through breast fondling alone or simply by stroking their sensitive spots, but it sure does help.
- A man should ask the woman to show him what she wants.
- If the man comes before the woman, he should try to help her climax by kissing and stimulating her continuously.
- The man should always help her feel safe. He should try his very best to provide an atmosphere of love, romance, security and compassion.

How You Can Help Bring Orgasms

A woman who experiences none or only a few orgasms can learn to bring herself to climax with patience and self-stimulation. It takes time to learn the sensitive spots, the best touches, interpret feelings and understand thoughts that arouse to the point of climax. These techniques can be practiced alone, and later with your lover.

1. Don't try so hard.

When you focus on the goal of orgasm, you risk increasing your anxiety and short-circuiting your pleasure and orgasmic responses. Instead of enjoying pleasure you'll become consumed with fear and you might not achieve your goal. Relax and focus on the pleasures of lovemaking.

2. Explore your body.

When alone touch and stoke yourself in ways you would like to be caressed by your lover. Learn to enjoy those things that really stimulate you.

3. Share your experiences.

Once you know what stimulates you communicate these things to your lover. Guide him to parts of your body that become aroused when stimulated - then let him find other ways to arouse you too.

4. Let him stimulate your love button.

During foreplay, until you find yourself on the brink of orgasm.

5. Move into intercourse.

After your lover has caressed your love button move into intercourse, remember to stimulate your love button.

6. **Add toys to your pleasuring moments.**

   Try the Hitachi Magic Wand. The intense vibrations are sure to help you along. It can help increase the number of orgasms you achieve. (See Part VI, Battery Operated Boyfriends).

7. **Practice your Kegel exercises.**

   Exercising your pelvic floor muscles makes your vaginal muscles and increases the blood flow to your pelvis. You orgasms are more intense when your pelvic muscles are stronger.

8. **Be patient.**

   Sex improves over time. The more comfortable and relaxed you are, the better the sex.

9. **Release and let go.**

   Practice breathing in a relaxed state. Accept pleasure. You deserve it. Love it.

Get an Orgasmic State of Mind

Some philosophies have two ideas about orgasm -- the physical orgasm and the heart orgasm. At first appearance they may seem dualistic and contrary, but on closer inspection one supports the other perfectly.

The orgasmic state of "being," which is considered the bliss-state can be equated with the energy transferred to all that we are and do during the day. On the "other hand," however, sexuality itself is used to reach the deepest spiritual levels a woman can attain. The orgasm is used as the gateway to recognize this bliss-state. Modern women recognize that there are several forms of orgasm. Let's discuss them.

- **Love button (clitoral) orgasms** tend to be more localized to the genitals. The vagina orgasm mostly involves the G-spot and a few other locations in the vagina. As implied, love button (Clitoral) orgasms come from direct stimulation of the love button and surrounding area. Most women only experience love button orgasms
- **Blended orgasms** involves both the love button and the G-spot, as the love button splits into two roots under the skin, wrapping around either side of the G-spot and stimulating it directly.
- **Energy orgasms** or heart orgasm are a result of superior sexual health. If a woman has good sexual health she'll experience amazing, frequent and intense energy orgasms.

- **Full body orgasms** lend themselves to full-body orgasmic potential when the breath, the mind and the orgasm itself come together. With this full-blown experience with different breath patterns, sounds and techniques, a woman has the potential to move into multiple orgasms and out-of-body sex. Going even further into this practice, she is able to have full-body orgasms, or energy orgasms, simply by deep breathing -- and small amounts of physical touch.
- **Vaginal orgasms,** including G-Spot orgasms. This type of orgasm occurs during intercourse or by direct stimulation of the G-Spot. It is often described as deeper and more intense that love button orgasms. Many women have never had a vaginal orgasm. Just like a love button orgasm, if you have good sexual health you'll experience
- **Multiple orgasms.** This is the ability to have repeated orgasms within a short period of time, e.g. a single lovemaking session. In order to achieve multiple orgasms during intercourse good vagina health is essential!

- **Ejaculatory orgasms** are known as natural occurrences for some women when coupled with incredibly intense orgasmic pleasure. There is one constant with women who experience ejaculatory orgasms; they have great sexual health.

Some Orgasms Are Difficult

Any times a woman will not be able to experience orgasms, no matter how hard she tries. Here are some possible reasons an orgasm might be difficult to achieve.

- **Fear**. You're afraid that you won't have an orgasm. So you don't even bother trying and end up completely repressing your sexual responses.
- **Physical factors**, such as fatigue. Your body and mind are tired and you need rest.
- **You think too much** about whether you will have an orgasm or not or about how aroused you are or aren't. You wonder what your lover thinks of you. These concerns make it difficult to climax. Focus on the sensations of your sexual encounter and stop thinking about all the would of, should of and could of's? Try not to over think things.

- **Length of time since last orgasm has been too long.** In order to reach climax it's important that you have regular sex. The more time that passes between sexual encounters makes it harder to become aroused, and less likely for an orgasm.
- **Pressure and tension.** You might be afraid or ashamed of asking your lover to arouse you and as a result you end up being unsatisfied. Also you're afraid that if your lover concentrates on your pleasure only, you'll feel pressured to do the same for him, which leaves you incapacitated sexually.
- **You rush into sex with your lover.** You're not leaving yourself enough time to get fully aroused to climax and your orgasm ends up getting pushed aside during sex.
- **Psychosocial factors.** This includes your mood, relationship to your lover, activity before sex, expectations, and feelings about the overall experience can leave you frigid.
- **Family, religious and moral values** often shape beliefs about sex. You've always thought of sex as something dirty or something that you shouldn't

enjoy. The guilt gets in the way of your true enjoyment of the experience.

- **Low self-confidence and feelings** about self may be opposing your efforts to feel good about sex. Some women are so ashamed of their body they are not comfortable while making love. They simply don't enjoy the thought of sex even though they do want it.
- **Past relationship trauma** can play an important role in whether or not you can relax, make love. If you are traumatized enjoying the entire sexual experience can be difficult.

Open Your Orgasm Door

Being able to achieve a satisfying climax is in your mind. You have to relax and focus completely on the sexual act. The following are things that will help you open the door to sexual satisfaction and pleasure.

- **Resolve your conflict.** Communication is very important because you know your body and what stimulates and turns you on. If you have a problem you must speak up. Get in the habit of talking about all facets of your relationship with one another. Unresolved conflicts can put the damper on sex and orgasm.

- **Let go of your inhibitions.** Fear, embarrassment, shyness, mental blocks etc., are factors that keep you from having an orgasm. Keep your mind clear and enjoy sex instead of depriving yourself of pleasure.
- **Know your body.** You have to be sufficiently aroused to reach orgasm, but to get sufficiently aroused you need to know what makes you feel good. Find out by exploring your body. To start, set aside 20 minutes of uninterrupted time. Take a relaxing bath and then look at yourself naked in a mirror. After looking at your physical body close your eyes for a while and quietly examine the mental picture you receive. Once you're comfortable put some lubricant on your finger and touch your vagina lips, love button (clitoris) and inside of your vagina. Find out which areas are most sensitive and what touch feels good. Touch yourself in ways that heighten your arousal to the point of orgasm. Understand what you're doing to excite

yourself and know how to make it happen again. Know more about your body than he does.

- **Try new positions.** Trying new positions helps you achieve different kinds of orgasms. To achieve an orgasm your G-spot needs stimulation. Try a position that will stimulate this spot leading to an orgasm. If you try many positions, you'll find the ones most likely to lead you to orgasm.

A Sensual Note:

For some women, difficulty in experiencing orgasm is the result of physical problems, chemical or hormonal imbalance, drug or medical side effects or even previous psychological trauma. Such situations may require more extensive sex therapy or treatment.

Heated Pleasures

Think of your sexual accessories in the same way you would add a framed picture to your wall or a piece of jewelry or a scarf to your wardrobe.

Note: To better understand your problems you should discuss them with your doctor or therapist.

Part 5

Pleasure Containers and Sexual Supplies

Chapter 24

Using Containers and Sex Supplies?

This chapter will introduce you to everyday items that can be used to enhance your sexual appetite.

S**exually** active woman should have a pleasure container that they refer to as their sexual hope chest, prop box, pleasure bag or goodie drawer.

Pleasure containers hold your favorite sexual accessories, sexual toys, sex props and sexual supplies and are used as sensuous supply holders. You can make your own from a variety of small decorative cardboard boxes, straw baskets, plastic, cloth, or metal containers.

Use your imagination and decorate your pleasure container to your own liking. Make it very personal. Your pleasure container could even be an extra drawer that's used for nothing except sexual supplies and toys. This container or drawer should safely store, hide and preserve your sex toys, and should always be clean and sanitary.

Let's face it, every woman needs a place to store their sexual items and the best way to hide or conceal them is to create a handy container just for your own personal items.

Exploring the use of sexual props and supplies doesn't mean you won't be able to have heated passionate experiences without them. Think of your sexual accessories in the same way you would add a framed picture to your wall or a piece of jewelry or a scarf to your wardrobe.

Your sex life won't be complete until you accessorize it. Using sex toys, games and accessories adds spice and excitement to your lovemaking. Every woman should have some sort of sexual accessory.

Sensuous Items for Every Woman

Listed below are thirty sensuous items that can be used along with your pleasure container. Whether you name it goodie bag, prop box, or sexual hope chest there's probably something in your home you can use create your own sexual accessory container. Why don't you try a few or all of the listed supplies? You'll be surprised at the fun you'll have.

1. **Whipped cream** can be used on all parts of the erogenous zones. Some favorite places are: nipples, stomach, navel, neck, ears, toes, buttocks, male identity, fingers and any other hot spots you can think of. Be careful not to get it inside the ears. This seduction is very inviting because the whipped cream can be eaten from your lover's body.
2. **Assorted lingerie** is nice to wear on almost any occasion. Men won't always admit that a woman in beautiful lingerie is a turn on. Watch the sparks fly when you approach him or unveil your body dressed in beautiful attire. Make sure bras and panties match, are fresh and sexy when you're going to be with your lover. It adds flavor to the mood.
3. **Sunglasses** in assorted styles with beautiful frames are glamorous when worn correctly. When wearing casual clothing, wear your favorite casual sunglasses. When wearing your most glamorous attire wear a pair that will fit the occasion. Every woman should have more than one pair of sunglasses in her wardrobe.

4. **Men suits** are hot on a sexy and sensuous woman. Wearing a man's suit adds flair and helps the man to chill out. Women in sensuous suits turn men on. Accompany the suit with a low cut blouse or no blouse at all. Accessorize with small delicate jewelry and sexy underwear.
5. **Nail polish** adds allure and beauty to a woman's nails. Clear polish is sensuous on clean, manicured hands. Color can send sexy messages to men.
6. **Fruits** like bananas, strawberries, cherries, and pineapple chunks are nice additives to oral sex. If you like to have your sex and eat it too try tasting pieces of fruit before, during and after sex.
7. **Long coats** are nice when you want to visit your man wearing nothing except your underwear. Wear the coat with nice lingerie or a teddy in his favorite color. Think of these coats as long dresses, and you'll be able to pull it off.
8. **Oils and lotions** are enriching to the skin when you're available for a nice massage before or after sex. Men love sensuous massages at any time.
9. **Toiletries** are great when your lover sleeps over. Having a few items of his favorite brands accessible

is being considerate and in tune with his needs. Keep a little container or basket under your counter for him with toothpaste, colognes, shaver/razor, comb, brush, after-shave, etc. Have the things your man needs so that he'll feel more comfortable and connected. Make sure he does the same for you.

10. **Aprons** are great when you need to sensuously greet him at the door. Wear nothing except an apron tied around your waist and watch his excitement grow.

11. **Popsicles** are a terrific turn-on as he watches you use them to penetrate, lick and penetrate again. Use this as erotic foreplay. It works wonders. Assorted popsicles are best.

12. **Chilled wine or champagne** is stimulating when poured over his body and licked off. Champagne can also be used for dipping pleasures. Dip his male identity into a glass of champagne and lick it off. He'll get goose bumps and you'll get turned on as you turn him on. He'll immediately rise to new heights.

13. **Mr. Good-Bars** are given as a sexual gesture to tell him he's good. The best time to send him a giant Mr. Good Bar is the day after sex. Personally

deliver it to him wrapped in gift paper or in a gift box, or have it delivered to him by a delivery company. He'll be ringing your phone off the hook after he receives this delightful message. You don't have to write a note or send a card with it unless you want because the candy bar will say it all.

14. **Breath mints** are a handy necessity for any woman who kisses and talks to someone up close and personal.

15. **Fresh condoms** are mandatory for every sexually active woman and man. Having fresh condoms is not only smart, but wise. Don't expect your lover to provide this protection for you. A smart and sensuously mature woman will be responsible for her own sexual protection. Condoms have a life span. Make sure your condoms are not old and outdated. This has influence on the effectiveness of your protection. Remember to use spermicidal jelly with condoms, because twice the protection is just as nice.

16. **Incense, potpourri or other aromas** can set the mood and enhance the atmosphere. The aroma creates waves of feelings and erotic moods. It's all in your thought process, so think sexy thoughts.

17. **Candles are romantic**, soothing and alluring whether used alone or with your lover. When alone, candles add a special and personal atmosphere that helps you enjoy time with yourself. They lull you to moments of subtle interludes. Watch television, take baths or just sit and talk by candlelight. Who can resist being romantic when the setting is so mellow.

18. **Lights and illuminations** are nice peeking in from other rooms. Dimly lit or colored light bulbs add romantic overtures and decrease electric bills if you're living on a budget. Enjoy the magic of subtle lighting in any atmosphere.

19. **Tape measures** come in handy when playing measurement games with your lover. If he's confident about his sensuous area, it's fun to measure the length and width of him. Don't use this as a ridicule tool. This is used to get a rise out of his male identity and your temperature.

20. **Costumes** are a nice turn on for men. Keep him at home by changing your look for his pleasure. Men like the idea of having more than one woman. So why don't you be that multiple person. Change your hair, clothes and any other features from time to time to add spice to an otherwise routine

relationship. Dress up to look like his favorite starlet or sex goddess, or create your own look for him. He'll be pleasantly surprised at your efforts to please him.

21. **Handkerchiefs** squirted with a little perfume are nice to carry in your bra, purse or pocket. It makes for a beautiful scent on your body.

22. **Love notes** are great messengers. Leave them everywhere he'll be. Keep them simple and personalized. Be sure to say little things in your notes that push his erotic buttons. Jot down something that only you and he can relate to in your notes. He'll understand the message you're sending.

23. **Create scenes** by decorating your home or apartment for a romantic trip to your favorite vacation place. If your favorite place is Rome, do as the Romans do and invent your pleasures from the scenery to the food you eat? Create a wonderful and romantic atmosphere of love for two. Stop by a travel agency and pick up brochures and travel information to your favorite vacation spot. Add the little things like the souvenirs. The key is to escape entirely by playing the role completely.

24. **Sweet additions** like syrups, jellies, honey, sugar, chocolate, and other delights can add tasty pleasures to your appetite. Use slow, seductive licks to eat it off. Alternate your tongue motions by slipping and sliding your tongue in continuous lavishing licks. This one will send chills throughout your lover's body and his excitement will arouse you.

25. **Balloons or flowers** are fantastic when trying to make up or add cheer to your lover's day. Keep some balloons in your prop box or send balloons or flowers and a message to let him know that you are thinking of him. He'll be a little shy at first, but the idea sends happiness to his brain.

26. **Picnics** don't have to be in the park. Why not have one for two in your living room, your back yard, on a patio or even in your bedroom. Fireplace picnics are a favorite also. Simply prepare a picnic basket with your favorite wine, cheese and foods, and select a place to enjoy it. Indulge in the fun of it all. Try a nude picnic at home? Try it and don't forget to add your own sensuous and spicy ideas.

27. **Pearls** are nice when worn alone. Greet him at the door wearing a single strand of pearls. Make sure he's the only one who gets a glimpse of you. If he

can guess how many pearls are on the strand, he'll be able to choose his sexual pleasure for the day.

28. **Silk scarves** should touch him lightly all over his naked body. You can also use silk scarves as halters, aprons, and veils or maybe even a G-string before stripping in front of him to music.
29. **Read Heated Pleasures**. Recite the parts that you know are sure to turn him on. If he gets turned on before you finish, and you have to make love don't worry. You can always start over when you need to excite him again.
30. Be sure to keep your copy of my first book **Will the Real Women Please Stand Up** nearby. It's also filled with many romantic games, props and supplies.

You might need more than one pleasure container for all of your props and supplies. One box can be used for sexual items and the other can be used for those things that you would eat or put in your mouth. Another one could be used for things you have to replace or clean on a regular basis like toothbrushes, soaps, lotions etc. Whichever way you decide to separate your items be sure to keep them clean, handy, out of sight and away from children. Don't forget to add your own special prop or accessory to this list. Have fun with your toys and experiment with your toys in wholesome and safe ways.

Every woman should have her own props and supplies on hand in addition to ordinary sex.

Chapter 25

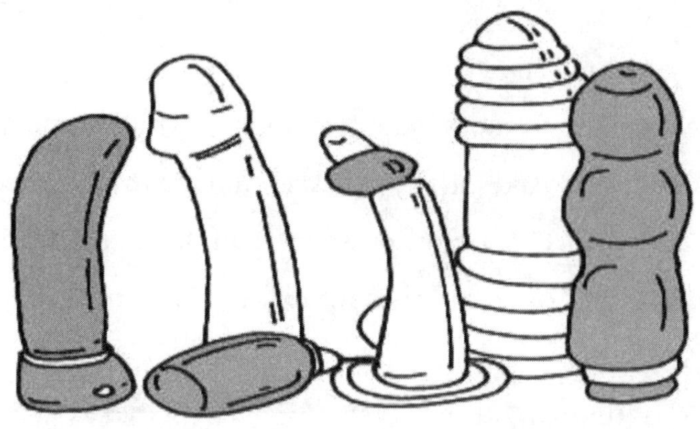

Using Vibrating Sex Toys

(Aka Battery Operated Boyfriends)

This chapter will introduce you to a world of battery and non-battery operated sex toys that most women adore.

Every woman should also own a few sex toys (Aka battery operated boyfriends) for private pleasure and sex play. Owning a few sensuous toys can help you gain a better understanding of your body and heighten your overall sexual experience. While the majority of sensuous toys basically look like male identities in different sizes and colors, there's a wide variation available. Sensuous toys that penetrate the vagina are available for all size preferences, from extra thick and stubby, to long and slender.

Some are smooth and featureless, while some have detailed veins and family jewels. Some are designed to stimulate the G-spot or prostate, and have undulations, bumps, angles or corkscrews for extra sensation.

When a woman wants a tune-up or an extended sensual session, her battery-operated boyfriends (BOB) known as vibrators are the ideal sex toys to get a woman's motor revving and send her racing to a 400-horsepower orgasm. Battery-operated boyfriend's come in a phenomenal array of types and sizes.

You Should Know

Use the battery-operated boyfriend to achieve multiple orgasms and learn how to enjoy your body and your sexuality.

Using battery-operated boyfriends (BOB) is great if a woman wants to learn her own sexual likes and dislikes. Vibrators are among the most widely used and widely available toys, and because they come in such a variety of sizes, shapes, colors and materials, you're sure to find one that you're comfortable with. They're great for vaginal, clitoral, or anal stimulation and can be used internally, externally, or both.

Some vibrators serve as body massagers, relieving more than your sexual tension. There are vibrators that work by battery and there are those that plug into the nearest electrical socket. There's even a model that can be plugged into the cars cigarette lighter.

Selecting Battery Operated Toys

Finding the best model may take a little self-love making research. Should you decide to look at a variety of toys, think about what you like sexually and then ask yourself a few questions?

1. **Do I like penetration, love button stimulation or both?** Do you find it more stimulating when your partner plays with your love button, penetrates your vagina, or both? Your answer will help you determine which type of vibrator you'll like best. Some vibrators are made for external use only to stimulate your clitoris; others are designed to enter your vagina; and some can stimulate both at the same time.

2. **Will I need a lot of power or something with more intensity**? All vibrators offer something different. Before you buy one consider the intensity of the vibration that will please you. An electronic vibrator produces strong vibrations and won't run out of energy as a battery-powered device, and may be worth its money in gold if you plan to use it often or for long periods of time. The best way to find what is best for you is to visit a retailer that has a multitude of different models.
3. **What toy can be aesthetically pleasing**? It's best if you're attracted to your toys. If you don't like the way a vibrator looks it's going to be very difficult for you to get comfortable using it. A woman who wants to be more discreet can find something as unassuming as a tube of lipstick.
4. **Learn what you like and dislike.** Using a battery-operated boyfriend is great for a woman to learn her sexual likes and dislikes. She can use them with relaxing music and an erotic atmosphere.

Remember to relax and breathe deeply. Concentrate on what you're feeling. Use the battery-operated boyfriend in different positions and you'll receive different degrees of stimulation. Use it until just before climax, take it away, relax, and begin again. Use the battery-operated boyfriend to achieve multiple orgasms and learn how to enjoy your sexuality. Men are not the only ones that can masturbate.

Keeping your battery-operated boyfriend clean is the ultimate way to practice safe sex. All you really need to know about using a battery-operated boyfriend is "Do what feels good to you," "Keep it clean" and if it is not waterproof don't put it in water. Now that you have the very simple rules - understand that a vibrator is designed to stimulate. It does a better job of stimulating than a tongue, fingers, or any inanimate object. It is a perfect masturbation tool for both women or men and can greatly heighten sexual intensity for couples. There is a definite difference between battery-operated-boyfriend induced-orgasms and orgasms produced by other means. A BOB orgasm is more intense and it's common for women to have multiple orgasms while using it. Consistent and intense stimulation of the love button is normally required for a woman to climax. The BOB is great at that.

What Sex Toys Are Made of

Your garden-variety sensuous toys are usually made out of rubber and/or vinyl, but the higher quality toys are

made out of silicone. They're nice, firm and a little more expensive. They feel good, and silicone is more durable and easier to clean than other materials. They require careful handling, but can be worth it for the realistic sensations. What's your preference?
When you visit your favorite sex shop, you'll see sensuous toys made of everything from plastic and rubber to glass and steel. How will you know which to select? You should consider your comfort, how realistic it will be, how pleasurable it is and how easy it will be to take care of. Here's an easy guide to help you:

- **Cyberskin** feels and looks like the real thing and isn't very high maintenance. Toys made of this material are very porous, difficult to clean and get a little sticky after using. To maintain the soft skin like feel, it helps if you cover them with a small amount of cornstarch before storing them. Bacteria and yeast can get trapped in them and may cause chronic vaginal infections. Your best bet is to use condoms on vibrators or dildos made of jelly rubber or cyberskin. You may need to replace these toys more often than toys made of other materials. And again always cover with a condom and keep them sanitary and bacteria free.

- **Glass** is used most often for dildos, a type that is great for G-spot stimulation. They can be warmed and chilled for different sensations, and the nonporous material is easy to clean. Most claim to be shatterproof, but be careful because rough handling can cause them to break. Glass toys are often hand blown and quite beautiful. You could probably put one on your coffee table and no one would ever recognize it as a sex toy. Clean with hypoallergenic soap and water.
- **Plastic** is nonporous, hard, durable, and easy to clean. In the past plastic toys used to be simple, hard plastic, but they broke, developed stains or cracked when used. Now, however, there are materials available that are so life-like and comfortable, that if you couldn't see it, you'd be hard-pressed to tell if it was a live male identity or a gadget. You can warm plastic toys with water before you use them for a more realistic feel. Plastic is the best material for really intense vibrations, but they tend to be a little louder than other toys. Clean with soap and water.

- **Jelly and Rubber** could easily be picked out of a line-up with real male identities. Jelly vibrators nevertheless provide a variety of fun. Often coming (pun intended) in vibrant colors, their 'skin' is soft and jiggly - like a sort of aroused cup of' Jell-O. One bit of advice when using jellies: keep them in a plastic bag and try not to let them fall to the floor as they have a tendency to collect lint and dirt. Otherwise, they're truly fun to play with. Jelly rubber is a porous rubber blend that has a soft feel that many women like. Unfortunately, it can become difficult to clean over time since lubricants and body fluids can get trapped in the pores and create stickiness. It holds its vibrations better than rubber latex. Clean with soap and water and replace after a few months of use.
- **Steel** can also be warmed or heated, and is also nonporous, so it's easy to clean. However the feel is far from realistic.
- **Silicone** is the most popular material for sex toys perhaps because it warms up to the body's temperature, maintains heat and is easy to clean. If it's waterproof, you can boil it for three minutes to sterilize it or place it in your dishwasher. Toys made

of silicone can last a long time. I don't recommend using silicone based lubricants on silicone toys because they damage them.

Battery-Operated Boyfriends

There are also special BOB designed to fit perfectly between a woman's legs, around the head of a guy's male identity, or neatly in anyone's anus. The BOB can produce a soothing sexual feeling, or an intense one depending on how one uses the gadget - and, how one is sexually wired. Those adventurers who want their orgasms more portable will find a huge variety of battery operated vibrators that start to look more "penile." There are also a great number that look nothing at all like a male identity. Those that arc not so male looking are easier to travel with.

Thanks to recent developments in the kind of plastic that's used in vibrators, they are life-like and feel both "incredibly realistic and hot" and "more than a little creepy." There's even a new series of 'realistic' vaginas available (with or without vibration), so those who prefer to make love rather than be made loved to - share in new state-of-the-art technologies.

One thing that's great about modern sex toys is that while it's possible to make a toy that looks like a penis or vagina, they added a special feature that will also stimulate a love button or other private parts.

Top Toys Every Woman Needs

These toys are sexy, guaranteeing hours and hours of wild orgasmic fun, and at least with one of these toys you'll have your vagina tickled. There are other, sometimes even more surreal devices, as well. Additionally, there are specially ringed vibrators just for the guys as well as toys such as the panty vibrator (wearable vibrators). But first, let's take a look at the toys I recommend as some of the best.

1. **The Pocket Rocket** is a small rocket-shaped vibrator - looks like a little pocket torch in appearance. If you can only purchase one toy this is my recommendation. The Pocket Rocket is a tiny but powerful "massager" that's only about four inches long. You can fit it in your purse. It looks like a tube of lipstick. It transforms when the jelly rubber sleeves are put on it. It comes in delicious colors such as blueberry, grape, lime strawberry and tangerine. You can also add jelly rubber sleeves shaped like a bunny (with extra-long ears) or a

variety of other textures. Lubricate this one for wonderful pleasure.

2. **The Hitachi Magic Wand** is still the Bentley of vibrators. It is a large electronic vibrator that is just as effective when you need to relax your tired, sore back muscles as producing intense orgasms. It's sold in the small appliance section of many department stores as well as adult sex shops. This enormous, two speed; plug-in model possesses a sturdy wand handle and a huge vibrating type blowjob. What is new about it is that there are now attachments fitting onto the head that focus on love button stimulation. The Hitachi Magic Wand is the most popular, but other comparable handheld models are available.

3. **Jack Rabbit** is a more elaborate creation. It's sold under several brand names, but the name rabbit was made more popular by the Sex and City cable television show. It features multiple elements and moving parts. They do everything except sing. This dual vibrator is the ultimate sex toy. It's not recommended for beginners. Most feature a rotating chamber of beads, or "pearls," in the shaft, which tumble against each other, creating extra movement

and sensations inside the vagina. At the base of the shaft is a cute rabbit, beaver, or dolphin - that buzzes and bumps against the love button. Deluxe models feature a rotating male identity. Some come with an anal tickler. All of these elements have separate controls and varying speeds. This is one of the only vibrators that stimulate several areas of the vulva and the vagina at the same time. It runs on four AA batteries. The pearls near the base of the shaft tumble to stimulate the sensitive entrance and lower third of the vagina. The little critter attached at the shaft flutters and vibrates your clitoris. The combinations boggle the mind, not to mention the coochie. They cost a bit more, and are generally well made and worth it if you want the ultimate vibrator experience.

4. The Dildo is a basic penis shaped toys. You can use it to practice fellatio and perfect your hand job. It can be used alone or with a partner to stroke your cervix or penetrate your vagina. They are cast from molds of real penises complete with veins and testicles.
5. The G-spot Vibrator is easy to detect due to the curve at the top of the shaft. The curve allows the

top of your vibrator to press against your G-spot when inserted in the vagina. You can also buy the G-spot vibrator dildo without the vibrations.

6. **The Finger Vibrator** is the perfect way to introduce toys to your male partner. It can be placed on his finger, allowing him to maintain control. It is, therefore less threatening for the man who has fears that toys will replace him in your life. The vibrations produced are perfect for stimulating your vulva and love button. It can be used to simulate his penis or perineum too.
7. **The Natural Contours Vibrator** looks more like a small medical device than a sex toy. It is sleek, smooth and designed to fit along the natural curve of the vulva. The vibrations are gentle and comfortable. It is perfect for the woman who is new to sex toys as well as for the more experienced woman.
8. **The Vibrating Bullet** is a tiny powerhouse and is capable of creating pleasurable sensations for both you and your partner. It's made to stimulate your clitoris and fits on top of or between your outer labia. You can simply drop the bullet into your panties and sit back and enjoy your private party.

The bullet is also great for partnered sex. Place it against your love button while having intercourse for erotic pleasure.

9. **The Strap on Vibrator** makes it easier for women to reach climax during intercourse. The straps hold it in place against your clitoris while leaving your vagina and anus free for intercourse. It provides additional stimulation for ultimate pleasure.

10. **The Cock Rings** as their names suggests are rings that fit over the penis shaft, encircling the base of the penis, or the penis and the testicles. Cock rings restrict blood flow out of the penis which keeps it engorged and helps the erection last longer. Rings may be made of plastic, rubber, leather, or metal. One word of caution is if he's using the cock ring make sure he doesn't limit blood flow out of the male identity for an extended period of time. (No more than twenty minutes). Choose rings that can be adjusted with snaps or ones that are made of stretchy rubber so they can be removed easily (and quickly in case of an emergency). Don't use the ring if it's too tight or causes pain.

11. **The Vibrating Cock Ring** is a stretchable cock ring that's placed at the base of the erect male identity. The attached vibrating egg should be rotated at the top of the ring. That way when you have intercourse, the vibrating egg has contact with your love button, providing additional stimulation during intercourse. The man can feel the vibrations at the base of his penis and scrotum. To increase clitoral stimulation you should assume the woman-on-top position and grind your hips against the egg attachment.
12. **Butt plugs** are designed and worn for the feeling of fullness. They are essentially small dildos designed to fit and stay in the anus. They have a flared bottom that prevents them from sliding too far up your rectum. They are made of silicone or rubber and are easier to use than what they sound like. They are also easy to clean. Some butt plugs come with heart shaped bases and the silicone is excellent for transmitting vibrations - all you have to do is apply a vibrator to the base. The plugs come in a variety of shapes and sizes. There is the long, thin, pointed plug; the shorter, flatter, slightly curved version; and the small, squat, fat beaded

version. Never use plugs that are more than 4 inches long, they could cause internal damage.

13. **The Flex-O-Pleaser** has a small battery pack, a long neck, and a vigorous head - just the thing to get to the small of your back; or prostrate; or G-spot, for that matter.
14. **Ecsta-Sleeve Vulva** is a stretchable sleeve made of cyber skin that fits over the male identity. It includes a vibrating egg for stimulating the sensitive head of the male identity.
15. **Ball Collar** attaches around the man's family jewels and he can add weights to it. Men love this kind of pressure.
16. **Neptune Ring Valve** is a tiny vibrating dolphin attached to a male identity ring. This works either by giving your lover a solo buzz or by stimulating the love button during intercourse.
17. **Gummy Bear Ring** is a jelly rubber male identity attachment that fixes at the base of the male identity (or dildo). The blue model comes with a mini-probe for focusing on the G-spot, and the red model comes with little side flaps that tickle the love button.

18. **Raspberry Ring** is a raspberry-shaped stimulator fitted to the front of the ring and said to be the most effective shape for love button stimulation. The ring is made of aqua-blue silicone.
19. **The Sensa-Touch Wand** by Dr. Scholl's. Dr. Scholl has graduated from sandals and is now selling his own version of the Magic wand.
20. **Attachments.** What is special about the last two vibrators is that there are some cute pink or purple G-spot attachments than can also be used to give the prostate a massage. Plus one has a slender curved tip specially shaped to give maximum pressure on the front wall of the vagina where the infamous G-spot is located. The latest models do more than vibrate - they pulsate which a woman might recognize as integral to a woman's style of orgasm, especially for G-spot stimulation. They are a lot quieter and can be turned on without everyone knowing.
21. **The Pulsatron** has several different speeds. It throbs and pulsates. You can pick and choose which speed you want by the touch of a switch.

22. **The iSurge Vibe** has several variations, which include vibration, pulsation, escalation, and roller coaster.
23. **Spiral Plug** comes in metallic black that includes a removable itty-bitty vibe. It which nestles perfectly into cord free base; is a quiet and reliable vibrator made of good-quality silicone and is excellent for prostate or vagina sensation. It includes three watch batteries (included) and has one strong speed.
24. **Rub My Duckie** looks like a rubber Duckie, and it floats like a rubber Duckie, but when you squeeze - it buzzes and vibrates. It's the ultimate vibrator disguise. The beak and tail stimulates the love button.
25. **Bottoms Up Kit** includes a book title 'Anal Pleasure and Health' by Jack Morin, which is considered the bible of anal stimulation. Also included is a lavender jelly rubber Arrow Twist Vibrator, which probes and promotes thrilling interior sensations. It comes with batteries and a bottle of special lube.
26. **Fukuoku** is a small, quiet vibrator designed to fit neatly over the end of a finger, basically turning the woman's finger into a tiny vibrator. The Fukuoku

can reach all those hidden areas - and quite a few obvious ones too.

27. **Fukuoku gloves** are also available, making each fingertip into an epicenter of tiny tremors.
28. **Fukuoku 9000** is one of the newest vibrators. Working off tiny watch batteries, it fits over your finger like a tiny finger sheath and vibrates. There is no battery pack and no cord. Perfect for surprises during intercourse, since it is virtually undetectable. The kit includes textured rubber pads to fit over the device so that you can vary your finger sensation.
29. **Thai beads** are a string of three small pearly-pink beads to be inserted into the anus and then pulled out slowly. They are used to accentuate stimulation or in a rush for a great climax.
30. **Jumbo beads** are a graduated larger version of Thai beads.
31. **Jelly beads** are spongy ruby-colored, equally sized jelly beads with a ring pull that offers a firm jelly-like sensation.
32. **Double delight** is a hands-free two-ended BOB that is supposed to be worn by heterosexuals when the man enjoys anal penetration.

33. **Mini-hummer** offers targeted vibration for women who find it difficult to climax. Wear it strapped into place over the love button, held on by an elastic waist strap and leg straps. Great during sex because it hits the right spots.
34. **Triple stimulation** is a male identity ring with a flexible dildo for penetration of the anus while the vagina is being penetrated.
35. **Bullet vibes** are small vibrators encased in an egg or bullet-shaped capsule and because of their compactness and the punch they pack for their size. they can be used directly on the love button. Many BOB's, butt plugs, male identity rings and are designed so one of these mighty mites can infuse them with a jolt of juice. The vibe is attached via a small cord to a handheld battery pack/controller.
36. **Wireless versions** are also available; just make sure you don't lose track of them in an orifice. Other very small vibes run off watch batteries, which are enclosed in their case. These little guys may look small, but they really do work.

Joy Buzzers

These are on the go vibrators that are small, can be hidden and fun to own. They are great when you have to sneak away to get off.

1. **Vibrating panties.** Underwear with a mini-vibe tucked inside, which can be worn without detection under your regular garments. Get one with a remote control unit and give it to your lover to add spice to a night on the town.
2. **Butterfly, Scorpion, or Dragonfly** are wearable units, that feature probes and plugs combine with a small vibe to tickle the love button, vagina and butt. Tiny clip-on vibes can be clamped to the nipples, love button, or labia for intense sensations.
3. **Tongue-Joy** is for those who like to give more than receive. The mini-vibe that straps onto your tongue, to give a little oomph to your oral sex. Put it on a single finger and it becomes an instrument of exquisite pleasure.
4. **Buzzing' buddies vibrators** are NOT just for the ladies. Vibrating jelly male identity rings slide over his male identity and sit snugly at the base. They

usually feature nubs or probes that contact his lover's love button during intercourse. For a real hummer, try putting a vibe under his ball sack, against his perineum (the spot between your family jewels and anus), or if you're really adventurous, slide one up his butt.

5. **Strap it on.** For no-hands with a lover, use a strap-on dildo. These are strap on's that are suitable for use by women, as well as men who want to enhance or maintain an erection.
6. **Ride that dong.** To make love and really grind on that male identity, get a dildo with a suction cup base that you can attach to the wall, shower tiles, floor or other smooth surface. Some women stabilize dildos by bracing the base with pillows.
7. **Get a buzz.** A vibrating dildo or multi-function vibrating dildo can provide extra stimulation along with penetration. These vibrators can also be used externally on the vulva, love button, or male identity and testicles for masturbation.

Batteries Not Always Included

They plug in too. The classic BOB is battery powered, phallic shaped and made of plastic, silicone, or a similar material. It can be stroked, inserted or held against the genitals. The most basic of these is the standard smooth plastic vibe. They used to sell these in the back of magazines as "facial massagers." They come in a dazzling rainbow of candy colors, neon, and glow-in-the-dark and light-up models. These aren't your mom's massagers. Don't even believe they are!

Heated Pleasures
Although two people can bang away on opposite ends of a dong, it works best if one lover remains more or less stationary.

Other insertables incorporate the vibrator into a realistically detailed dong made of rubber, jelly-rubber, vinyl, or silicone. With so many sizes, colors and styles available, even if you're a prissy girl you're bound to find something that appeals to you.

Avoiding Damage

A tiny nick on the surface of a jelly rubber, silicone, or Cyberskin dildo can turn into a big tear that will ruin the toy. Take care to keep your dildo away from sharp or pointy objects or abrasive surfaces and prolong its life by storing in a box or protective cloth or bag when not in use. Less common are "Swedish" type massagers that can be strapped onto the back of your hand, thereby turning your whole palm and fingers into a vibrator/massager. These produce a very intense vibration that some find wonderful and others find overwhelming.

Security Checks and B-O-B's

Speaking of embarrassment, everyone's heard horror stories about someone getting pulled out of the airport screening line because there was a vibrator hopping around in their luggage.

There's a simple way to avoid this embarrassment: remove the batteries before you pack. If you're still concerned about discretion, consider getting a vibrator that isn't shaped like a male identity or the standard vibrator.

There are lots of non-phallic vibes designed to fit the shape of a woman's vagina, resembling a high-tech electric shaver instead of a sex toy. Others are shaped vaguely like

You Should Know
The classic BOB is battery powered, phallic shaped and made of plastic, silicone, or a similar material. It can be stroked, inserted or held against the genitals.

flashlights, while some are disguised as rubber duckies or small dolls. Mini or finger-sized vibes are a good choice because they can easily be slipped into a pocket or purse.

Battery Operated Boyfriend Tips

- Experiment with positioning to get the best sensations. Going straight for the sensitive areas may not work best. Vary pressures and, if the vibrator permits try changing the speeds.
- Try using the vibe on the outside of clothing or through layers if it's too intense.
- Watch out for "vibrator dependency." Vibes won't deaden your sensations, but you may get used to them and find it difficult to come with other stimulation.
- Lube can reduce friction and intensify sensation, whether you're inserting the vibe or just stroking your spot.
- Test the vibe on other body parts (thighs, buttocks, breasts, etc.). Sensuous ripples of pleasure are great.
- If you plan to use your vibe in the bath, be sure to get a waterproof model. Don't use electrical vibrators near water.

- ❖ Clean your battery-operated boyfriend's regularly with soap and water, or according to its directions.
- ❖ Remove the batteries during cleaning and don't get water in the battery compartment. It will rust the inside metal parts.

Dildo: It's a Versatile Toy

The double dildo is one of the more exotic sex toys. The double dildo is a standard prop in girl-on-girl porn scenes, but it's actually a versatile toy that can be used by couples of either gender, or individuals for solo masturbation. Here's a rundown of the many ways it can be used:

1. **A double dildo** is designed to allow two people to be penetrated simultaneously. You don't even need two people to play with a double dong; it can be used for solo masturbation.

2. **Vagina to vagina** is when two or more women use a double dong for simultaneous vagina penetration. A man and a woman can use it to find more pleasures that stimulate his prostate and her G-Spot.

3. **Vagina to butt:** The female is penetrated in her vagina while her lover takes the other end of the dildo in the butt.

4. **Butt to butt:** Two lovers of either sex can use a double dildo for simultaneous anal penetration.

5. **Double penetration:** If the dong is flexible enough, a woman can insert one end in her vagina and the other in her anus for double penetration.

6. **Solo masturbation:** A double dong can be used like a regular dildo.

7. **Penetration during masturbation.** The user grips the free end as a sort of "handle."

If you use your creativity juices, you can come up with many more possibilities. Ever wanted to suck male identity and eat vagina at the same time? Have the female lover insert a double dildo and then go down on her.

1. **Face to face:** Lean back and insert the dong. Best for vagina-to-vagina.

2. **Side by side:** Lay side-by-side, prop one leg up slightly and insert the dildo. Lie face to face for vagina-to-vagina sex.

3. **For vagina-to-butt,** the lover receiving the dildo anally should lie with their back to the other.

4. **Back to back:** Both lovers kneel on all fours facing in opposite directions. They back up toward each other as they insert the dildo. Works best for butt-to-butt, but can also work for vagina-to-vagina or vagina-to-butt.

Getting started is easiest if one person inserts the dildo first, and the other moves toward them and inserts the other end. The act of making loving can be a little tricky, as it's easy for the dildo to slip out while you're both pumping on it. During sex, one person may have to hold the dildo in place to keep it

> **You Should Know**
>
> Take care to keep your dildo away from sharp or pointy objects or abrasive surfaces and prolong its life by storing in a box or protective cloth or bag when not in use.

steady. Although two people can bang away on opposite ends of a dong, it works best if one lover remains more or less stationary. One person can grip their end of the dong and grind into the other person, or they can hold it in place while the other person rides their end. One of the great things about a double dong is that it's an equalizer, and you can both take turns being active and passive.

Watch Your Behind

A few cautionary words are necessary concerning the use of double dongs for anal penetration. If one end of a double dong is used in the anus that same end should never go into a vagina without being thoroughly cleaned first. Inserting an object in the vagina after it has been in the butt spreads germs that can cause yeast and internal bacterial infections.

- As with any sex toy, take precautions when sharing so you don't transmit infections or STDs. Don't insert a dildo into one person and then insert it into another without cleaning it between lovers. Be sure to clean your toys thoroughly after use, or cover them with condoms for easy clean up.

- Be sure not to push it so far into your butt that the whole thing slides up and gets stuck. It's best to only insert toys in your butt that have a flared base, like butt plugs, to keep them from slipping in past the anal sphincter.
- Most double dongs are long enough that if you keep a grip on the free end, you're not likely to lose the whole thing. But if your hands are slick with lube, and you push a little too far...you may find yourself stuck in a very embarrassing predicament. If you're concerned about your double dong getting lost, you can get a model with a flange or family jewels in the middle that will stop it before it goes too far. Scary, but true.

Other Doubles

If the double dong isn't your style, or you're looking for something more ergonometric for dual penetration, you could try a strap-on with a vagina plug in the harness. The harness holds the smaller dildo inside.

Other double dildos like the Feeldoe, the Nexus, the Boomerang, and the Super Penetrix are V-shaped dildos designed to have one end held in place by the wearer's vagina muscles. The other end of the dildo sticks up out of her crotch at an angle like an erection, allowing the woman to make love as if she were wearing a strap-on.

The vagina dildo is usually a bit larger and thicker, while the anal dildo is smaller and curved to meet the inner contours of the body. These toys are suitable for masturbation rather than with a lover. To help you use your double remember this:

- **Use a water-based lube.** A water-based lube like KY Jelly or Astroglide will make insertion easier. Water-based lubes are compatible with all sex toy materials and clean up easily.
- **Start with one end.** Let one lover get the dong inserted before the other tries to get their end in. Trying to get both ends inserted at the same time will result in the dong slipping around too much.
- **Take turns with your lover.** Double dongs are great equalizer for heterosexual couples because you can both get make love at the same time. You can take turns being the active or passive lover. One of you can hold the dong in place inside you and make love the other with it.
- **Double your pleasure with double penetration.** A woman can insert one end of a flexible double dong in her vagina and one end in

her butt. This works best with dongs made of jelly rubber that are 16 inches or longer. Get one end inserted and hold it in place, then push the free head into the other hole.

- **Use the free end.** While masturbating with a double dong, rub the other end on your love button, or give it a hand job. You've got a whole 'other male identity sticking out there so put it to work.
- **Grip the end to use the double dong as a make love tool.** You know those dildos with a handle or grip on one end? You can use one end of a double dong for the same purpose. The nonlubricated free end of makes a convenient "handle" for loving yourself or a friend.
- **Use separate ends of the dildo for anal and vagina insertion.** If you use one end of a double dong anally, be sure not to use that end for vagina insertion until it has been thoroughly cleaned. Inserting anything in the vagina after it has been used anally can result in transmitting germs that cause bacterial and yeast infections.

Sex Toy Warnings

1. **Don't use oil or petroleum-based lubricants** (like Vaseline or Crisco) if your rubber male identity is made of rubber or Cyberskin; use a water-based lube (like Astroglide). Greasy stuff will cause rubber male identities or BOB's to disintegrate.

2. **Don't hide the toys.** If you use a rubber toy for anal pleasure, be sure it has a flared base big enough to keep it from disappearing up your butt.

3. **Don't let your eyes be bigger than your, um, orifice.** To get an idea of how much you can comfortably handle, test-drive a cucumber or zucchini. Whittle it if needed until you get the right proportions, and then measure the length and circumference. Put a condom on the vegetable for added protection of infections. Remember that pesticides are used on fruit and vegetables. Can you imagine explaining pesticide infection in your vaginal area to your doctor?

4. **Guard against germs.** If you're sharing the toys with a lover, or using it in more than one orifice (e.g., the vagina and the anus/butt), either clean the dildo thoroughly between insertions, or use condoms on it and change them between insertions to avoid STDs or germs that cause infections.

5. **Always keep it clean.** Clean your toys after every use by washing with mild antibacterial soap and hot water, or use a disinfectant sex toy cleanser. Sticky dildos can breed germs and attract dust and dirt that can cause serious infections.

Vagina Dildo Warning:

Be careful about inserting one of those slick plastic numbers. If there's nothing at the base to keep it from slipping up inside you may be embarrassed if an ER doctor has to extract a still-buzzing sex toy from your body cavity.

Soap and water is an acceptable way to clean sexual toys after use. Other disinfectants may cause irritation of the genitals. If you are sharing toys with other partners you can place a condom over it to prevent transmission of fluids

Chapter 26

Using Sensuous Clamps

This chapter will introduce you to toys that clamp down and amplify sensuous sensation.

W**omen**-owned-and-operated sex businesses have made it their mission to take sex toys out of the dark and into the light. If you think sex toys are just for men, think again. They aren't! There's a whole new non-biased world for the sexually interested female and she has many kinds of sex toys to choose from. It seems that women have always possessed needy orifices and there are many new sensuous toys that have been added to the list of toys that probe (the kind that vibrated). There are those that gently constrict and amplify (male identity rings), those that imitate (false vagina's, plastic tits), and those that restrict (bondage implements). Yet, for the most part, sex toys basically buzz or get inserted wherever it feels good.

Most any woman can find a reason to use sensuous clamps. They add excitement to lovemaking. They are used in addition to the sexual hope chests, props and supplies. Most adventurous low-key toys are included in the clamp category. They might consist of: (a) handcuffs, in black leather and fluffy trimmings, (b) self-adhesive diamante' tattoos, (c) PVC blindfold (kinky heart-shaped bottom paddle); (d) fur collars and leads, and (e) nipple chains.

You Should Know

Piercing can stimulate growth of nerve endings in the nipples, increasing sensitivity. You may need to use less pressure with the clamps.

There are two kinds of clamps: the wand and the coil. Wands are powerful, and have multi-speeds like large plastic flashlights with a vibrating head at one end. The coil type usually has a much higher vibrating rate and is smaller, with a pistol grip. Neither of these types of toys look like something you'd clench between your thighs, but don't let that change your mind from giving them a try.

Buzzing Clamps

There is some special buzzing devices that come with gentle and not-so-gentle clamps . These are tiny vibrators that work directly on the nipples - fed by a small controller and battery pack. In their simplest form, nipple clamps are a variation of an alligator clamp with an adjustable spring or locking device. Each of the clamps is attached to a chain in such a way that pulling on it tightens the grip of the clamps. The tips should be covered with cork, soft vinyl or rubber, both for traction and to give some cushioning to protect the skin and tissues.

- **Forceps** designs are great if you're into doctor/nurse fantasy or medical fetishes. They look like a pair of scissors, and have a locking device between the arms to hold them in place.
- **Tweezer clamps** are just miniature tweezers or tongs encircled by a metal band that slides upward to tighten them. Their ends are covered with rubber or vinyl cushions.
- **Clovers clamps** resemble a pair of pliers with two rounds, flat pads that compress the nipples.

Nipple Clamps

Nipple clamps have a chain that keeps the clamps together as a set, but also looks and feels good to women who use them. The chain adds a little weight, and gives couples something to tug on to manipulate the clamps. Sexually submissive types get excited at the thought of being lead around by the tits.

Nipple clamps are ranked highest among the best selling by several erotica companies. Despite their name and appearance, nipple clamps are not torture devices. They have a reputation as sadomasochism toys, but couples don't have to be into heavy kink to enjoy them.

Heated Pleasures
Sexually submissive types get excited at the thought of being lead around by the tits.

The main purpose of nipple clamps is not to inflict pain, but to provide constant, intense nipple stimulation and heightened sensitivity. They actually squeeze the nerve endings.

Both men and women, get some level of erotic response from having their nipples squeezed, played with, bitten or sucked. Nipple clamps provide that stimulus while freeing up your hands and mouth to do other things. They put constant pressure on the nipples, which can be intensified with added weights, vibrators, or manual tugging. This heightens the nipples' sensitivity during play.

Nipple Jewelry

This kind of jewelry combines form and function. These trinkets are mostly for women and are worn by women, but men like them too. One type is a sort of mock – a springy open metal circle with covered ends that tweak the nipple between them. Tension holds it in place, and the effect is like a nipple ring without the piercing.

- **Elastic loop or adjustable lasso** goes around the nipple, often with beads, feathers or tassels attached.
- **Weights and vibrators** are another add-on that heightens the effect by pulling on the nipple. They swing as you move.
- **Deluxe nipples clamps** come with mini vibrators attached for really over-the-top stimulation and are a great multipurpose toy as well. The clamp can be used on the love button and family jewels, and can be clipped either directly onto those body parts or

onto your underwear so they nestle against your private body parts.

If you have pierced nipples, you may need to remove the piercing jewelry before attaching the clamps, or you can position it perpendicular to the piercing. Because piercing can stimulate growth of nerve endings in the nipples, increasing sensitivity, use less pressure with the clamps.

Nipple Clamp Application

Nipple clamps need to be applied with care. Take the time to get them properly adjusted and placed.

- ❖ If the nipple clamp has a screw adjustment, tighten it slowly until you achieve a pressure that will hold the clamp in place without causing too much pain. If the clamp has a simple spring mechanism, place the open clamp around the nipple and release slowly, so pressure is applied steadily to the nipple. Don't let it snap shut.
- ❖ The initial pressure of the clamp may feel intense, and may even be slightly painful for the first couple of minutes. If you can tough it out, the pain will gradually dull and give way to a warm throbbing and tingling, especially if you are already aroused.

At this point, you may find that your nipples are hypersensitive, so that the slightest brush or tug on the clamps produces overwhelming sensations.

- ❖ Nipple clamps compress delicate tissue and restrict blood flow. They should never be used for more than 15 minutes at a time.
- ❖ Discontinue use and remove the clamps if you experience real pain (as opposed to pleasurable pain), if the skin becomes broken, or if the nipple turns blue or purple. If you do sustain a nipple bruise or injury, ice it to reduce swelling and discoloration.
- ❖ For some people, nipple clamps are part of a more involved nipple play scene, which may involve nipple bondage (tying ropes or cords around the breast or nipple) and pumping (using suction pumps or snake bite kits to pump up and enlarge the nipples). Please read all directions on the clamps before use. Use caution.
- ❖ If you use nipple clamps occasionally, it's unlikely you'll experience any permanent changes in your nipples as a result. However, frequent tweaking may cause slight enlargement of the nipples and prolonged heightened sensitivity.

- A woman's nipple sensitivity varies during her menstrual cycle. Adjust the pressure of the clamps as desired.
- Vibrating nipple clamps are nice on your love button or family jewels. Attach to the inside of undergarments for an undercover buzz.
- When the clamps are taken off, brace yourself. Removing them can actually be more painful than putting them on, because the sudden rush of blood circulation back into nipple brings back feeling to the area. The nipples will be extremely sensitive for a while. Try having your lover blow on them, or brush them lightly with their lips or a feather and see what happens. Later, massage gently with some lotion or have your lover help to ease the sting.

Warning for Pregnant Women

Pregnant women should use caution when engaging in clamped nipple play. Stimulation of the nipples releases the hormone oxytocin, which causes uterine contractions and may induce early labor in the later stages of pregnancy.

To love oneself is the beginning of a life-long romance.
~ Oscar Wilde

Chapter 27

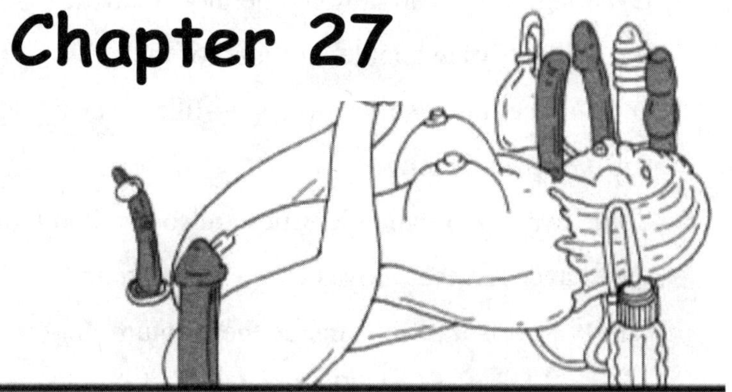

Using Cyberskin Toys

This chapter will introduce you to toys made of soft like materials that warm to the body's temperature.

Toys made of Cyberskin and similar soft flesh like materials go by various names: Softskin, Ultraskin, Futurotic, and so on. They're made from a high-tech rubbery polymer, or thermal plastic, whose silky texture and pliable consistency is amazingly lifelike. Unlike regular rubber or silicone, cyberskin does not feel cold to the touch and it quickly warms to body temperature. It's very stretchy, soft, and flexible, which makes it an ideal material for a wide range of sex toys.

- Cyberskin dildos are among the most realistic penis-like toys available, not just for their appearance, but also for their skin-like surface and soft-yet-firm density.
- Some cyberskin male identities are so detailed that they have skin that moves along the shaft and family jewels that shift inside the scrotum. If you want a dildo that feels like the next best thing to a real male identity, cyberskin is the way to go. And if you want to use it with a friend, you can get a cyberskin double dong.
- The skin-like texture of cyberskin male identity makes them a pleasure not only to make love, but also to suck and touch. Just be aware that cyberskin requires special handling. Take care not to nick the surface of it, because it is delicate and can tear very easily. Imagine that it's actual flesh and treat it with sensitivity. Because it is semi-porous, it's more difficult to clean than other materials.
- You may want to cover your cyberskin dildo with a condom before inserting it, especially if you are using it for anal penetration or if you are sharing it. And as with all cyberskin toys, use water based lube only. Oil-based or silicone-based lubes will destroy cyberskin material.

Watch Out
_Don't use talcum powder or baby powder to dust your cyberskin. Talcum has been linked to cervical cancer.

If you're rough on your toys, or you prefer a harder and hassle-free kind of love making, you're better off with a dildo made of rubber, latex, or silicone. Cyberskin vibrators and vibrating dildos are exceptionally kind to your delicate areas. Be aware that because cyberskin is so soft, it can absorb vibrations.

A small vibrator inside a thick cyberskin casing may produce a barely perceptible buzz. For more powerful sensations, look for larger vibrators with thinner cyberskin surfaces.

Cyberskin Vaginal Stimulators

Cyberskin is also a popular material for strap on vibrators that focus directly on the love button. Elastic straps hold these small vibrators over the love button, as the cyberskin casing stimulates the love button, labia, and vagina. Although most are too large and

Watch Out
Be aware that because cyberskin is so soft, it can absorb most of the vibrations.

awkwardly shaped to wear under clothing, the soft material is comfortable against the skin.

- ❖ The lifelike properties of cyberskin as well as its stretchiness and pliability make it an idea material for vagina simulators and masturbator sleeves. Simulated vagina's are molded to resemble the female genital area and are modeled to accept a male identity for more simulated intercourse.
- ❖ The cyberskin replicates the feeling of flesh, and stretches to accommodate and hug the inserted male identity. For those who are more interested in the male anatomy, there are cyberskin male identities and anus simulators.
- ❖ Many vagina simulators come with an anal aperture as standard equipment, so you can pick the orifice that you want to stimulate.
- ❖ Male masturbator sleeves differ from realistic vaginas in their size and design. Vagina sleeves give you a little more to grasp onto and are made for simulated lovemaking. The masturbator sleeve is held in one hand and used as sexual accessory. They may be molded in the shape of a miniature vagina or lips, to simulate the man's head. But rather than make love to them per se, you insert the

male identity into the snug sleeve and stroke it up and down.

- Cyberskin masturbators may not look like much, and you may look at the tiny hole in the end and wonder how even a modest-sized male identity could get inside. Cyberskin proves to be a wonder material with an amazing ability to stretch, without tearing or losing its shape.
- Find a male identity mold maker in your city and make arrangements to visit it with your lover so he can get a mold made of his male identity.
- Male identity extensions fit over the male identity to add length and girth. Cyberskin extensions have the benefits of feeling lifelike and being comfortable to wear. There are strapless and strap-on.
- Handle your cyberskin extension carefully when you put it on and take it off. It is flexible and stretchy so you can roll it on and off as you would a condom. Don't tug or pull at the end or the edges.
- Most cyberskin male identity rings are designed to fit around the base above the family jewels. They help maintain an erection by slowing the flow of blood of the male identity.

- Cyberskin male identity rings also lend themselves well to the addition of love button stimulating knobs or vibrators. Because it restricts blood circulation, never leave a stretchy male identity ring on for more than half an hour.

Cleaning /Storing Cyberskin Toys

- After using sex toys, wash them with warm water and mild or antibacterial hand soap. Pat dry with a clean cloth or paper towel.
- Don't rub cyberskin toys roughly, as this may abrade the surface or rub lint onto it. If it's an extension, masturbator sleeve, or vagina simulator, wash and dry it inside and out.
- Take a Ziploc baggie or Tupperware-type plastic container with a lid, and put about a quarter cup of cornstarch in the bag or container, then drop in your cyberskin toy. Seal it up, and shake thoroughly till it is coated. The cornstarch keeps the surface of the cyberskin from getting sticky and prolongs its life. If it's a sleeve or extension, make sure the cornstarch gets inside as well. If the toy is too big to fit in a bag or container, apply a light coat of cornstarch with your fingers.

Important Note:

Don't use talcum powder or baby powder to dust your cyberskin. Talcum has been linked to cervical cancer. Even though cornstarch will cake on, it can be brushed with a tissue or cloth, and your cyberskin will be smooth as a baby's bottom. You can store the toy in the cornstarch container until the next use. Or you can dust it off and wrap it in a clean, dry cloth or place it in a clean Ziploc bag for storage in a secure place.

Using sex toys are really a matter of personal preference.

Chapter 28

Using Lubricants, Gels, Oils and Creams

This chapter will introduce you to many sexual lubricants that women prefer.

Did you know that the lack of lubrication is the number one reason condoms break? If you're looking for personal lubricants or wonderful sexual lubricants, look no further. There are a wide variety of sex lubricants that will help you slip and slide your way to safe sex.

Women and men love lubricants. Even though natural lubrication is the preferred fluid, it's always nice when a woman has options. There are times that a woman's vagina becomes dry, which make it difficult to receive easy penetration during lovemaking.

Watch Out

Lubricants such as Vaseline or baby oils can cause holes in latex condoms, so it's best not to use them.

Dry vagina is a common problem for many women who are experiencing menopausal symptoms or some kind of hormonal problem. Because of the reduced levels of estrogen women may not secrete enough fluid to have normal lubrication so lubricants are great sex aides.

Lubricants such as Vaseline or baby oils can cause holes in latex condoms, so it's best not to use them. If you must use oil try coconut oil. The major complaint about lubes that have artificial ingredients is they taste bad and leave a numbing effect. Here's a list of popular lubricants, oils, creams or pills. Take a look, maybe you'll find one you'll like.

Lubricants, Gels and Jellies

1. **Sensual Organics** offer's the world's first all organic personal lubricant, made from whole, certified organic food-grade ingredients. The Peach and Raspberry formulas have a light, fruity scent and a mild, all-natural taste. The unflavored formula

is odorless and tasteless. In addition to being the healthiest choice, Sensual Organics innovative formulas allow for continuous rehydration by using the body's own moisture.

2. **Homeopathic Luscious Flower Libido Formula.** The Original Organic™ Homeopathic Personal Lubricant. Specifically designed to increase desire and sensation, while promoting a healthy response in women.

3. **K-Y Jelly** safely replaces personal moisture in a way that feels natural and helps enhance sexual pleasure. KY lubricants are condom safe, rinse off easily, and can be used every day. KY lubricants are thoroughly tested and proven safe to use.

4. **Bliss Lube** is not only natural it does not numb the mouth. It's lightly flavored liquid with vanilla, not overwhelming, has a bit of sweetness (without sugars) and it doesn't have that chemical-soapy smell that other lubes have. It has nature's purest ingredients. It's a personal lubricant that couples with the body's natural chemistry to enhance moisture and glide. This water-based formula is

non-irritating and long lasting for naturally pure pleasure. If a woman is concerned with the effects that chemical lubes might have on her body, Bliss lubricant is water-based, pH balanced, and made with minimal, natural ingredients without any harsh petroleum derivatives. There are also no paraben preservatives or propylene glycol. It's a bit more expensive than some lubes, but in lubes, as in life, you largely get what you pay for. Bliss Lube contains natural aloe Vera, which has been known to be a natural spermicide. However, it's probably not wise to use it as a spermicide. It's 100% natural, PH balanced, Petroleum-free, water based, Paraben-free, sweet tasting, non-sticky, latex friendly.

5. **Very Private** is a daily intimate moisturizer created specifically to counteract vagina dryness. Very Private also helps ease the beginning of intimacy and gives maximum tissue protection, literally cushioning the vagina tissue with moisture so sexual activity is completely comfortable and can last as long as desired. It's extremely effective and consumer friendly and feels as natural as a woman's own moisture- no stickiness, no residue and no superfluous ingredients to change the natural vagina

environment. It's used by thousands of women for vagina dryness with great satisfaction. Very Private is also recommended by several teaching hospitals such as MD Anderson, and Cedars Sinai departments of gynecology, FDA approved to be marketed as a 501 (K) medical device. It feels as natural as a woman's own fluid and adapts to her body's temperature.

6. **Astro-Glide Sex Lube** is a favorite that's sure to please. Astroglide lubricant is water based and water soluble, petroleum free, light, odorless, colorless, tasteless, non-staining, and long-lasting. It contains no spermicide and won't harm your condoms! What more could a woman ask for in a sex lube? Astroglide is second only to nature. Astroglide lube now comes in a Sensual Strawberry Flavored lube and it fights HIV in lab tests.

7. **Venus for Women** is a clean, safe, highly concentrated, moisturizing massage lubricant designed especially for women. Venus pampers the body, leaving skin velvety soft and smooth. Venus is composed of the highest quality clinically tested ingredients. Safe to use, nontoxic and

hypoallergenic. Perfect for women with extra sensitive skin. Venus is extremely long lasting and does not block pores. Contains no preservatives and it's oil, water, fragrance and taste free. Never dries out or gets sticky. Latex safe. Venus is perfect for body massages and moisturizing.

8. **Aqua Lube** is from the makers of Kimono brand condoms. Specially formulated to enhance sensual pleasure by supplementing the body's own lubrication. Aqua lube is odor free, non-staining and won't harm condoms. If you're looking for frictionless pleasure, this is the product for you! Aqua-lube is available without spermicide in two convenient sizes.

9. **Foreplay** is a sensual water based lubricant. It's one of the most advanced lubricants available. Non-staining, completely edible, and has a pleasant taste. It is safe to use on condoms. Forplay is also pH balanced for sensitive skin. Regular or with Aloe Vera and Vitamin E. 9.0 oz. Bottle.

10. **I.D. Glide** is a water-based lubricant that stays slick longer and doesn't gum up or get sticky. ID

Glide is unflavored, non-staining and fragrance free. This product is safe to use on your favorite condoms!

11. **Wet Light Lubricant** is the longest lasting, most dependable personal lubricant available. Its colorless, greaseless and odorless and a favorite among lubricant lovers. Water based, oil free and safe to use with condoms. Wet Light is a lighter, thinner LIQUID version of WET Original. Both are without spermicide.

12. **I.D. Millennium Never-Drying and Super Slick**. I-D Millennium is the leader in long lasting Lubricants. Using a special silicone-based formula, I-D Millennium is Latex-Friendly and will stay slick even under water. Available in 2 oz. and 8 oz. sizes, the Advanced Formula makes I-D Millennium the Preferred Choice in High-End Lubricants.

13. **Eros Body Glide.** A revolutionary new moisturizing lubricant from Germany, recently introduced to the U.S.A., Eros will never get sticky, never dry out and will not absorb into your skin.

One drop is all it takes. It takes less and cost less. Eros is hypoallergenic, tasteless, fragrance free, oil free, no staining and protects the skin without blocking pores. Eros will enhance anybody-to-body experience and is produced under the strictest European clinical standards and completely safe with latex.

14. **Sylk** is tasteless, odorless and non-greasy. Sylk mimics the natural vagina juices. Sylk is safe to use with condoms.

15. **Wet Platinum** is the top quality lubricant. It comes in a sexy black bottle and stays wetter and slipperier for longer than any lubricant tested in clinical trials. It can be used by men and women and is safe to use with condoms.

16. **Spike**. Anal lubrication. Also by Dr. Johnson. It comes in a concertina-shaped squeeze bottle with long probe applicator for delivering deep inside.

17. **Small gelatin-filled capsules** that you bite during oral sex to flood your lover's genitals with

sweet smelling edible gel. Chocolate flavored gels and soft candies are great.

Sex Oils

Even when your sex life is going good, you can find ways to make it better. The following lubricants will add positive spice to your lovemaking.

1. **Zestra** is plant-based oil that increases arousal, vaginal lubrication and sexual pleasure in some women. The oil is massaged into the love button, labia and opening of the vagina prior to sex. The effects begin five minutes after application and last up to forty-five minutes.

2. **ProSensual** is a soy-based lubricant that is described as a topical sexual stimulant for women. When applied to the vulva it may increase arousal and sexual pleasure. Some women describe a warm tingly sensation after application.

Sex Creams

For women who want to give their man the pleasure of a lubricant there is the ever popular, most familiar and reliable of sexual pleasures - men cream. Men creams enhance the sensation and augment the pleasure to satisfy a man's personal and sensual needs.

1. **Avanti Men Cream** lubricant is oil based and only safe to use with polyurethane condoms such as Avanti and Supra. It should not be used with latex condoms.

2. **Forever Yours** is a prolonging emollient. It makes pleasurable moments last. This amazing cream temporarily desensitizes and will increase any man's staying power for prolonged sexual pleasure. Mild, yet cool and fresh, Forever Yours is vitamin E enriched, water-soluble, condom safe and made from pure food ingredients. Comes in 2oz jar. Two flavors to choose from Crèmes de Menthe and Passion Fruit.

3. **Durex Maintain Sex Cream** is for the man who desires a little extra staying power. A desensitizing lubricant to prolong sexual pleasure for both lovers. Maintain is water based, clear, odorless and safe to use on condoms. Put a little dab on your lover's

male identity and he'll stand at attention all night. It comes in a one-ounce tube.

4. **Viacreme** offers women enhanced physical sensation. It's safe and natural and made just for women!

5. **Vivid Virility** is an fast-acting supplement that creates longer, stronger, harder erections within minutes! Vivid heightens sexual drive and desire as a man's penis engorges with increased blood flow.

Because reduced levels of estrogen in women may cause a lack of secretion or limit normal lubrication lubricants are great sex aides.

Note: There are many other lubricants available that you can try: www.annsummers.com and www.goodvibes.com

"Sensual and spiritual are not easy words to use; that there are, perhaps, not two"

Using Electricity

This chapter will introduce you to electrical sexual devices.

There's always the emotional intensity that sparks electricity between two lovers. There is also the kind of electricity that's used to excite lovers with safe low voltage mini bolts of electricity. It's known as Faraday Electricity. It's better known as the infamous TENS unit machine which is a small box like piece of equipment used in physiotherapy to send small electrical charges into the skin to relive physical pain.

The electricity I'm speaking about in this chapter is for the enhancement of sexual pleasure. It comes in minimal doses and believe it or not couples that use it really like it.

They give it their stamp of approval. To be honest I've never tried it, but I couldn't resist including it in this book. The lengths people will go to find and get pleasure fascinated me. This is purely for your information and curious nature.

The Violet Wand

The Violet Wand is the sexual version of the TENS unit. It's been on sale since the 1930's and is presently a highly interesting sexual toy. When it's held near the body it sends out a continuous stream of tiny electrical charges and sends a spark to the recipient that is worth more than its weight in gold. I've never tried it because I'm not into electrical sex, but I thought I would mention it because it sounded so interesting.

Butt Plugs, Rings and Shields

Other electrical stimulating toys are butt plugs, male identity rings, and vagina shields. To become better informed about electrical sex I suggest you buy the Guide to Electrical Sex Book. It explains the sexual electricity phenomenon.

Electric-powered vibrators are as far as I go. They are the kinds that have cords you plug into an outlet and are the largest and most powerful vibrators available. They tend to be a bit more expensive, but then again, you'll never have to buy batteries.

Warning:

Research the do's and don'ts and hazards associated with any electric toys before use. Understand them before you use them.

What really makes sex great - is love.

Part 6

Indulging In Sensuous Foods

Chapter 30

Pleasure Foods

This chapter will discuss foods that are considered sensuously good.

Let's face it, good food, good sex and good times go hand in hand Food, sex and romance have been linked for centuries. Every meal gives you a chance to cherish your mate and express your love and sexuality.

Cooking and eating is a lot like making love because you use all of the same senses: smell, touch, taste and sight. The science of sex through food like making love, are pleasurable, fun experiences that ignite the flame of romance.

When you cook for someone you provide nurturing at the most basic level. When you make love the two of you are providing sustenance for your souls. Couples who cook together have strong relationships in most cases. Candlelight, romantic music and good food always add up to amour.

The erotic power of food has been celebrated for centuries. Casanova was said to share oysters with his paramours to whet their sexual appetites. Greek and Roman cultures enjoyed a parade of ripe fruits and exotic dishes before engaging in sensual pleasures. It has even been said that a delicious meal is the quickest way to a man (or woman's) heart. After all, what courtship would be complete without a romantic dinner?

Heated Pleasures

Nutritious foods can stir libido, revive sexual function and enhance health, especially when served in a sensual way.

Nutrition plays a vital role in love and lovemaking. The quality of our diet has a great deal to do with the quality of our sex-life. Nutritious foods can stir libido, revive sexual function and enhance health, especially when served in a sensual way.

Eating Erotic and Exciting Foods

When I think of eating and eroticism, I feel that the most erotic and beneficial aphrodisiac is a woman's mind. What a woman eats can enhance or diminish her sexual arousal. Because your brain releases chemicals that send messages of well-being, motivation, and arousal - the feelings that put you in the mood for making love.

Heated Pleasures
Take the ice cube into your warm mouth while wrapping it around his male identity. The simultaneous sensations of hot and cold will have an indescribable effect on his male identity.

One of the worst and best hormones that enhance desire is fat. A diet rich in essential fatty acids found in nuts, vegetable and fish oils is essential for these hormones. The mineral zinc, found in pumpkin and sunflower seeds, mushrooms, and seafood, especially oysters.

Once you are turned on and ready for sexual intercourse, you need long-lasting energy. This is where the carbs come in: the fruits and grains you eat are what give you energy that's needed for sexual stamina. Everything you eat or drink affects your motivation or desire for sex, your ability to respond to sexual stimulation, and the intensity of your response.

Exciting Frozen Treats

Ice cubes, for instance, can be used for stimulation by inserting one into your mouth before giving oral pleasure. If you can't take ice in your mouth for too long, just hold it in your hand and let the iced water drip onto the nipples and/or other sensuous parts of the body?

On the flip side, why not ask for some reciprocity? Take the ice cube into your warm mouth while wrapping it around his male identity. The simultaneous sensations of hot and cold will have an indescribable effect on his male identity.

Heatology
Although it can get quite sticky, what's wrong with being "glued" to someone whose sexually intrigues you?

Kissing each other while exchanging frozen treats is exciting. Hold it in your teeth and outline his lips and face with it. Sex is all about fun, and a little cold water never hurt anyone.

Sensuous Dream Creams

Everyone has heard of using whipped cream to add a little sweet to the treat, but there's more to this condiment than placing it his genitalia and licking it clean. Let him hold the bottle and place the cream wherever he wants you to lick him? It's a fun way to discover his erogenous zones or see how far he is willing to take this creamy delight.

Once again, for the men who want equal treatment; why not turn your member into a whipped cream heaven? If he likes dessert, and enjoys sucking on your nipples place some whipped cream on your nipples and watch him turn into a wild tiger.

Sinfully Sweet and Sticky

Not only can chocolate add some color to your sex lives, it is also believed that chocolate stimulates the production of endorphins, which provide a sense of pleasure or pain. The rich, delicious decadence raises the body's natural antidepressants. Enjoyed in moderation, a few morsels can lift libido, providing a tantalizing prelude to sex.

Apparently, chocolate contains a natural substance that allegedly stimulates the same reaction in the body as the feeling of falling in love. So don't be shy; pour some chocolate syrup all over your lover and lick until there's no trace of chocolate anywhere - then start all over again!

Why not dip his male identity in some chocolate and have a taste of his Mr. Good bar? You'd be surprised at how enjoyable fellatio can feel when a woman has the pleasure of devouring a chocolate-covered male identity. If chocolate doesn't tempt your palate, then why not make like a bee and provide some honey? By using a squeeze bottle, you can make a path down his body leading to the end of a trail where you'll ultimately spend most of your time. Although it can get quite sticky, what's wrong with being "glued" to someone who sexually intrigues you?

Healthy "Gourmet Love"

The dietary ingredients for a lifetime of wonderful sex include a variety of fresh, wholesome fruits and vegetables, and lean proteins. Complex carbohydrates should be the centerpiece of a healthy sex diet, with lean proteins comprising about 20% to 30% of daily calories, advises Chris Meletis, N.D. Chief Medical Officer at the National College of Naturopathic Medicine.

Meals rich in fruits and vegetables provide beneficial nutrients that keep organs in peak condition and energy at maximum levels, both of which are essential for lovemaking.

Although some foods arouse, others can impair sexual function. Fried foods and rich cream sauces can leave you feeling more sluggish than sexy. What's more, excessive sugar, salt, saturated fat and highly processed foods are linked to frigidity, difficulty reaching orgasm and lack of interest in sex. Cutting back on these foods will help revive and preserve sexual vitality and enhance overall well-being. It's a good idea to limit consumption of alcohol and coffee, and to skip tobacco altogether. These "pleasure drugs" can dampen sexual desire and leech beneficial nutrients vital to your sexual health.

You Should Know

Meals rich in fruits and vegetables provide beneficial nutrients that keep organs in peak condition and energy at maximum levels, both of which are essential for lovemaking.

The Erotic Power of Food

The following is a selection of high vitality, fresh foods that supply nutrients essential for a healthy sex life. Keep in mind that any food can be an aphrodisiac.

- **Feast on fruits.** Bursting with fiber and antioxidants, and thought to be imbued with aphrodisiac properties, many fresh fruits are as sensual as they are nutritious. Apples, apricots, bananas, cherries, coconut, dates, figs, grapes, mangoes, papayas, peaches, pears, plums, pomegranates, quince, raspberries and strawberries are celebrated in erotic literature throughout the world. Whichever fruits you choose, enjoy them often, and with a new appreciation of their sensual attributes.
- **Devour delicious vegetables.** Celery, corn, cucumbers, carrots, eggplant and several other phallic-shaped vegetables have long been prized for their aphrodisiac effects. Although it may be hard to think of them as "erotic", these earthly delights certainly invigorate the body with vitamins and minerals. The avocado, on the other hand, is undeniably sensual - so much so that the Spanish conquistadors helped spread its reputation throughout the world as a powerful stimulant.
- **A juicy tomato**, or "love apple," a potent source of the powerhouse antioxidant, lycopene. It was once a highly sought-after libido enhancer. Other

veggies reputed to turn up the heat and fortify the body, include: beans, garlic, leeks, onions, (yes onions) parsley, peppers, soybeans, spinach, truffles, turnips and watercress. Serve these foods often for optimal sexual health.

- **Savor fruits of the sea and lean proteins.** Shellfish including abalone, oysters, clams, scallops, shrimp, lobster and deep, cold-water fish like cod and halibut, fuel the body, brain and the sex drive. Oysters, for instance, are rich in zinc and iodine. Zinc, a vital sexual nutriment, is essential for testosterone production in men and women.
- **Eat lean meats.** Meats such as chicken and turkey are healthful in moderation. "Good protein intake is important, but excessive amounts can interfere with sexuality," warns Elson Haas, M.D., and author of "Staying Healthy with Nutrition". If possible, choose organic meats to avoid hormones, antibiotics and other additives typically found in these foods. Nuts, seeds and beans are also excellent sources of protein. Both pine nuts and pumpkin seeds are sexual adjuvants.

- **Multi-Vitamins.** Although a healthy diet provides most of the nourishment necessary for sexual wellness, a multivitamin / mineral supplement offers extra health insurance. Vitamins including A, the B group, C and E are necessary for sexual functioning. Vitamin E, for instance, supplies the sex organs with sufficient oxygen. B vitamins, including niacin and B-5, can help men and women reach orgasm and improve sexual stamina. Selenium, manganese and zinc, are also vital in regulating hormones and revving up sex drive. Rather than taking these individually, take a multivitamin/mineral to ensure correct dosages. Check with your doctor to learn which brands are recommended.

The Erotic Elements of Food

Now that the erotic food ingredients are in place, it's time to have some fun! Start by taking time to savor each meal. Nutritious foods fuel sexual energy, but it is the art of eating that can be truly erotic.

A lovely prepared meal served in the proper ambience can precipitate passion. To help set the mood for a night of romance, try some of the following:

- ❖ Prepare a dinner for two in sexy costumes or in the nude with your lover.
- ❖ Spread a blanket on the floor. Decorate with candles and flowers, and then eat with no silverware.
- ❖ Serve finger foods such as olives or raw vegetables and dip. Dim the lights and play music that sets the right mood.
- ❖ Sip champagne, wine or drink seltzer water.
- ❖ Feed your partner a juicy slice of mango, a delicate sliver of pear, or sweet juicy grapes.
- ❖ Take turns feeding each other in creative ways. Offer to nibble ripe raspberries from your lover's chest.
- ❖ Finish with an arousing massage or a warm bubble bath or both.

For a real adventure, enjoy a picnic in a secluded park, on the beach, or even in the bedroom. Pack light foods that can be fed to each other; such as strawberries and chocolate, hard-boiled eggs, yogurt, French

<u>Heated Pleasures</u>

Try to experiment with food from appetizers to dessert (dessert means YOU), and be sure to use proper kitchen etiquette (cleaning up means showering together).

bread and string cheese. Wear something sexy. And don't forget the blanket. Treat each course as an overture to lovemaking. Most importantly, eat well and with pleasure.

Soul Nourishing Foreplay Foods

If the sizzle in your relationship has started to fizzle or you're looking for a new playmate to heat up your love life, then create your favorite dish and use food as foreplay. Creating recipes for romance can definitely heat up your love life. Why not? Use the sensual philosophy of food, romance and relationships to contribute to the health and wealth of your soul.

Using food as foreplay will get you out of the kitchen and into the bedroom. Try to experiment with food from appetizers to dessert (dessert means YOU), and be sure to use proper kitchen etiquette (cleaning up means showering together). Discover why cooking is like making love. Stock your passion-filled pantry with things both of you will love to eat." Make it more than just a meal. Use it as a great aide to keeping the home fires burning. Food has many sexual advantages. Just to mention a few…

- It is a scientifically proven aphrodisiac.
- Creates a culinary fantasy that will capture your lover's - body, heart and soul.

- Seals the relationship with a kiss and a home-cooked meal.
- Cooking for the person you love or lust after is a great way to get things moving in the right direction.
- You and your home will become romantic gardens of sensual delight (edible of course).

Aphrodisiacs: Fact or Fiction

Many foods have developed a reputation as aphrodisiacs over the centuries. Favorite love foods include: chocolate, basil, oysters, shrimp, honey, donuts, black licorice and champagne. Blindfold your partner, feed him tidbits and discover what foods really turn the two of you on. Many people swear by the sex-enhancing effects of certain foods, but can what you eat really help boost your libido?

> **You Should Know**
> Because procreation was an important moral and religious issue aphrodisiacs were sought to insure both male and female potency

Aphrodisiacs were first sought out as a remedy for various sexual anxieties including fears of inadequate performance as well as a need to increase fertility. Because procreation was an important moral and religious issue aphrodisiacs were sought to insure both male and female potency.

Despite long-standing literary and popular interest in internal aphrodisiacs, almost no scientific studies of them have been made. Scientific research is limited to occasional tests of drugs or hormones for the cure of male impotence. Most writings on the subject are little more than unscientific compilations of traditional or folkloric material.

You Should Know

Undernourishment creates a loss of libido as well as reduces fertility rates.

Of the various foods to which aphrodisiac powers are traditionally attributed, fish, vegetables, and spices have been the most popular throughout history. It must be concluded that the reputation of various supposedly erotic foods is based not upon fact, but upon folklore. With the exception of certain drugs such as alcohol or marijuana, which may lead to sexual excitement, modern medical science recognizes a very limited number of aphrodisiacs.

Why Certain Foods?

In ancient times a distinction was made between substances that increased fertility versus those that increased sex drive. One key issue was nutrition. Food was not as readily available as it is today. Undernourishment creates a loss of libido as well as reduces fertility rates. Substances that "by nature" represent "seed or semen" such as bulbs, eggs, snails" were considered inherently to have sexual powers. Other types of foods were considered stimulating by their "physical resemblance to genitalia"

It's important to realize these food substances were identified and documented by the likes of Pliny and Discords (ancient Greeks) first century AD and later by Paul of Aegina from the seventh century. Later more credence was given to foods that "satisfied dietary gratification".

Other foods deemed to have these aphrodisiac qualities were derived from mythology. Aphrodite, the love goddess was said to consider "sparrows" sacred because of their "amorous nature" and for that reason were included in various aphrodisiac brews.

Aphrodisiac Food List

There was not always agreement upon what foods were actually aphrodisiacs or "anaphrodisiacs" (decrease potency). But the ancient list included Anise, basil, carrot, salvia, gladiolus root, orchid bulbs, pistachio nuts, rocket (arugula), sage, sea fennel, turnips, skunk flesh (a type of lizard) and river snails. The ancients suggested you steer clear of dill, lentil, lettuce, watercress, rue, and water lily. Here is a list of many of the foods that are believed to be a source of erotic stimuli. Let me know what you think.

- **Aniseed**

  A very popular aphrodisiac with many culinary uses. It has been used as an aphrodisiac since the Greeks and the Romans, who believed aniseed, had special powers. Sucking on the seeds is said to increases your sexual desire.

- **Asparagus**

  This vegetable earned its reputation as a sex enhancer because of its shape. Given its phallic shape, asparagus is frequently enjoyed as an aphrodisiac food. Feed your lover boiled or steamed asparagus spears for a sensuous experience. The vegetarian society suggests "eating asparagus for three days for the most powerful affect".

- **Almond**

  A symbol of fertility throughout the ages. The aroma of almond is thought to induce passion in a female. Try serving Marzipan (almond paste) in the shapes of fruits for a special after-dinner treat.

- **Arugula**

  Arugula or "rocket" seed has been documented as an aphrodisiac since the first century A.D. This ingredient was added to grated orchid bulbs and parsnips then combined with pine nuts and pistachios. Arugula greens are frequently used in salads and pasta.

- **Avocado**

  The Aztecs called the avocado tree "Ahuacuatl which translated means "testicle tree". The ancients thought the fruit hanging in pairs on the tree resembled the male's testicles. This is a delicious fruit with a sensuous texture. Serve in slices with a small amount of Balsamic vinegar and freshly ground pepper.

- **Bananas**

  The banana flower has a marvelous phallic shape and is partially responsible for popularity of the banana as an aphrodisiac food. An Islamic myth tells the tale that after Adam and Eve succumbed to the "Apple" they started covering their "nudity" with banana leaves rather than fig. From a more practical standpoint bananas are rich in potassium and B vitamins, necessities for sex hormone production.

- **Basil (sweet basil)**

  Basil is said to stimulate the sex drive and boost fertility. It is also said to produce a general sense of well-being for body and mind.

- **Broccoli Rabe (And Other Mustard Greens)**

  The ground seeds of various plants in the brassica family were believed to increase vitality. In the case of broccoli rabe it's more likely a myth created to get people to eat this bitter vegetable.

- **Chocolate**

  The Aztecs referred to chocolate "nourishment of the Gods". Chocolate contains chemicals thought to effect neurotransmitters in the brain and a related substance to caffeine called theobromine. Chocolate contains more antioxidant (cancer preventing enzymes) than does red wine. The secret for passion is to combine the two. Try a glass of Cabernet with a bit of dark chocolate for a sensuous treat or let us temp you with our recipe for chocolate espresso pots de crème.

- Carrots

Another good reason to eat carrots is it's believed to be a stimulant to the male. The phallus shaped carrot has been associated with stimulation since ancient times and was used by early Middle Eastern royalty to aid seduction. High vitamins and beta-carotene is perhaps a justification for a piece of carrot cake?

- Coffee

Caffeine is a well-known stimulant, too much and it becomes a depressant. Serve small amounts of rich dark coffee in special little demitasse cups. Coffee stimulates both the body and the mind so taste a little in preparation for an "all-nighter". It may boost your energy, but has no real effects on your sexual prowess or stimulation.

- Coriander (Cilantro seed)

The book of The Arabian nights tells a tale of a merchant who had been childless for 40 years, but was cured by a concoction that included coriander. That book is over 1000 years old so the history of coriander as an aphrodisiac dates back far into history. Cilantro was also known as an "appetite" stimulant.

- Figs

An open fig is thought to emulate the female sex

organs and traditionally thought of as a sexual stimulant. A man breaking open a fig and eating it in front of his lover is a powerful erotic act. Serve fresh Black Mission figs in a cool bowl of water as it is done in Italy and be sure to eat with your fingers!

- Garlic

  The 'heat' in garlic is said to stir sexual desires. Make sure you and your partner share it together. Garlic has been used for centuries to cure everything from the common cold to heart ailments. This is a good time for moderation. Enjoy pasta with a lightly garlicky sauce and it and lead up to something spicy in the bedroom later. Eat too much of this and you might not ever get or keep a lover. Eat a very, very small amount.

- Ginger

  Ginger root raw, cooked or crystallized is a stimulant to the circulatory system. Perhaps a stir-fry with freshly grated ginger can stir something spicy up in the bedroom later.

- Honey

  Many medicines in Egyptian times were based on honey including cures for sterility and impotence. Medieval seducers plied their partners with Mead, a fermented drink made from honey. Lovers on their "Honeymoon" drank mead and it was thought to "sweeten" the marriage.

- Licorice

The Chinese have used licorice for medicinal purposes since ancient times. The essence of the Glycyrrhizin glabra (licorice) plant, glycyrrhizins, is 50 times sweeter than sugar. Chewing on bits of licorice root is said to enhance love and lust. It is particularly stimulating to woman.

- Mustard

Believed to stimulate the sexual glands and increase desire. Prepare a tenderloin roast (filet mignon) for two with a mustard and peppercorn sauce.

- Nutmeg

Nutmeg was highly prized by Chinese women as an aphrodisiac. In quantity nutmeg can produce a hallucinogenic effect. A light sprinkling of the spice in a warm pumpkin soup can help spice up your evening.

- Oysters

Oysters were documented as an aphrodisiac food by the Romans in the second century A.D as mentioned in a satire by Juvenal. He described the wanton ways of women after ingesting wine and eating "giant oysters". An additional hypothesis is that the oyster resembles the "female" genitals. In reality oysters are very nutritious and high in protein. It doesn't carry the power to increase sex, but because it is loaded with zinc it increases testosterone in men, which is the hormone responsible for sexual desire.

- Pine Nuts

  Zinc is a key mineral necessary to maintain male potency and pine nuts are rich in zinc. Pine nuts have been used to stimulate the libido as far back as medieval times. Serve pine nut cookies with a dark espresso for a stimulating dessert.

- Pineapple

  Rich in vitamin C and is used in the homeopathic treatment for impotence. Add a spear to a sweet Rum drink for a tasty prelude to an evening of passion.

- Raspberries and Strawberries

  Raspberries and strawberries are perfect food for hand feeding your lover. Both invite love and are described in erotic literature as fruit nipples. Both are high in vitamin C and make a sweet light dessert.

- Truffles

  The Greeks and the Romans considered the rare truffle to be an aphrodisiac. The musky scent is said to stimulate and sensitize the skin to touch.

- Vanilla

The scent and flavor of vanilla is believed to increase lust. According to the Australian Orchid Society, "Old Totonac lore says that Xanat, the young daughter of the Mexican fertility goddess, loved a Totonac youth. Unable to marry him due to her divine nature, she transformed herself into a plant that would provide pleasure and happiness." Fill tall Champagne glasses to the rim and add a vanilla bean for a bubbly treat.

- Wine

A glass or two of wine can greatly enhance a romantic interlude. Wine relaxes and helps stimulate the senses. Drinking wine can be an erotic experience. Let your eyes feast on the color of the liquid. Caress the glass and savor the taste on your tongue. Do remember that excessive alcohol can make you drowsy for the after-dinner romance. A moderate amount of wine has been said to "arouse" but much more than that will have a reverse affect. Wine just as any other alcoholic beverage should be drank in moderation. It may make you feel relaxed and reduce inhibitions, however it may also make it difficult for you to become aroused or achieve orgasm.

Your Brain

If you truly believe a particular food will enhance or increase your sex drive, it probably will. Your brain is the most powerful aphrodisiac you own. There you have it, the great sensuous aphrodisiacs. Enjoy.

How to Use Aphrodisiac Foods

Create an evening revolving around a menu of delicious aphrodisiac foods! It is important that you are both rested, and ready to enjoy a relaxed evening. This will not work if you are tired or stressed or under time pressure.

Ms. Real Suggests
To appreciate the evening fully, consider serving the meal in courses - one course at a time over a two or three hour period.

The evening must be relaxed and pressure free. Neither of you should be concerned about work, kids, phone calls, or needing to be somewhere by a specific time - the focus should be on each other, enjoying the "special" meal, and soaking up the pleasures of the evening.

To appreciate the evening fully, consider serving the meal in courses - one course at a time over a two or three hour period. This will give you lots of time to spend

Heated Pleasures

Place fresh clean sheets on the bed, make sure the bathroom is sparkling with towels and toiletries laid out for your lover.

together, and makes it easier for you to enjoy the evening and prepare the foods without pressure. The food is more special if served gradually over the course of your special romantic evening. Here are the steps to make it easy!

Extend the Invitation Early

Create anticipation by extending the invitation for a very special romantic evening at least a week in advance. Planning an evening in advance lets your partner know that the evening you are planning for them is something very special. There is power in creating expectations! Anticipation should be created for your lover. They will feel very loved and special knowing that you are putting so much time and energy into an evening just for them.

Clean and Sparkling Is Sexy!

You should have a pristine home. Don't overlook any details. Every room in the house should be spotless. Look at it with a new eye. Get rid of clutter. Add candles, natural scents, flowers etc. to make the room feel romantic and ready for your special evening. Place fresh clean sheets on the bed, make sure the bathroom is sparkling with towels and toiletries laid out for your lover.

The kitchen and living areas should be clean and organized and have romantic touches. Everything should be ready for your romantic evening a day ahead of time, so you are not rushing around stressed at the last minute.

Creating an Appetizing Mood

Set your dining room table in advance, with your good china and crystal, and decorate the dining room, living room, and bedroom with candles and flowers. Put on your favorite romantic music, and turn off the phones.

Greeting Your Lover

Wear something exotic and sexy. When the big day arrives, greet your lover at the door wearing something sexy - and, if possible, have something comfortable and sexy for them to slip into also. If not, you should let your lover know what the proper attire will be for your evening. You don't want them to show up in a sweatshirt and jeans for your special evening.

Popular Erotic Recipes

These aphrodisiac dishes are nutritious, low fat and easy to prepare.

Oyster Pleasure

- 1-1/2 pint shucked oysters
- 1 cup finely chopped onion
- 2 tsp. butter
- 1/2 tsp. salt
- 2 cups skim milk
- 1 cup half and half
- 1 Teaspoon of fresh parsley
- 1/4 tsp. white pepper

In a large saucepan, cook onion in butter until tender. Stir in oysters and salt. Cook over medium heat for 5 minutes, until oysters curl around the edges. Stir in milk, cream, parsley and pepper. Heat thoroughly. Serves 4 to 6.

Acorn Squash with Apricot Glaze

2 medium acorn squash

- 1 medium apple, sliced
- 2 apricots, sliced. or 1 peach, peeled and sliced
- 1/4 cup apricot nectar
- 2 T honey

- 1/4 tsp. ground nutmeg
- 1 T butter

Cut the squash in halves and discard seeds. Place squash in a baking dish with about one-quarter inch of water. Bake at 350 degrees until tender (usually 30 to 45 minutes). Or, microwave for 12 minutes until tender. In a small bowl, combine apple, apricots, nectar, honey and nutmeg. Turn squash over and spoon mixture into the cavities. Cook until hot. Garnish with nutmeg. Serves 4.

Sensual Asparagus Delight

1 to 1 and 1/2 lbs. fresh asparagus

2 tsp. olive oil or butter

2 Teaspoons snipped fresh chervil or 2 tsp. tarragon

A dash of course salt

Preheat oven to 475 degrees. Cut woody bases from asparagus. Combine oil and 1 T chervil or 1 tsp. tarragon. Drizzle over asparagus. Toss to coat. Roast 4 to 6 minutes in greased baking pan until tender. To serve, place upright in a jar. Sprinkle with remaining chervil. Serves 6.

Sensual Lemon Tart

This dish, if you buy the pastry shell ahead of time, takes only twenty minutes to prepare and is a great sensual experience both to cook and to eat. Experiment with different amounts of lemon juice to get your desired tartness. Light enough to leave you fulfilled but not FILLED. I guarantee the tart in you will savor this one!

1 1/2 cup water

3/4 cup sugar

1 tsp. grated lemon peel

1/4 tsp. salt

5 tbs. corn starch

Cook and stir in double boiler (or place sauce pan in larger pan of heated water) until thick. Then add 2 beaten egg yolks and 6 tablespoons lemon juice. Pour into a pre-baked pie shell and let cool in fridge for two hours. For extra sweetness, you may add meringue. Sensuously delicious.

There are no good girls gone wrong - just bad girls found out." - Mae West

Protecting Yourself

Safe Sex Reminders

This chapter will help you understand the importance of abstinence, easy methods of birth control and safety against sexually transmitted diseases.

What is the most sexiest thing in the world to you? Is it when you get up from a wonderful lovemaking session you feel good inside and outside. Knowing that I am completely satisfied don't have a sexually transmitted disease is high on my list too.

It's sad, but true ... the days of completely carefree sex have come to an end. Though there are cures for certain sexually transmitted diseases with medical treatment -

penicillin and other antibiotics provide no cure for genital herpes or AIDS.

Part of being a great lover means taking responsibility for your personal protection from any serious incurable diseases. Even though total abstinence is one means of protection, it is not the most enjoyable solution for the sexually active women.

If you and your man have had sex with each other for at least five to ten years, and neither of you use drugs intravenously or haven't had a contaminated rating blood transfusion you can happily and safely enjoy most all of the sexual treats in this book. This is often the case for the vast majority of monogamous couples who read my books.

Heated Pleasures

Some of the best sex in the world is the kind that happens when you are relaxed, confident, and sure it will be pleasurable and safe.

Usually, when I ask women what the sexiest thing in the world is they don't immediately say birth control. It should be. Some of the best sex in the world is the kind that happens when you are relaxed, confident, and sure it will be pleasurable and safe. Nothing is tenser for a woman than worrying about an unwanted pregnancy and a sexually transmitted disease. Nothing is more bothersome than the worry associated with ..."Am I ovulating? Did I take my birth control pill? Did I bring a condom? Did I bring my diaphragm? Was that a sore on his penis?

You Should Know

Take the time to get to know one another, then establish the fact that you're concerned about each other's health and well-being.

When you are prepared and have effective contraception you can focus on the pleasure of your sexual experience more than the negative association that comes with forgotten birth control of unprotected sex.

Thank God we have become scientifically and technologically advanced in the both areas and we have many options. Because birth control is safe, easy to use and effective you and your partner can fully focus on the pleasure sex provides. The methods provide little or no effort and the protection is long lasting.

Share Your Moments

I'm not going to lecture you, but if you and your lover are relatively new to each other, there are plenty of safe ways to share some very sensuous moments. Take the time to get to know one another, then establish the fact that you're concerned about each other's health and well-being. Verbally share with one another any sexual and intravenous drug use and what you'd like to do to protect each other. At the very least use condoms as a natural part of your lovemaking each time you decide to have sex. It's better to be sensuously safe than seriously sorry.

Easy Methods of Birth Control

Depo-Provera

What it is and how it works: Depo-Provera is a prescription injection known by most women as "the shot," containing a progestin hormone that is given every three months at your doctor's office. This injection prevents ovulation and changes a woman's cervical mucus and lining of the uterus to help prevent pregnancy.

Side effects: It has a few side effects. The most common complaint is spotting and irregular bleeding during the first year. Over time there is no period at all while using this method and it might possibly take several months for your cycle to return after discontinued use of the Depo-Provera. It’s 99 percent effective for preventing pregnancy, but does not protect against STD's.

Intrauterine Device:

What it is and how it works: An Intrauterine Device (IUD) is a small, thin device that is placed in your uterus by a healthcare provider to prevent pregnancy. There are two types of IUD's: The T-shaped Copper-T IUD (Paragard) is a device that prevents the man's sperm from fertilizing the woman's egg. It provides up to ten years of protection. The Mirena IUD is made of plastic and works by releasing a progesterone-type hormone in continuous low doses. It provides five years of experience.

Side effects: The IUD is 99 percent effective and is very safe. It can be easily inserted and removed by your doctor. It provides long-term trouble-free protection. It does not protect against STD's so it's best to use a condom with it.

NuvaRing

What it is and how it works: The NuvaRing is used in the same way a diaphragm is used, but it remains in place for three weeks. The NuvaRing is 2 inches in diameter and is a one-size-fits-all, flexible transparent ring that is placed into the vagina for three weeks. The ring is removed during the fourth week, causing the woman to have her period. While inside of the woman it releases a steady dose of estrogen and progestin to prevent release of an egg and reduce the mobility of sperm. The ring contains the same hormone as the birth control pills. Then you insert a new ring. The ring is 99 percent effective.

Side effects: It doesn't protect against STD's so it's best to use a condom with it.

Orthro Evra

What it is and how it works: The Orthro Evra is a small thin patch that releases a continuous dose of estrogen and progestin, which are absorbed through the skin, to prevent ovulation and thicken the cervical mucus. The hormones are the same ones in birth control pills. Patches are changed once a week for three weeks. Users do not wear a patch on the fourth week. You can place them on your body anywhere you feel comfortable, including the outer upper arm, butt or stomach. The patches stay in place during physical activity and the once a week dosage is easy to remember. They are 99 percent effective.

Side effects: Risks and side effects are the same as the birth control pill. The patch may cause skin irritation in some women and does not protect against (sexually transmitted infections). Not recommended for women who weigh more than 190 pounds.

Sterilization

What it is and how it works: Sterilization is a permanent form of birth control. In women doctors perform a surgical procedure called a tubal ligation to block the fallopian tubes and permanently prevent sperm from accessing the egg. When your tubes are tied doctor’s burn, cut, tie, or block them. A new apparatus Ensure, is a small soft metal device that is placed in the fallopian tube by way of the vagina, the non-surgical procedure causes your body to form scar tissue around the device blocking our tubes so eggs can't pass through them.

Side effects: The tubal ligation is permanent and difficult to reverse. It is not a viable option for women who want to have children in the future. It does not protect against STD's so it's best to use a condom with it.

Hormone Free Birth Control

Barrier methods of protection are great contraception that release hormones to prevent pregnancy. Using these methods is better when planned so as not to interrupt sexual play.

Diaphragm

What it is and how it works: The diaphragm is used before sexual activity. Apply spermicide inside the dome of the diaphragm. Place the soft dome-shaped latex cup securely in your vulva so it completely covers your cervix and blocks his sperm. Your doctor must fit diaphragms.

Side effects: To prevent pregnancy your diaphragm must remain in place for at least six hours after sex. It can remain in place for up to twenty-four hours. If you use the diaphragm every time you have sex it's 94 percent effective. With usage of the diaphragm your risk of contracting gonorrhea and chlamydia is decreased.

Cervical Cap

What it is and how it works: Before sex, your place this small latex cup over your cervix to prevent sperm from reaching your uterus. Cervical caps come in different sizes and must be fitted by a physician or nurse practitioner.

Side effects: For effectiveness, a cervical cap has to remain in place for eight hours after sex. It can remain in place for up to forty-eight hours, allowing sexual spontaneity while it is in place. When used consistently, the Prentif cervical cap is 91 percent effective in women who have never had children but drops to 74 percent for women who have given birth. The cap is not recommended for women who have poor vaginal muscle tone, cervical inflammation, a current reproductive tract infection, or any other type of vaginal bleeding. Using the cap may decrease your risk of contracting gonorrhea and chlamydia.

FemCap

What it is and how it works: FemCap is a hat-shaped silicone rubber cap that is placed in your vagina before sex. It covers the cervix, preventing sperm from entering your uterus, and has a strap for easy removal.

Side effects: It must remain in place for six hours after sex but can be worn for up to forty-eight hours. You can also use it during your period to allow comfortable sex play. It should be fitted by a health care professional.

Lea's Shield

What it is and how it works: You place this dome-shaped disc, made of silicone rubber in your vagina before sex. It operates by creating a suction that traps air between the shield and your cervix. The Lea's Shield covers your cervix and blocks sperm from entering your uterus. Like the Fem Cap, the shield has a strap for removal. Once one-size-fits-all no pre-fitting is necessary, but you need a prescription from a physician.

Side effects: Leave the shield in place for eight hours after intercourse to prevent pregnancy. It can be worn for up to forty-eight hours. The shield may reduce your risk of contracting gonorrhea and chlamydia. It is approximately 85 percent effective in preventing pregnancy.

Condoms

What it is and how it works: the male condom is a sheath that covers the penis and catches the sperm, preventing it from entering your uterus. For full effectiveness, condoms must be placed on the penis at the beginning of intercourse and should be used every time that you have sex. The Reality female condom is a soft plastic pouch that is placed inside the vagina before sex. It also prevents sperm from entering the uterus.

Side effects: If used correctly, the Reality female condom is 95 percent effective in safeguarding against pregnancy. It also protects you from may sexually transmitted infections, including HIV. All male condoms - latex, polyurethane and natural lambskin - are 98 percent effective against pregnancy. Only latex and polyurethane condoms protect against HIV infection. Condoms are the best method we have to prevent sexually transmitted infections.

Other Birth Control Methods

Abstinence

What it is and how it works: This depends on a woman's personal preference; this can mean saying "no" to anything sexual or avoiding vaginal intercourse. True abstinence, however, safeguards you from a potential pregnancy and sexually transmitted infections because it requires that you avoid vaginal intercourse, anal intercourse or any other act that might put you in contact with his sperm.

Side effects: Abstinence is the only method that has proven to 100 percent effective against pregnancy and sexually transmitted infections.

Birth Control Pills

What it is and how it works: Oral contraceptives contain the hormones estrogen and progestin. The most common type, the combined synthetic pill, suppresses ovulation. The progestin-only variety, the mini pill alters the cervical mucus to make it difficult for the sperm to enter the uterus.

Side effects: Some women complain of side effects such as weight gain, breast tenderness, moodiness, vaginal dryness and a decreased sex drive. Often changing the prescription takes care of the problem. Uses of the mini pill tend to have fewer side effects. The pill does not prevent sexually transmitted diseases. It is 99 percent effective in preventing pregnancy.

One of the most buzzed about parts of the Affordable Care Act is the contraceptive mandate, which requires private health insurance plans cover birth control without a co-pay or deductible. In other words, for free.

Chapter 32

Understanding Sexual Diseases

There are more than 25 diseases that are transmitted through sexual activity.

Sexually transmitted diseases (also called STDs, or STIs for sexually transmitted infections) are infections that can be transferred from one person to another through sexual contact. According to the Centers for Disease Control and Prevention, there are over 15 million cases of sexually transmitted disease cases reported annually in the United States. There are more than 25 diseases that are transmitted through sexual activity. Other than HIV, the most common STDs in the United States are chlamydia, gonorrhea, syphilis, genital herpes, human papillomavirus, hepatitis B, trichomoniasis, and bacterial vaginosis. Adolescents and young adults are the age groups at the greatest risk for acquiring an STD. Approximately 19 million new infections occur each year, almost half of them among people ages 15 to 24.

Some STDs can have severe consequences, especially in women, if not treated, which is why it is so important to go for STD testing. Some STDs can lead to pelvic inflammatory disease, which can cause infertility, while others may even be fatal. STDs can be prevented by refraining from sexual activity, and to a certain extent, some contraceptive devices, such as condoms.

> **You Should Know**
>
> There are more than 25 diseases that are transmitted through sexual activity.

Now that you've read and understand more about all the sexy exciting and wonderful things you can do to improve your intimate relationships you're probably ready to dive right in and have some fun. I'm the first to say, "Get busy girlfriend." But before you get busy you have to stop long enough to give thought to how to really enjoy safe sex.

It's important to learn as much as you about sexually transmitted infections and how to prevent them. It starts before you have sex of any kind, with anyone.

The good news is that, with the wide variety of fun safety gear that's available, there is no reason not to have safer, healthy, wilder, more fabulous sex every time.

Sexually transmitted diseases (also called STDs or STIs for sexually transmitted infections) are infections that can be transferred from one person to another through sexual contact. According to the Centers for Disease Control and Prevention, there are over 15 million cases of sexually transmitted disease cases reported annually in the United States. There are more than 25 diseases that are transmitted through sexual activity. Other than HIV, the most common STDs in the United States are chlamydia, gonorrhea, syphilis, genital herpes, human papillomavirus, hepatitis B, trichomoniasis, and bacterial vaginosis. Adolescents and young adults are the age groups at the greatest risk for acquiring an STD. Approximately 19 million new infections occur each year, almost half of them among people ages 15 to 24.

Some STDs can have severe consequences, especially in women, if not treated, which is why it is so important to go for STD testing. Some STDs can lead to pelvic inflammatory disease, which can cause infertility, while others may even be fatal. STDs can be prevented by refraining from sexual activity, and to a certain extent, some contraceptive devices, such as condoms.

STI's: You Need To Know

Bacterial Vaginitis

What it is and how it works: Bacterial Vaginitis infection is sometimes characterized by vaginal irritation and discharge. It results from a change in the different types of bacteria in the vagina. Although it's not always due to intercourse, sexually active women run a higher risk of developing this condition.

Do you have it? Your gynecologist can be your best friend in times such as this. He or she can determine if you have BV by performing a pelvic exam, testing your vaginal secretions and examining a sample of your vaginal tissue under a microscope. Although many women have no symptoms, the most common are vaginal discharge and a strong unpleasant vaginal odor.

How to treat it: BV is treated with antimicrobial creams. Condoms may reduce the risk of developing BV.

Chancroid

What it is and how it works. Chancroid is a condition caused by bacterium, Hemophilus ducreyi. It is common in the United States.

Do you have it? You might notice one or several painful ulcers on the opening of your vagina or vulva. Also, you might have swollen lymph nodes, (glands) seven days after contact. Your doctor will diagnose you by performing special cultures.

How to treat it: Treat it with antibiotics. Patients are usually examined 3-7 days after treatment to see if it has successful. Uncircumcised men usually have difficult time curing the Chancroid. All sexual partners that have in contact with the affected person must be treated with antibiotics whether they have the symptoms or not.

Chlamydia

What it is and how it works: Chlamydia is caused by an organism called Chlamydia trachomatis. It is most common sexually transmitted infection in the United States. Most women infected with chlamydia do not have symptoms. A few women have a heavy yellow discharge from the vagina.

Do you have it? The diagnosis is made when your doctor performs a culture. You should specifically ask to be tested for chlamydia, as it may not be a part of your routine exam. Chlamydia may infect your cervix, anus, throat or urethra.

How to treat it: Both partners must be treated with antibiotics. Follow up testing should occur three or four months after treatment. If untreated, chlamydia may cause pelvic infections, damage to fallopian tubes, ectopic pregnancy and infertility. Condoms will decrease your risk of infections.

Gonorrhea

What it is and how it works: Gonorrhea is caused by a bacterium called Neisseria gonorrhea. It is the second most common sexually transmitted infection in the United States.

Do you have it? Most women who are infected by gonorrhea do not have symptoms. Those with symptoms may have a heavy yellow discharge, burning while urinating, or abnormal menstrual periods. Gonorrhea can affect the anus, throat, cervix and urethra.

How to treat it: The diagnosis is made once the doctor has taken a culture of any of the affected areas, and the infection is treated with antibiotics. Since chlamydia often accompanies gonorrhea you and your partner should be treated for both infections. If left untreated, gonorrhea may cause pelvic infections and infertility. Using condoms may decrease chances of infection.

Hepatitis

What it is and how it works: Hepatitis B infection is caused by the hepatitis B virus (HBV), which is spread through semen, blood, urine and saliva. HBV, however, can be prevented with vaccination. The sexual transmission of the hepatitis A virus (HAV) and hepatitis C (HCV) is less common.

Do you have it? Many people with hepatitis have no symptoms. Those with symptoms may experience headaches, fever, extreme fatigue, nausea, vomiting, lack of appetite and tenderness in the abdomen. They condition is diagnosed by having a blood test.

How to treat it: There is no treatment for hepatitis infection; however your immune system will most likely fight the infection successfully. Sexually active women should get the vaccine to protect from possible infection.

Herpes

What it is and how it works: The herpes simplex virus types 1 and 2 cause genital herpes infections. Herpes type 1 typically infects your mouth but can be spread to your genitals. Herpes type 2 more typically infects the genitals. It is estimated that one in four Americans are infected with genital herpes. Most women and men affected are not aware that they are infected yet are able to transmit the virus to others.

Do you have it? If you have symptoms you may notice a sore, blister or an ulcer on your vagina or vulva. The lesion could appear as a cluster of blisters or a tiny spot the size of a pinhead. The lesions may be painful or itch and can last a few days or weeks. The diagnosis is made when your doctor performs a culture or blood test looking for antibodies to the virus.

How to treat it: There is no cure for herpes, and the virus remains in your body. There are several antiviral medications that can treat herpes symptoms. If you have an outbreak you should refrain from sexual activity with another person. Using condoms may decrease the spread of the virus, but will not eliminate the risk completely because the lesions can exist in areas not covered by a condom.

HIV

What it is and how it works: The HIV infection is caused by the human immunodeficiency virus, which attacks your immune system and eventually, causes AIDS. The virus is transmitted through direct contact with blood, semen, vaginal secretions, breast milk, and to a smaller degree, saliva. The greatest risk of transmission is with anal intercourse. But the virus can also be transmitted through vaginal sex and, to a lesser degree, oral sex. Your risk of contracting HIV from an infected person is increased if you have other sexually transmitted diseases.

Do you have it? Two to four weeks after exposure to HIV, 70 percent of HIV infected people will develop flu like symptoms in the early phase of the infection. But many will not have any symptoms. More advanced symptoms include unexplained rapid weight loss, diarrhea, fevers, night sweats, headaches and lack of appetite. The diagnosis is made by blood tests used to detect the HIV antibody. It could take up to six months after exposure before you actually test positive.

How to treat it: There is no cure for HIV, but there are retroviral medications that can delay the progression of AIDS, a fatal disease. Using latex or polyurethane condoms every time you have sex will reduce your risk of contracting the AIDS virus.

HPV (Human Papilloma Virus)

What it is and how it works: Human Papilloma virus infection may cause either genital warts or an abnormal pap smear. Virtually all cases of cervical cancer are caused by HPV. There are hundreds of different types of human Papilloma virus. Fortunately most HPV infections are benign and cause nothing more than genital warts. It has been estimated that more than 80 percent of sexually active women will be become infected with HPV during their life span.

Do you have it? If you are infected with HPV, you may develop warts on your vulva or vagina that may or may not cause symptoms. When the virus affects your cervix you may get an abnormal pap smear. Most of these infections will spontaneous resolve themselves, within a year. In a small number of cases the virus will persist and cause cervical cancer or a lesion that may lead to cervical cancer over time. If you have an abnormal pap smear your doctor will follow you closely and may recommend further studies to evaluate your cervix. See your doctor regularly until all signs of the infection are resolved. Condoms reduce the risks of acquiring HPV, but are not 100 percent effective.

How to treat it: Warts can be treated with laser, freezing, cutting or several medications that you and your doctor can apply. Often your immune system will kick in and rid your body of the virus altogether.

Molluscum Contagiosum

What it is and how it works: This is a skin infection transmitted by intimate contact. You can catch it through sexual contact, nonsexual skin-to-skin touching or sharing towels.

Do you have it? Symptoms include small flesh colored, waxy, dome-shaped bumps that typically appear between two and twelve weeks after exposure. A doctor can determine if you have Molluscum Contagiosum by evaluating the infected tissue under a microscope.

How to treat it: Your doctor can remove the growth by using chemicals, electrical current, or freezing. Though condoms reduce the risk of Molluscum Contagiosum, the virus maybe in areas not covered by the condom.

Syphilis

What it is and how it works: Syphilis is caused by a tiny spiral-shaped parasite called Treponema pillidum.

Do you have it? The most common symptom is a painless ulcer on your genitals that appear from three weeks to three months after exposure to the infection. The ulcer typically disappears without treatment. Symptoms of advanced syphilis include rashes on the palms of the hands and soles of the feet, mild fever, weight loss, headaches, muscle pain, hair loss, fatigue, and a sore throat. Your doctor can make a diagnosis by performing blood tests.

How to treat it: Antibiotics can be used to successfully treat both partners. If caught early, syphilis is fully curable. In late stages, however damage caused by the disease is completely irreversible. Using condoms may decrease risk of infection during vaginal, oral, or anal sex.

Trichomoniasis

What it is and how it works: Trichomoniasis (trich) is very common. It is caused by a parasite Trichomoniasis vaginalis. Though considered a sexually transmitted infection, trich can be transmitted by non-sexual acts as well.

Do you have it? Trich often causes a heavy, frothy yellow or green vaginal discharge that may be foul smelling. You may also experience severe itching or burning on your vulva and vagina, particularly when you urinate. Your doctor can diagnose you by examining your vaginal discharge under a microscope or by sending your specimen to a laboratory for examination.

How to treat it: Your physician can treat trich by prescribing an antibiotic, metronidazole, in a single dose or several days' worth. Your partner should also be treated. Using condoms prevents the infection.

Safe Sex Reminders

Here are nine things women should remember about safe sex.

1. Obey the sexual privilege rules. These are rules that you design and place enforcement upon.
2. Never violate your lover by doing something he doesn't want.
3. When in doubt about sex it's best to ask for permission.
4. Do not get involved with sexual acts that will harm anyone.
5. Practice birth control regularly.
6. When playing games that involve restraint or pain decide upon a safety word that will let your lover know you want to stop. This word is to be taken serious and should never be used to joke with.
7. If you lack trust in the person that wants to play the game, trust your gut instinct and suggest you get to know each other better before you move forward with any games.

8. Ask and discuss HIV exposure with your lover before any sexual activity takes place.
9. Always... always practice safe sex.

In the heat of the moment it's easy for a man to forget the consequences of unsafe sex. If he takes responsibility for remembering to protect his partner every time, she will trust him, be grateful to him and appreciate the intimacy during sex.

Information Is Available

There are much excellent information and many resource books in print that will help you find basic facts about sexually transmitted diseases and how to protect yourself. I've listed several in the appendix of this book. I recommend that you read one or more of these books and educate yourself.

When you are armed with facts you can make an informed decision about your sexual activities. Once you are armed with this powerful information feel free to enjoy yourself. Having sex with a man whom you feel comfortable and safe with will create some of the hottest moments you'll experience during sexual activity.

It is especially important for women to practice safe sex because in a heterosexual relationship, women are at a higher risk than men who are exposed to the AIDS virus. During intercourse the virus if it is present in the man's semen can enter into the bloodstream through tiny tears in your vagina, tears that commonly occur during intercourse. Some women find it very difficult to insist a man use a condom every time they have sex to protect her because men say condoms reduce pleasure during sex. The woman is involved and concerned with what the man thinks and feels that she will risk her health and life.

Some condoms can limit the loss of sensitivity, which makes it more enjoyable to incorporate condoms into sex. If wearing a condom reduces a man's sensitivity he can hold back from ejaculating before the woman is satisfied. When holding back - his orgasm may become stronger.

For most women, including women who want to have children, contraception is not an option; it is a basic health care necessity

Ella's Final Note

Writing this book has been the most difficult, yet wildest, wackiest, exhilarating and most fulfilling adventure I have ever had.

As I conclude this book; I would like to share my own personal convictions on what I believe to be correct sexual principles. I believe that correct sexual principles are whatever feels most natural and comfortable to you and whatever contributes to your overall good health and happiness. I understand that a woman gets older her views and lifestyle changes and she becomes wiser in life and in love.

I wrote Heated Pleasures: A Sassy, Down To Earth Sexuality Guide about Self-Esteem, Sensuality, Sex and Self-Discovery out of my sincere desire to help consenting adult women accept their sexuality in wholesome and nurturing ways.

This is my personal attempt to assist women in their quest for romance, sex, and intimacy. Sex and sexuality is not about performance or who has the most orgasms; it's about a woman's personal sexual healing moments. Taking the time to understand what you like and want from your sexual experiences will make you feel better about your sexuality. Learning what turns you on, what satisfies you and doing wonderful things that enhance your sexual experiences is what I hope this book will do.

Every growing, maturing adult woman deserves sexual pleasure and satisfaction. Learn about it, embrace it and then use it to empower. Giving and receiving pleasure has many facets; there's no right way or wrong way to do it. It basically boils down to "what you like." You have to take time to discover for yourself what makes you feel good before, during and after sex.

I would suggest is that you communicate with your partner by letting him or her know what you enjoy and also understand that sensual improvement is a never-ending process. So, as my knowledge deepens, more books will be published appropriately. Meanwhile visit some of the websites I mentioned in the back of this book for the latest news, updates and sensuous adventures.

Feel free to contact me. I am open to your opinions, views and criticisms. As always, I am delighted to hear from you. Share your experiences with me. Tell me what chapters were particularly helpful and give me feedback on how you put these ideas into actions. Offer your suggestions to help others improve. Let me know what still perplexes you. Although I can't guarantee your total sexual success, the principles offered here, is my attempt to help move you toward a more positive sexual awareness. These tips, treats and techniques have worked successfully for many who use them.

Ella Patterson

As my knowledge deepens, more books will be published appropriately. Meanwhile, visit some of the websites I mentioned in the back of this book for the latest news, updates and sensuous adventures.

I have withheld nothing as my special secret. I've shared sensuous victories and disappointments. And as always I wish you a lifetime of positive heated pleasures.

I delight in your sexual happiness and improvement; however I extend this warning, "Be careful." If you follow the guidelines set forth in this book, you could outgrow the status of a beginner.

I invite and encourage you to share with me your own safe, insightful pleasure experiences. I look forward to seeing you at my seminars. My seminars are geared to educating women and helping them explore their own sexuality as well as improving their understanding. For information about conducting girl's night out, pampering parties, seminars, event pricing, or purchasing any items listed in this book please email, write, or call us at:

You Should Know

Best place to find information on sexually transmitted diseases is Centers for Disease Control and Prevention
1600 Clifton Rd. Atlanta, GA 30333, USA
800-CDC-INFO (800-232-4636)
TTY: (888) 232-6348 - Contact CDC–INFO

email, write, or call us at:
Ella Patterson
ellampatterson@aol.com
P. O. Box 973
Cedar Hill, Texas 75106
1-972-854-1824

Appendix A

Questions for Women Who Read This Book

This questionnaire is anonymous, so you don't have to sign it. Every question does not need to be answered. Answer only the questions that you are interested in. You don't even have to complete it. Just reply as you wish to. You may not choose to answer any of the questions. You may want to create your own. Send it in. Mail questions, answers and comments to:

Attn: Heated Pleasures
Questionnaire Dept.
P.O. Box 973
Cedar Hill, Texas 75106

1. Have you had the opportunity to read Heated Pleasures? Which sections, chapters or issues do you agree with? Disagree?

2. Which part of this book is the most important to you? Least important? Most emotional?
3. Has your sensuality changed since you read this book? In what way?
4. Is orgasm easier for you since reading this book?
5. Are orgasms important to you or do you enjoy sex just as much without orgasms?
6. When do you have orgasms? During intercourse? Masturbation? Love button stimulation? Other sexual activities? How often?
7. Do you have orgasms during intercourse? Never? Sometimes? Rarely?
8. Remembering your most favorite orgasm, give a description of how your body is stimulated to orgasm.
9. Give ways that you and your partner practice direct stimulation.
10. What kind of stimulation do you prefer? Do you prefer hard, medium, or soft massage? Do you like continuous movement? Do you like your positions varied?
11. Do you like intercourse? Physically? Psychologically? Do you have any physical discomfort?

12. Do you enjoy masturbation? Physically? Psychologically? Is it more intense with or without a partner?
13. Do you enjoy rectal contact? What kind? Do you enjoy penetration? How often do you do it?
14. What do you think about during sex?
15. Do you have fantasies? What about?
16. Do you look ugly or beautiful during orgasms?
17. Do you think that most men are uninformed about what pleases women?
18. How do you feel about your sexuality since reading this book?
19. Did you learn anything positive while reading this book?
20. Do you like objects in bed with you?
21. Do you like to use sensual toys while making love?
22. Do you have intercourse during your period?
23. Do you have oral sex during your period?
24. What are your best sex experiences?
25. How long do your sexual encounters last?
26. Do you have sex with the strangers?
27. Do you usually initiate the sex or the sexual advances?
28. Do you enjoy touching?

29. Who do you touch-men, women, friends, relatives, children, yourself, animals, and pets?
30. Do you feel politically inclined to have sex?
31. Do you masturbate with your partner during sex?
32. During general caressing was it difficult to do the first time that you did it? How did you feel about it?
33. Have you discussed your sexual relationship with any other women?
34. Have you discussed masturbation with them or not? What did she say? What did she think?
35. Do you like this questionnaire?
36. What else would you like to find out about sex?
37. Why did you answer this questionnaire?
38. Are you in love?
39. Does being in love make you happy?
40. What makes you happiest in life?
41. What sex is the person that you are closest to?
42. What is your biggest sexual problem?
43. What is your favorite way to spend time alone?
44. Does having children increase or decrease your sex drive?
45. How do you feel about pornography?
46. Have you ever had an affair or sex with a married man?

47. How often do you have sex with your partner?
48. Would your relationship be in danger if sex decreased?
49. How often do you want or like to have sex?
50. Does sex with you lover change for the better? The worst? Does it become boring or more pleasurable?
51. Do certain conflicts in your relationship tend to last for years or over long periods of time?
52. Have you found that the same problems keep cropping up even after you've talked about them or thought that they were worked out?
53. What do like most about your man? Least?

Be present within your mind, body and soul
and then allow the energy of the universe
to flow through you to your lover.

Appendix B

Helpful Resources

Institute for Advanced Study of Human Sexuality
1523 Franklin St.
San Francisco, CA. 94109

Information on Sex and Disability
It's okay! A magazine on sexuality and disability.
Linda Crabtree, Phoenix Counsel, Inc.
1 Springbank Drive
St. Catherines, Ontario,
Canada, L2S 2K1, $23.95 a year.

Erotic Aids for Women: Eve's Garden
119 West 57th Street, Suite 420
New York, NY 10019
1-800-848-3837
www.evesgarden.com Catalog for $3.00

Good Vibrations
938 Howard St.
San Francisco, CA 94103
Catalog $1.00 of aids, books, and videos
(Arrives in plain packaging)
1-800-buy-vibe www.goodvibes.com

Passion Parties
To find a consultant go to ...
www.passionparties.com

Appendix C:

Organizations Dedicated to Sex Ed.

National Society for Scientific Study of Sex (SSSS)
P.O. Box 208
Mt. Vernon, IA 52314

Sex Education and information Council of the US (SEICUS)
130 West 42nd Street, 25th Floor
New York, NY 10036

American Association of Sex Educators, Counselors and Therapists (AASECT)
435 North Michigan Ave. Suite 1717
Chicago, IL. 60611

The Kinsey Institute for Research in Sex, Gender and Reproduction
University of Indiana Morrison Hall 313
Bloomington, IN 47405

Appendix D:

Sensuous Internet Sites

- Products - www.easypleasers.com
- Products - www.stockroom.com
- Products - www.fourcuples.com
- Products - www.annsummers.com
- Vibrators - www.goodvibes.com
- Lubricants - www.passion8.com
- Sex Art - www.eroticat.com
- Sex Art - www.bettydodson.com
- E-cards - www.kinkycards.com
- Condoms - www.ripnroll.com

Appendix E:

Weights for Kegel Exercises

- www.aswechange.com
- www.goodvibes.com or 1-800-buy-vibe
- www.bettydodson.com

Appendix F:

Recommended Reading
Men and Relationships

How a Man's Mind Really Works,
By Michael Gurian

Courting a Woman's Soul: Going Deeper Into Loving and Being Loved
By John Lee

Why Men Don't Listen: And Women Can't Read Maps: How We're Different and What To Do About It, By Barbara Pease and Alan Pease.
Keys to the Kingdom, By Alison A. Armstrong

Be Loved For Who You Really Are: How The Differences Between Men and Women Can Be Turned into the Source of the Very Best Romance You'll Ever Know
By Judith Sherven and James Sniechowski

Opening to Love 365 Days a Year,
By Judith Shervan, Ph. D. and Jim Sniechowski. Ph. D.

Women Can't Hear What Men Don't Say: The Myths That Divide Couples and Poison
By Warren Farrell

The Maiden King: The Reunion of Masculine and Feminine
By Robert Bly, Marion Woodman.

What Women and Men Really Want, Creating Deeper Understanding and Love in Relationships, By Aaron Kipnis Ph.D. and Elizabeth Herron M.A.

Men Talk: How Men Really Feel about Women, Sex, Relationships and Themselves,
By Alvin S. Baraff.

Space for Notes

Acknowledgements

This book is a personal retrospection of the author; however I attribute experiences gained while doing my research to many people who had the courage to tell me their stories. I am indebted to women who over the past twelve years knowingly and unknowingly contributed to this data. Numerous others helped by encouraging me to keep at it. They gave me honest and open criticisms every time I threw something new at them.

They allowed me tremendous freedom of speech and without their faith in me I would not have been challenged to dig so deeply, probe so many crannies or look beyond readily available answers. Without their knowledge and experiences this book would not exist.

In many of my books, I’ve tried to use this page to thank people who have helped me keep it together. As I wrote this book I recall wonderful words of wisdom received from people who empowered me. These gracious experts inspired me with their sensuous stories, wholesome levels of sensuality and fun loving comments. I’d like to say thanks to each of them.

My gratitude goes to single and married women, lesbians, transvestites, exotic dancers, teachers, coaches, bartenders, managers, doctors, lawyers, college students, and preachers for their undying support and encouragement to this project.

To my husband Martin Jr., thanks for being the one to say, “Keep at it baby, you’ll get it done.” I love and appreciate you so much.

To my children Juanna, T’Juanna and Martin III, I continue to love each of you and I thank you for showing me support in everything I set out to do.

To Robert Corley, this book would not be if it were not for your insight, true opinions and support. Thanks for traveling this road with me. You are my friend for life.

Herbert Jones, my oldest brother, thanks for being here - seen and unseen to give me love, strength and encouragement. Also, thanks for helping me find my way. You nurtured my spirit and gave me support when I needed it most. You have never let me down and I am so proud of you. I love you dearly.

My brother Richard in love and spirit, I miss you so much. I miss having someone around that looks like me. I know that God and his angels are in great company. I'll be seeing you one day.

My sister Evelyn (Muff) may God be with you in all that you do. I love you dearly, even though we don't see each other much.

To my eternal friends Marva Houston and Carol Murray you have been there with me from the very beginning. I appreciate you both. Thanks for keeping it real and telling me like it is. Only true friends would do that.

My friend, Betty Artis, thanks for bringing the undying support. You are a lifesaver. You stuck with me when I needed a friend most.

My friend, Denella Ri'chard, thanks for your loving support and wild ideas. You gave me inside knowledge about the universe. We have laughed, stressed, cried and planned our life together. Thanks for being there in good and bad times.

My Soror, Brenda Brown, thanks for being an inspiring wild woman. You reminded me… that if I don't watch out my stock would go down. Girl you are wild and smart and always on target. I love you Soror.

My special Soror, Debra Martin, you always keep in touch, by sending an email; make a phone call or just popping up. Thanks for reaching out to me, and thanks twice as much for showing the love. You have been so loyal to me and I really appreciate you.

Big Boom; thanks for awakening my writer's spirit. Ghostwriting your books 'If You Want Closure in Your Relationship, Start with Your Legs' and 'How to Duck a Suckah' has helped me get back on track. I have respect for your forward thinking. Congrats on your book deal.

For Creamola, who's always been here with me and for me. You understand my plight. Thanks.

Jan Miller-Rich, my literary agent, thanks for not pressuring me when I was going through some life changing ordeals. Time has passed and things have changed, but your patience is my blessing in disguise. We have had times that we misunderstood one another, but that's okay because our lives have purpose, and a whole lot of other stuff we can't explain. I really do love you for the lessons. I never forgot that we are joined at the hip. Thanks for your unwavering support. You have greatly contributed to my growth and I thank you for it.

My God, as always I thank you daily. I look to you for guidance, strength and wisdom while on my life journey. Thanks for shining your light on me. Thanks for wrapping your arms around me. I give thanks to you for my many opportunities to make a difference in this world. "God you are my light when the world seems dark."

INDEX

1

15 calories, 314, 316

2

2 types of orgasms, 382
26-degree pelvic tilt, 359

4

400-horsepower orgasm, 408

5

501 (K), 460

A

a final note, 529
a man's heart, 115
a note for men, 324
a note for women, 323
a woman's erotica, 352
a woman's touch, 176
abandon inhibitions, 11
abnormal pap smear, 523
abrasion, 148
abrasive stubble, 125
abstinence, 502, 511
accessories, 218
achieve a pouty, sexy mouth, 136
acid, 316
acidic taste, 314
acids, 122
acknowledgements, 544
acorn features, 255
additional resources, 538
adjustable lasso, 445
adult toys, 408
advance your knowledge, 11
African American men, 317
African drums, 218
afterglow, 341
aides and lubrication, 456
airport screening line, 430
Alan Hirsch, 106
alcohol, 128, 147, 314, 477, 484
Algae Body Wrap, 206
allergic reactions, 144
alleviating cramps, 294
allure, 146
almond, 487
aloe vera, 459
American Association of Sex Educators, 539
american association of sex educators counselors and therapists, 539
American's favorite pastime, 118
ampullae, 97
anal cleansing, 112
anal pleasure and health', 424
anal sphincters, 84
analyzed, 20
anaphrodisiacs, 486
angles, 116, 117
aniseed, 486
ankles, 145
answers, 533
antibiotics, 502
antiperspirant ads, 77
anus, 75, 108, 112, 113, 260, 286, 298, 310, 313, 319, 415, 425, 428, 433, 435, 452
anvil stroke, 279
aphrodisiac, 359
aphrodisiac dishes, 497
aphrodisiacs, 483
Aphrodite, 485
appeal to her senses, 58
appearance, 114, 115, 119, 172, 362, 387, 416, 444, 450
appendices, 533
apple, 478

application of fragrances, 145
apply lipstick, 135
apply perfume, 147
apply your knowledge, 253
applying mascara, 131
appreciating each other, 190
apricot squash with apricot glaze, 497
apricots, 478
aprons, 158, 400, 405
aqua lube, 461
arcade, 191
areola, 95
armpits, 310, 313
arms, 140
aroma, 147
aromatherapy, 207
Aromatherapy Body massage, 206
arouse your sexual appetite, 189
art, 124, 139, 175, 193, 213, 339, 415, 480
Arugula, 487
ascorbic acid, 315
ashamed of how your body looks, 28
ask for permission, 526
asparagus, 314, 486
asparagus delight, 498
astringent, 133
astro glide lube, 460
Astroglide lubricant, 460
attitude, 28, 50, 114, 168, 193, 330
authentic sexual fulfillment, 38
author
Ella Patterson, 303
authors final note, 530
Avanti men cream, 465
avocado, 478, 487
dildos, 429
awareness, 189
Ayurvedic leg/foot ritual, 206
azooapermia, 99

B

B-5, 480
baby oil, 236
baby powder, 127
baby talk, 164, 166
back of your knees, 145
back yard, 49
background music, 169
bacteria, 112
bacterial putrefaction, 313
bacterial vaginitis infection, 516
bacterial vaginosis, 514
bad breath, 195
bad times, 61
baggy pants, 116
balloons, 404
balloons and flowers, 404
balsamic vinegar, 487
banana, 487
banana leaves, 488
bananas, 478
barbecue odor, 107
bare feet, 209
barrier methods, 508
base clutch, 281
base of the throat, 145
basic hygiene, 108, 119
basic stroking, 269
Basil, 488
bath, 110
bath gels, 145
bath oils, 146
bath together, 190
bath treatments, 103
bathing therapy, 103
batteries, 429
battery pack, 443
battery-operated boyfriend, 408, 410, 411, 429, 430, 432
battery-powered vibrators, 415
be careful, 440
beautiful features of your face., 123
beauty treatments, 207
becoming sensuous, 62
bedroom, 16, 22, 193, 208, 209, 210, 211, 212, 213, 214, 215, 216, 217, 218, 220, 221, 224, 343, 344,

345, 364, 370, 371, 404, 481, 482
compliment, 210
exotic, 217
bedroom activities, 22
bedroom door, 193
bedroom pressures, 34
bedrooms
making it passionate, 218
bedspreads, 221
beer, 314, 319
behind the ears, 145
bell weather, 133
bells and whistles, 28
bend of your elbows, 145
beneficial nutrients, 477
benefit of sensuous ideas, 62
Bentley of vibrators, 417
berries, 320
best fit forward, 282
bikini's, 125
birth control, 134, 147, 502, 526
birth control pills, 134, 506
bistro table, 219
bitch, 16, 148, 341
bite, 297
blacksmith duos, 280
bladder, 84
blanket, 482
blankets, 223
blemish fighter, 134
blemish free skin, 138
blindfold your partner, 483
bliss lube, 458
Bliss lubricant, 459
bliss-state, 388
blocking the tubes, 507
blood flow, 96
blood pressure, 96
blood transfusion, 502
blowjob, 295, 298
blowjob dong, 436
blowjob., 255
blowjobs, 303
body, 143
body chemistry, 144
body fluids, 77, 414
body massagers, 409
body odor, 108, 145
body oils, 223
body treatments, 104
body, balances, 103
bondage implements, 442
book, 19, 27, 50, 63, 108, 148, 165, 258, 303, 348, 424, 502, 527, 530, 531, 532, 534
book ends, 280
boomerang, 253, 436
bosom, 145
boutiques, 116
bowel movement, 112
bra, 143, 146, 355
brandy, 357
bras, 118, 355, 398
breast, 105, 143, 177, 242, 320, 333, 367, 385, 447
breasts, 85, 96
breath savers, 321
bringing out deep-set eyes, 131
brittle lashes, 131
broccoli rabe, 488
brochures, 403
brow bone, 131, 132
brows, 131
brush, 400
brush your hair, 128
bumping and grinding, 34
Butterfly, 427
buttery/fish taste, 313
buttocks, 75, 319, 333, 337, 398, 431
buying sexier shoes, 62
buzzin buddies, 427
buzzing devices, 443
BV (bacterial vaginal infection), 516

C

caffeine, 489
calcium, 315
caloric content of an average ejaculate, 314, 316
camisoles, 348
camouflages, 134

candle, 104, 190, 223
candlelight, 106, 192, 219, 222, 402
candles, 402, 481
canoe ride, 191
cardamom, 361
careaholic, 26
career, 62
carefree sex, 501
carrots, 188, 478, 489
carvings and woodwork, 218
Casanova, 472
castor oil, 130
Caucasian penis, 317
celery, 478
Celsius, 93
Centers for Disease Control and Prevention, 513
cervical cancer, 451, 455, 523
Cervical cap, 509
cervix, 81
chaffing, 148
champagne, 192, 202, 319, 366, 400, 481, 483
Chancroid, 517
change your thinking, 50
charades, 191
cheap and dirty, 162
cheap imitations, 144
chemical, 394
chemicals, 145
cherries, 320, 478
chest, 105, 129, 143, 153, 177, 240, 345, 346, 481
chewing,, 122
chicken, 479
chilled wine, 222, 366, 400
chills, 154
chipped nails, 122
chlamydia, 514
Chlamydia, 517
chlorine, 315
chocolate, 288, 299, 404, 475, 476, 481, 483, 488
chocolates, 348
choices, 42
cholesterol, 128, 315
Chris Meletis, N.D, 476
cilantro, 489
cinnamon, 361
cinnamon-based ointment, 278
circumcised, 255
circumcision, 257, 306
clamp pressure, 446
clamps, 442, 443, 444, 445, 446, 447, 448
clarifier, 128
clean an uncircumcised male identity, 257, 260
clean the anus, 112
clean your face, 133
cleaning toys, 440
cleaning sex toys, 454
cleaning the sex organs, 111
cleanliness, 119
climax, 384
clip-on vibes, 427
clitoral cleansing, 111
clitoral orgasms, 388
clitoris, 72, 108, 474
clothes, 116, 117
clothing, 116, 117, 120, 146, 159, 170, 223, 348, 357, 360, 366, 431, 452
clover clamps, 443
cluttered, 210
cock, 67, 68
cock rings, 420
coconut, 478
coconut oil, 457
coil, 442
coitus interruptus, 99
cold cuts, 202
cold temperatures, 179
cold towels, 134
collagen, 136
colognes, 134, 144, 145, 400
colonies of beneficial bacteria, 110
color of your eye shadow, 131
colored contacts, 131
coloring hair, 128
comb, 400
comments, 533
common sense, 313
common symptom of syphilis, 524

communicate, 129, 149, 153, 163, 172, 176, 338
communicating, 22
communication, 47, 157, 241, 347
completeness, 44
complexion, 132, 133
complicated sex, 334
concealer, 130
concentration, 242
conditioners, 126
condom, 368
condoms, 223, 401, 435, 440, 456, 457, 460, 461, 462, 463, 465, 504, 528
condoms reduce pleasure, 528
connoisseurs, 342
consenting adult lovers, 26
construction worker, 349
contact Ella, 531
conversationalist, 160
conversations, 14, 22, 219
cooking, 192, 482
cooking and sex, 471
cooking oil, 264
cool cotton sheets, 209
cool running water, 122
cool sex, 334
copyright page, 2
coriander, 489
corn, 478
corns and calluses, 119
cornstarch, 454, 455
corona, 255, 276, 305, 306
coronal area, 307, 312
coronal ridge, 311
corpora cavernosa, 87
cosmetic labels, 134
cosmetic surgery, 70
costume jewelry, 147
costumes, 402
cotton ball, 146
cotton balls, 127
cotton cycle, 359
cotton pad, 128
cotton straps, 143
cotton swab, 111
couch, 296
cough drop, 318
cough drops, 318
cover cream, 134
cradle of the phone, 133
cream, 475
creamy delight, 475
create sexy moods, 360
creative ways to enhance your sensuality, 27
Crèmes de Menthe, 465
criticized, 20
crotch area, 159
crushed ice, 134
cucumber, 366
cucumbers, 131, 188, 478
culinary fantasy, 482
cunnilingus, 238, 286, 288, 291, 294
cunt, 67, 68
cupboard, 359
Cupping, 206
cure for herpes, 521
curling the lashes, 131
curly permed hair, 128
cuspids, 140
cuticle cream, 122
cuticles, 122
cyberskin, 412
cyberskin extension, 453
cyberskin toys, 449
cysts, 134

D

daily calories, 476
dairy content, 314
dairy products, 313
damp sea sponge, 139
dandruff, 127
dandruff shampoo, 127
dark shade of lips, 137
darker skin complexions, 135
dartos fascia, 93
dates, 26, 478
day-old make-up, 119
deadlines, 176
decorating, 403
decorating scenes, 403
decylo-leate, 134
deep breaths, 11

deep massaging thrusts, 359
deep-blue color stick, 131
deodorant, 77
deodorant,, 145
deoxyribonucleic acid, 315
department stores, 116
Depo-Provera, 504
designer clothing, 124
diagnosis
  gonnorrhea, 519
diagnosis chlamydia, 518
diaphragm, 293, 294, 508
diaphrams, 457
diet, 109
difficult intimacy, 18
diffuse stress, 133
dildo
  solo masturbation, 433
dildo tips
  astroglide, 439
dildos, 407
  cheek to cheek, 433
  double penetration, 433
  germs, 440
  get a buzz, 428
  ride that dong, 428
  sticky, 440
  strapping it on, 428
  vagina to ass, 433
diner in bed, 192
dingy clothing, 117
dinner, 60
dip the tip, 359
dirty, 210
dirty laundry, 211, 212
dirty movie, 364
dirty underwear, 118
disclaimer, 11
discolorations, 117
discount stores, 116
divine purpose, 333
DNA, 315
doggy style, 282
cyberskin toys, 450
double dildo, 432
double dong, 432, 435, 450
double pleasures, 437
double whammy, 279
douche, 110, 112
douching, 109
down comforters, 209
drab eyes, 131
Dragonfly, 427
dramatic effects, 121
draped penis, 256
dressing tables, 219
drink, 173, 222, 314, 356
drugs, 502
dry vagina, 457
drying, 124
dull hair, 124
dull, lifeless hair, 128
durex sex cream, 465

E

e cards, 540
E. Mediterranean, 257
ear lobes, 367
earlobes, 199, 310, 313
early labor, 448
Easy Pleasers, 540
eating fruit, 320
Eau De Perfumes, 146
e-card, 358
Eclipse Magazine, 33
ecstacy, 162, 306, 322, 339, 340, 363
ectopic pregnancy, 518
educate yourself, 527
educational, 20
eggplant, 478
eight hours of sleep, 133
ejaculation, 161
ejaculatory abstinence, 98
ejaculatory orgasms, 390
elastic straps, 451
electric, 153, 402, 430
electricity, 467, 529
  violet wand, 467, 529
Electric-powered vibrators, 469
electrolysis, 125
Elson Haas, M.D, 479
emails, 108
emery board, 123
emission, 97
emotional needs, 17
emotional sensations, 56

enjoy your own body, 105
epididymis, 88, 97
epithelium, 82
equilibrium, 89
erection, 89, 298
during, 96
Eros body glide, 462
erotic, 126, 149, 156, 157, 158, 161, 163, 167, 170, 221, 223, 249, 299, 313, 319, 334, 346, 347, 349, 350, 353, 357, 360, 363, 366, 400, 401, 403, 410, 444, 472, 478
erotic aids for women, 538
erotic colors, 360
erotic food, 480
erotic foods, 480
erotic magazines, 157
erotic moments, 156
erotic part of her body, 156
erotic photos, 221
erotic recipe swapping, 206
erotic stories, 349
erotic things, 157
erotic toys, 205
erotic turn on's, 161
erotica, 352
eroticism, 473
escta sleeve vulva, 422
exercise program, 109
exfoliate, 132
exfoliating products, 132
exhaustion, 344
exotic plants, 221
exotic rug, 217
exotic sexual treats, 12
expert oral love making, 311
exploration, 47
explore, 20, 35, 304, 313, 386, 532
exposed to the AIDS virus, 528
exposing skin, 135
exposure to sex, 161, 162
external vagina, 110
eye bags, 130
eye contact, 129
eye drops, 132
eye shadow, 129
eyebrow pencil, 130
eyebrows, 129
eyelash curler, 131
eyelid crease, 131
eyelids, 367
eyes, 105, 129, 131, 139, 151, 159, 176, 188, 189, 203, 216, 244, 295, 299, 313, 320, 332, 333, 354, 355, 393, 439
eyes appear whiter, 131

F

fabric, 217
fabrics, 221
sensual, 213
facial contours, 139
facial redness, 134
fake earrings, 119
fake orgasms, 351
false lashes, 129
false vagina's, 442
family jewels, 256, 276, 277, 279, 280, 281, 297, 298, 301, 305, 310, 313, 408, 428, 436, 445, 448, 450, 453
fantasies, 167, 192, 346, 349, 364, 535
fantasy party, 204
Faraday Electricity, 467
fashion, 115
fashion conscious, 116
fashion magazines, 115
fast food, 330
faulty areas, 115
favorite song, 148
fear, 390
fear of inhibitions, 393
feathers, 445
Feeldoe, 436
feet, 142, 203, 333
felatio, 323
fellatio, 295
female ejaculation, 245
female genitals, 246, 247
female homologue, 93
female pros, 153
female sexual juices, 321

female sexuality, 45
FemCap, 509
feminine accessories, 219
feminine body odors, 109
feminine hygiene, 22, 110
fermented beer, 314
fertilizing the woman's egg, 505
field trip, 205
fig, 489
figs, 478
fine jewelry, 124
finger vibrator, 419
fingernail polish, 399
fingernails, 122
fingerprints, 108
fingers, 310, 313
fireman, 192
fireplace, 365
fireplace picnics, 404
fireworks, 53
first timers, 287
five senses, 147, 214, 370
flame, 281
flannel sheets, 209
flared base toys, 439
flavored cough drops, 318
flavored gels, 464
fleshlike materials, 449
flex-o-pleaser, 422
flick her tongue, 300
flicker, 256
flirting, 124, 349
fluffy skin, 111
fluffy throw, 221
fluids from sex, 111, 116
flush out impurities, 133
focus, 16, 121, 153, 214, 222, 307, 312, 313, 392, 417, 451
follicles, 134
food, 471
foods that arouse, 477
foolproof make-up, 131
forceps, 443
forearm, 346
foreplay, 328
foreplay before sex, 329
foreskin, 257
forplay, 461
foundation, 129, 139
fragrance, 104, 108, 134, 144, 145, 146, 461, 462, 463
fragrance questions, 144
fragrances, 107, 110, 134, 144, 147
frame of a woman's body, 121
frames
  sunglasses, 398
frenulum, 88
  stroking, 268
frenum, 88
fresh condoms, 401
frosted shadow, 131
fructose, 315
fruit, 319, 320, 399
fruit juices, 319
fruits, 222, 478
fruits and sex, 320
fuel sexual energy, 480
Fukuoku gloves, 425
full lips, 135
fun to have sex locations, 370
fur rug, 221
Futurotic, 449

G

gagging on penis, 317
game
  sprinkle, 319
games, 223
  creating your own, 49
garlic, 490
gels, 128
genders, 248
gene pool, 143
genital attitude, 289
genital herpes, 502, 514
genital ulcer, 524
genitalia, 72
genitals, 238, 242, 247, 251, 388, 429, 430, 463
  shaving, 126
gestures, 193
get in tune with your body, 109
ginger, 490

girls night out, pampering parties, seminars, pricing, 532
girth, 253
giving sex, 343
glans, 255, 256, 257, 276
Glass toys, 413
gloss, 136, 318
glossy, 137
glutathione, 315
goal oriented, 62
God, 203
goddess of love, 12
gonorrhea, 514
Gonorrhea, 518
good haircut, 122, 123
good health, 139
good love, 26, 327, 353
good vibrations, 538
goose head formation, 277
gourmet sex, 329, 330, 334
grade AA eggs, 277
Grafenberg spot, 237
grapes, 478
grass-cloth wall coverings, 217
great orgasms, 382
grocery list, 347
grocery shopping, 192
G-spot, 76, 237
G-spot orgasms, 389
G-spot vibrator, 419
Guide to Electrical Sex Book, 468
guilt, 21, 328, 329, 343, 392
gums, 139, 140
gut instinct, 526
gynecologist, 148

H

hair, 123, 124, 126, 128, 134, 146, 147, 148, 179, 247, 251, 281, 308, 346, 363, 402
hair products, 124
hair shafts, 127
hair sprays, 128
hair styling products, 134
hairbrush, 128
hairs, 125, 126, 148
hand job, 261, 263
handcuffs, 442
handheld battery pack, 426
handkerchiefs, 403
hands, 105, 117, 121, 124, 192, 206, 208, 222, 223, 242, 253, 254, 277, 279, 280, 281, 296, 297, 298, 300, 301, 302, 305, 310, 321, 346, 388, 406, 430, 438, 452, 454, 471, 474, 478
happiness, 16, 58, 213, 343, 404, 531
hard objects, 188
hard-boiled eggs, 481
hardened or gummy, 123
health spa, 203
healthy attitude, 115
healthy vagina, 109
heated moments, 47, 60
heated sex, 334, 338
heated sex skills, 335
heels, 119, 121, 158, 363
helping women, 62
Hepatitis, 519
hepatitis B, 514
Herpes type 1, 520
Herpes type 2, 520
heterosexual relationship, 528
highlight your lips, 136
high-tech electric shaver, 430
hips, 143
his nipples, 96
Hitachi Magic Wand, 417
HIV, 460, 521, 527
HIV symptoms, 521
HIV treatment, 522
holding back his orgasm, 528
holes in latex condoms, 457
Holistic, 206
Holistic facial, 206
Holistic pedicure, 206
home computer, 209
home-cooked meal, 483
homeopathic luscious flower, 458
homologous, 95
honey, 319, 404, 491

Hopi ear candles, 206
hormonal imbalance, 394
hosiery, 119
hot breath, 297
hot sex, 334
Hot stone massage, 206
hot temperatures, 179
hot water, 132
how your body feels during sex, 27
HPV, 523
http
//www.annsummers.com, 466
//www.goodvibes.com, 466
hugging, 47
hugs, 174, 190, 330
human immunodeficiency virus, 521
human life cycle, 51
Human Papilloma virus, 522
human papillomavirus, 514
human sexuality, 538
humidifier, 135
hyaluronidase, 315
hybrid, 129
hygiene, 108, 127, 257, 289
hymen, 74
hypoallergenic shaving cream, 148
hypospermia, 98

I

ibuprofen, 134
ice breaks, 134
ice cream lick, 320
ice cube, 354
ice cubes, 474
ID glide, 461
ID millennium, 462
illumination, 402
illuminators, 222
imperfections, 134
impotence, 98, 100
improve pleasure zone, 50
improve semen taste, 361
improving sex, 338
in black leather, 442
incense, 401
increase sexual aptitude, *50*
incurable diseases, 502
Indian head massage, 206
Indonesian massage, 206
infertility, 518
inflammation, 134
information, 16, 45, 108, 263, 288, 338, 403, 527, 532, 539
inhale slowly, 11
inhibition, 20
inhibitions, 328, 352, 361, 393
inner thighs, 110, 281, 288, 319
inositol, 315
inside your wrists, 145
intense orgasms, 381
intercourse, 261, 300, 350, 357, 386, 389, 422, 425, 426, 428, 452, 528, 534, 535
intimacy, 61, 169, 209, 212, 213, 214, 215, 224, 243, 329, 331, 340, 341, 344, 345, 346, 347, 362, 459, 527, 530
intimate relationship, 22
intimate relationships, 59
intimidation, 21
Intrauterine Device, 505
intravenous drug, 504
introduction, 47
involuntary rhythmic contractions, 381
irritating effects, 134
irritation-free, 127
isopropyl myristrate, 134
isopropyl palmitate, 134
IUD's, 505

J

jack-off accessory, 452
Jacuzzi, 102
jam, 288
jazz, 104
jelly, 414
jelly rubber penis, 422

jelly rubber tyoys. *See* Selecting Toys
jelly vibrators, 414
jewelry, 147, 361, 445
jewels, 277
journey of self-discovery, 18
judged, 20
junky, 210

K

Kama Sutra Honey Dust, 319
kegel exercises
for men, 248
kinds of vibrators, 429, 430
kinky heart-shaped bottom paddle, 442
kisses, 195
kissing, 198
kissing with ice cubes, 474
kissing your man, 157
kiwi slices, 131
Knead his nipples, 320
knob, 298, 299, 300, 301
know your body, 106
knowledge, 44, 49, 247, 317, 530, 531
Korean Hand massage, 206
K-Y jelly, 235
k-y jelly lubricants, 458
KY lubricants, 458

L

labia, 111, 239, 286, 427, 451
labia majora, 71
labia minora, 70
lackluster felatio, 324
lactic acid, 315
lactiferous ducts, 85
lambskin, 511
lamps, 211, 212, 218, 221
lanolin, 134
large lips, 136
latex plastic glove, 284
laundry detergents, 133
learn more about sex, 51
learning process, 19
Lea's Shield, 510
least erotic color, 360
leather or woven fabric, 120
leg hair, 124
legs, 121, 125, 141, 153, 282, 296, 333, 348, 355, 359, 415
lemon, 122
leper colony, 124
letter 'O' hand job, 271
letters, 108
lettuce, 486
levels of mind-blowing sex, 20
libidinous fervor, 345
libido, 472
licker, 317
licorice, 491
life altering problems, 52
lifestyles, 103
light color nail polish, 123
lights, 402
lingerie, 159, 192, 348, 398
lingerie drawer, 42
lip balm, 137
lip colors, 135, 137
lip line, 138
lip liner, 136
lip pencil, 135
lip shapes, 135
lip sizes, 135
lip textures, 135
lips, 129, 135, 136, 137, 138, 139, 141, 196, 247, 251, 254, 295, 297, 305, 306, 307, 308, 311, 320, 321, 322, 333, 354, 383, 393, 448, 452, 474
full, 136
thin, 137
lipstick, 135, 136, 137, 138, 139, 146, 219, 358
liquors, 314
live strip show., 364
living on a budget, 402
living room, 404
local pharmacist, 127
local stores, 132
locking device, 443
long coats, 399
long sex, 334

long-playing song, 169
loss of sensitivity, 528
lotion, 106
lotions, 106, 145, 399
love button, 111, 112, 116, 238, 239, 241, 243, 244, 245, 247, 251, 354, 360, 382, 384, 386, 388, 389, 393, 411, 416, 417, 418, 422, 423, 424, 426, 427, 428, 438, 445, 448, 451, 454
love button causing odors, 112, 116
love button cleaning, 111
love button orgasms, 388
love button stimulators, 454
love buttons (clitoris), 239
love foods, 483
love notes, 186, 403
love tug, 281
lovemaking, 28, 111, 161, 163, 179, 212, 222, 311, 344, 350, 362, 365, 367, 389, 442, 452, 457, 472, 477, 482, 504, 535
loving kisses, 186
loving sex, 334
low dose or triphasol birth control pills, 134
lower lashes, 132
low-fat cheese, 482
lubricant, 235, 240, 246, 278, 393, 458, 460, 461, 462, 463, 464, 465
lubricants, 456, 464
lubricates, 278
lubrication, 322
lunch box, 170

M

macrobiotic nutritionists, 313
magazines, 211
magical powers, 179
magnesium, 315
major complaint about lubes, 457
make, 105
make thin lips appear fuller, 138
make your relationships more sensual, 27
make-up brush, 134
male anatomy, 310
male condom, 510
male gonads, 91
male identities, 167, 279, 407, 414, 439, 452
male identity, 124, 125, 126, 177, 188, 244, 249, 253, 254, 255, 276, 277, 278, 279, 280, 281, 288, 295, 296, 297, 298, 299, 300, 301, 303, 305, 306, 307, 308, 309, 310, 311, 312, 313, 316, 317, 318, 319, 320, 321, 322, 323, 324, 354, 356, 358, 359, 360, 361, 363, 365,366, 367, 382, 383, 398, 400, 402, 413, 415, 418, 422, 426, 427, 428, 433, 438, 442, 450, 452, 454, 466, 468
male identity (penis), 322
male identity extensions, 453
male identity handler, 296
male urethra, 94
manganese, 480
mangoes, 478
manicure, 175
manicured and polished, 122
man's heat, 336
marbles, 283
marijuana, 484
marital tension, 344
mascara, 129
mascara drying out, 132
mascara remover, 131
massage, 106, 127, 175, 192, 203, 206, 207, 298, 354, 356, 358, 363, 364, 365, 367, 399, 423, 448, 460, 481, 534
massage, 339
massage your scalp, 127
massages, 104, 180, 202, 399, 461

masturbate, 167
masturbation, 71
masturbation habits and fluids, 109
masturbators, 452
matching bath and body products, 146
maturing women, 13
MD Anderson, and Cedars Sinai departments of gynecology, 460
meal, 471
meatus, 88, 256
mechanics of sex, 16
mechanics of sexuality, 27
medical circumcision, 259
medical fetishes, 443
medications, 52
Mediterranean colors, 218
mellow music, 190
memorize, 188
memory skills, 188
men suits, 399
menopausal symptoms, 457
menopause, 83
menstrual blood, 294
menstruating women, 77
menstruation, 147, 294
mental blocks, 44
mental foreplay, 156
mentholated, 318
messages, 60
messy hair, 124
microscopes, 333
mineral oil, 134
mineral water spray, 139
mini retreats, 191
mini vibrators, 445
mini-celebrations, 192
minor things, 121
mint, 357
mint flavored candies, 321
mints, 401
mirrors, 116, 117, 133, 219, 323, 393
missing buttons, 119
misty molecules, 146
moisture in the hair shafts, 127
moisturize your skin, 138
moisturized sunscreen, 135
moisturizer, 104, 106, 203, 459
moisturizing lotion, 278
Molluscum Contagiosum, 523
monogamous couples, 502
mons, 69
monthly period, 111
mood strike, 342
moral values, 391
mousses, 128
mouthwashes, 321
move forward, 526
movies, 118
Mr. Good Bars, 400
Mr. Goodbar, 476
mucous, 111
multi-floral scents, 146
multiple orgasms, 380, 389
muscle fibers, 83
music, 104, 105, 190, 192, 203, 207, 410
musky smell, 278
mustard, 491
mutual masturbation, 263
my lover, 22

N

N. Africa, 257
nail biting, 122
nail color, 122
nail polish remover, 122
nails, 122
naked, 49, 106, 133, 170, 190, 335, 358, 363, 364, 365, 393, 405
napkins, 222
national society for scientific study of sex, 539
natural beauty, 219, 220
natural body odor., 145
natural contour vibrator, 419
natural skin tone, 122
NavaRing, 505
navel, 313
neatness counts, 119
neck, 141, 310, 313
negative anchoring, 209
negative anchors, 212
neurotransmitters, 488

Nexus, 436
nickname, 170
nipple clamps, 444, 446
nipple rings, 446
nipple sensitivity and menstruation, 448
nipple swelling and discoloration, 447
nipples, 125, 177, 310, 313, 320, 353, 354, 358, 365, 398, 427, 442, 443, 444, 445, 446, 447, 448, 474, 475
nitrogen, 315
nocturnal emission, 97
nonporous toys, 413
non-sensuous women, 59
non-sexual activities., 353
noparaben preservatives, 458
normal vagina, 109, 110
nose, 146, 323, 354
Note From Ella, 45
nude photograph, 363
nude pictures, 362
number 2 pencil, 131
nurse, 192
nutmeg, 491
nutritionists, 313
nymphomaniac, 53

O

oasis, 179
obscene letters, 359
obscene messages, 359
odors, 109, 112, 125
bothersome, 286
odors and body functions, 109
odors and body oils, 109
odors and exercise, 109
odors and lotions, 109
odors and medication, 109
odors and menstrual cycle, 109
odors and powders, 109
odors and rest factor, 109
odors and sex, 109
odors and skin type, 109
odors and soap products, 109
odors and vaginal secretions, 109
odors and water source, 109
oil, 127, 133, 134, 138, 192, 358, 439, 457, 461, 462, 463, 465, 498
oil build-up, 127
oil-based, 450
oil-free, 134
oil-free foundation, 134
oil-free powder, 133
oils, 220
bath, 104
oils and lotions, 399
old make-up, 119
older women, 303
older worn teeth, 140
one-day mail services, 170
opposite sex, 141, 172
oral fun, 288
oral lovers, 318
oral sex, 56, 110, 179, 258, 287, 288, 317, 318, 320, 322, 323, 356, 357, 361, 364, 399, 427, 463, 535
oranges, 320
orchid bulbs, 487
orgasm cures, 342
orgasmic state, 388
orgasms, 111, 177, 246, 248, 260, 294, 303, 324, 381, 382, 383, 385, 388, 389, 390, 394, 408, 411, 415, 534, 535
full-body orgasms, 389
orgasms., 380
oriental scents, 146
Original Organic™ Homeopathic Personal Lubricant, 458
Orthro Evra, 506
O-shape, 300
ovaries, 83
ovary, 82
overall grooming experience, 141, 142
oviducts, 82
ovum, 83
oxytocin, 448

oyster stir, 497
oysters, 483, 491

P

pains, 425
palm of your hand, 321
palms, 145
palms of your hands, 360
pamper party, 203
pampering treatments, 207
panties, 125, 358, 365, 366, 398, 427
panty line, 110
panty sets, 355
panty vibrator, 416
Papilloma virus, 522
Paragard, 505
passion, 20
passion boudoir, 219
passion party, 205
passionate sex, 334
pasta, 490
Patches, 506
patio, 49
peaches, 219, 319, 346, 478
peanut butter, 223
pearls, 361, 404, 417
pedestals, 121
pelvic organ prolapse, 84
pelvic tilt, 359
penetration, 157, 382, 425, 426, 428, 432, 433, 435, 436, 437, 450, 457, 535
penetration during masturbation, 433
penicillin, 502
penile juices, 323
penile mutilation, 259
penile size, 252
penis, 87
penis sleeve, 283
penis spasms, 302
penis withdrawal, 99
peppercorn, 491
peppermint, 361
perfumes, 109, 110, 144, 145
perimeter of the penis, 255
perineum, 75, 90
period trash, 111, 116
perky posture, 143
personal accessories, 112
personal appearance, 22, 114, 143
personal lubricants, 456
pet name, 169
petroleum, 147
petroleum jelly, 136
phallic-shaped vegetables, 478
phase 2
  awaken your senses, 189
philosophy of food, 482
phimosis, 259
phone conversation, 165, 168
phone sex, 165, 166, 167, 168, 169, 355
phone sex business, 167
phone sex line, 169
phosphorus, 315
physical, 174
physical activity, 109
physical aspects, 333
physical problems, 394
physical self, 17
physical touch, 172
picnic, 222, 404
picnics, 404
pillows, 208, 216, 217, 218, 221, 223, 367, 428
pimples, 133, 134
pine nut, 492
pinnacle of sexual passion, 382
pistachios, 487
pistol grip, 442
pituitary gland, 83
places to have sex, 370
plant, 366
plastic containers, 454
plastic tits, 442
plastics, 413
Playboy pictorials, 247
playful sex, 334
playing games, 526
pleasure
  craving it, 316
pluck, 129
plucking, 130
plumber, 342

pocket rocket, 416
pole it, 136
policeman, 192
polish, 206
polymer, 449
pool table, 347
poopoo, 67, 68
poor diet, 128
popcorn, 193
popscicle game, 320
popsicle, 301
popsicle lick, 320
popsicles, 400
pornographic magazines, 363
pornographic story, 364
porous toys. *See* Selecting toys
positioning, 143
posture, 143
potassium, 315
potpourri, flowers, 211
pouty lips, 135
pouty, sexy mouth, 136
powder and blush, 133
powdered honey dust, 319
powdered sugar, 319
powders, 145
pregnant women warning, 448
Prentif cervical cap, 509
preparation for oral sex, 110
prepuce, 258
pre-seminal fluid, 278
pressure and tension, 391
prevent nail polish bottle tops from sticking, 123
prevent nail polish from thickening, 123
prevent running, 139
prevent smearing, 139
preventing ovulation, 504
preventing pregnancy, 504
primary sexual objects, 310
principlesips, 41
private notes, 11
private sanctuaries, 220
private sanctuary, 215
private time, 348
private time, 47
product build-up, 128
professional model's secret, 130
professional phone sex lines, 168
Prolong Emollient, 465
pronunciation, 165
props, 320
props and supplies, 223
ProSensual, 464
prostate, 94, 237, 238, 259, 408, 423, 424, 432
prostatic disease, 97
prostatic urethra, 95
protect against STD's, 504
protect skin against dry, cold air, 138
protect your eyelashes, 131
protect your lips, 137
proteolytic enzymes,, 95
provocative sounds, 165
psychiatrist, 106
psychological attachment, 253
psychosexual development, 76
puberty, 83
pubic bone, 68, 238, 240
pubic hair, 124, 125, 126, 308
pubic hairs, 125
puffiness, 130
pulse points, 147
pulse spots, 145
punanny, 67, 68
punk rock type person, 119
purine, 315
purity, 119
purpose of nipple clamps, 444
push-out contractions, 246
pussy, 67, 68
pyrimidine, 316
pyruvic, 316

Q

Q-tip, 136
quality time, 58
questionnaire, 533
questions, 533
quick strokes, 322
quickie, 179, 334, 345, 358, 408

quickies, 327
quiet surroundings, 105

R

radio, 118
random number, 342
Raphe, 88
raspberries, 478, 481
Raspberries and strawberries, 492
raw potatoes, 130
razor, 400
read quotes, 158
read this book, 62, 502, 534
reading
  participation, 19
reading the book, 20
reading this book, 11, 50
receiving sex, 343
recipes, 472
rectal exam, 94
refining the suck, 302
Reflexology, 206
refrigerator, 220
rejection, 331
rejuvenation, 47
relationship problems, 52
relax, 206, 207, 209, 308, 309, 343, 392, 410
Relax, 104
religious values, 391
removing make-up, 133
rescent, 146
rescue nail polish, 123
resentments, 44
residues, 112
resolving conflict, 392
resource books, 527
restaurant, 159, 176, 323
retreat, 213, 220
revealing too much gum, 140
revitalization, 134
revitalize, 209
revive tired eyes, 131
rhythmical contractions, 98
ridge, 255, 305, 311, 321
rituals, 103
Romans, 403
romantic cards, 192
romantic dates, 186
romantic dinners, 28
romantic interludes, 194
rough sex, 334
rubber sex toys, 411
rubber sheet, 358
rubbery, 449
rubbing alcohol, 127, 128
rubbing the clit, 241
rules, 526
running mascara, 119

S

S words, 165
sacrotuberous ligament, 90
sadomasochism toys, 444
safe sex, 22, 411, 456, 501, 526, 527, 528
safety pins, 118
sanctuaries, 220
sanitary napkin, 78
scents, 106, 145
Scorpion, 427
scrotum, 93
scrubs and creams, 345
scuffed handbags, 119
secrets, 42, 241
secrets of genital sex, 340, 341
security checks, 430
seductive colors, 219
  rouge red, lipstick reds, creamy peaches, and subtle pinks, 219
seductive tool, 132
seeds, 479
Selenium, 480
self touch, 262
self-adhesive diamante' tattoos, 442
self-indulgence, 348
semen, 88, 238, 256, 258, 260, 287, 302, 314, 315, 361, 528
  ejecting, 97
semen spouting, 302
seminal fluid, 258, 260
seminal vesicles, 95

semi-porous materials, 450
sensa touch wand, 423
sensitive awareness, 188
sensitive skin, 148
sensua organics, 457
sensual activity, 149
sensual allure, 110
sensual baths, 103
sensual delights, 483
sensual healing, 16
sensual moments, 370
sensual philosophy, 482
sensual recipes, 472
sensual self, 22
sensual sex, 334
sensual stimulation, 103
sensual style, 16
sensual surprise, 11
sensual techniques, 62
sensual treats, 28
sensuality, 22, 27, 50, 59, 60, 62, 104, 132, 153, 164, 165, 211, 212, 285, 332, 348, 353, 471, 534
sensuality adjustment, 60
sensuous, 103, 104, 105, 189
sensuous activities, 45
sensuous adventures, 47, 530, 531
sensuous appetizers, 360
sensuous attributes, 22, 62
sensuous drive, 340
sensuous foods, 472
sensuous hints, 11
sensuous needs, 17, 61
sensuous pleasures, 352
sensuous poem, 158
sensuous side, 340
sensuous talk, 186
sensuous thinking, 346
sensuous touching, 172
sensuous woman., 352
sensuous zone, 157
sex
  safety, 501
sex and disability, 538
Sex Art, 540
sex creams and pills, 464
sex drive, 342
sex education and information council of the US, 539
sex education organizations, 539
sex flush, 96
sex hormones, 83
sex quota's, 342
sex talk, 162, 163
sex tools, 147
sex toy, 435
sex toy warnings, 439
sex toys, 432, 441
  attachments, 423
  ball collar, 422
  beads, 425
  bottoms up kit, 424
  bullet vibes, 426
  butt plugs, 421
  fukuoku 90000, 425
  Hitachi wand, 417
  iSurge vibe, 424
  jack rabbit, 417
  jelly beads, 425
  joy buzzer, 427
  jumbo beads, 425
  mini hummer, 426
  pocket rocket, 416
  pulsatron, 423
  raspberry ring, 423
  rub my duckie, 424
  triple stimulator, 426
sex with your mate, 27
sex, photos, 364
sex-loving women, 349, 350, 351
sexual advantage, 347
sexual appetite, 340
sexual attributes, 62
sexual awakening, 112
sexual awareness, 331
sexual basics, 359
sexual books, 355
sexual confidence, 153
sexual desires, 59
sexual electricity, 345, 467, 529
sexual electricity phenomenon., 468

sexual encounter, 323
sexual encounters, 391
sexual exchange, 29
sexual failure, 295
sexual fantasies, 204, 349
sexual frequency, 383
sexual fulfillment, 335, 339
sexual goodies, 397
sexual habits, 45
sexual hang-ups, 352
sexual hope chests, 442
sexual intensity, 335, 411
sexual intercourse, 259, 382
sexual intimacy, 22
sexual journal, 186
sexual phenomena, 245
sexual pleasure, 161, 187, 316, 381, 405, 458, 465
Sexual pleasure, 54
sexual priviledge rules, 526
sexual relationship, 22
sexual satisfaction, 392
sexual sensation, 247
sexual speed, 339
sexual stamina, 248
sexual stimulator, 318
sexual tune-ups, 327
sexual wisdom, 51
sexuality, 20, 27, 45, 51, 58, 59, 61, 121, 147, 151, 189, 212, 252, 258, 330, 332, 353, 388, 408, 411, 479, 530, 532, 538
sexuality plan, 212
sexually active women, 502
sexually committed, 22
sexually transmitted diseases, 501, 527
sexually transmitted infections, 515
sexy clothing, 170
sexy piece of underwear, 360
sexy underwear, 159, 364
shades of lip color, 137
shaft, 253, 254
shame, 21
shampoo, 127, 128
shampooing, 124, 128
shampoos, 128
share erotic pictures, 157
share these tips, 44
sharing this book, 9
sharp blade, 126
shave, 126
shave hair, 125
shaver, 400
shaving cream, 126
shaving your pubic area, 148
sheer stocking, 355
shoe wardrobe, 120
shoes, 62, 117, 119
shoes that compliment your feet, 120
short sex, 334
shower, 147, 189, 190, 192, 288, 345, 363, 428
shrimp, 483
shuttle penis, 280
side effects
  abstinence, 512
  birth control pill, 512
  condom female, 511
  Depo-Provera, 504
  FemCap, 509
  Intrauterine Device, 505
  Lea's shield, 510
  NavaRing, 505
  Orthro Evra, 506
side of your eye, 132
Sigmund Freud's theory, 76
silicone, 412, 415, 449
silicone sex toys, 412
silicone-based, 450
silk, 348
silk scarves, 223, 405
silky texture, 449
silverware, 481
simple sex, 334
simulated vagina's, 452
six principles, 39
size, 143
skeletal muscle fibers, 94
skid marks, 112
skin, 133
skin cancer, 135
skin irritation, 126, 127
skin problems, 133
skin type, 135

slippers, 209
slut, 53
small eyes, 132
Smell and Taste Treatment and Research Foundation, 107
smells, 145
smile, 139
smoking, 173
smooth textured nails, 121
snake bite kits, 447
snatch, 67, 68
sniffing, 348
soaps, 145
socks, 119
sodium, 316
sodium laurylsulfite, 133
soft and sensuous music, 221
soft music, 203
soften your tone, 164
softskin, 449
soothing colored lights, 222
sorbitol, 316
soul, 105, 129, 173, 178, 220, 316, 336, 337, 348, 482
sounds, 203
speaking voice, 165
spell your name, 365
sperm, 259
spermatozoa, 278
spermicide, 508
spermidine, 316
spermine, 316
sphincter, 75
spike, 463
spine, 321
spiral plugs, 424
spirit behind eyes, 132
spiritual levels, 388
spiritual self, 51
spirituality, 22
sponge applicator, 136
spoon, 130
spritz, 146
squirms, 356
stains, 117, 413
static electricity, 128
STD testing, 514
STDs, 435
stearic acid, 134
steel, 414
sterilization, 507
STI, 506
stick shift, 346
stimulate her love button, 386
stimulating the G-spot, 238
stockings, 223
strap on vibrator, 420
strap on vibrators, 451
strategic places, 19
strawberries, 478, 481
streamlined lips, 135
strengthen your relationship, 43
stress, 173, 203, 209, 344
stressaholic, 26
strip domino, 366
strip poker, 191
stripping, 405
stroke dipping, 321
stroking hair, 124
stroking the love button, 383
style, 143
styling aids, 128
styling your hair, 124
sucking, 165, 256, 295, 300, 301, 302, 303, 312, 313, 318, 320, 324
sucking technique, 304
suction motions, 358
sugar, 404
summer switch, 138
sun block, 134, 135
sun blocks, 134
sun dries zits, 134
sunglasses, 398
Super Penetrix, 436
supply basket, 400
Supra men cream, 465
swallow semen, 315
Swedish" type massagers, 430
sweet additions, 404
switch hitter, 279
sylk, 463
symptoms
Molluscum Contagiosum, 524
synthetic materials, 120

syphilis, 514, 524
syrup, 319

T

table, 203, 218, 323, 363, 365, 372
taboos, 80
talcum powder, 127, 451, 455
talk show hosts, 118
tampon, 293, 294
Tampon, 78
tantric orgasms, 387
tape measures, 402
tape recorder, 158
taste
  oral sex, 287
  sex organs, 287
tea, 190
tearing the vagina, 528
techniques, 11, 16, 44, 124, 146, 312, 339, 362, 385, 389
teeth, 117, 136, 139, 140, 288, 297, 306, 307, 320, 321, 322, 474
television, 211, 212
television commercials,, 118
temperature, 179
tender sex, 334
TENS unit, 467
test your sensitivity, 188
testes, 91
testicles, 91, 93, 256, 297, 298
  licking them, 319
testosterone, 95
Thai seated massage, 206
that thing, 334
the barrel, 285
The Book of Heat, 405
thermal plastic, 449
thigh swatter, 281
thighs, 154, 177, 242, 333, 431, 442
thin lips, 135
throating cautions, 308
Tibetan head massage, 206
tickets, 192
tiny vibrating dolphin, 422
tips, 16, 43, 44, 131, 153, 412, 443
tips and techniques, 9
tips that improve sex, 359
tissue, 112, 136, 137, 447, 455, 459
tissues, 223
titanium dioxide, 134
toenails, 122
toes, 310, 313, 319, 367, 398
toilet, 113
toilet tissue, 112
toiletries, 399
tomato, 478
Tongue Joy Oral Vibrator, 360
tongue motions, 404
tongue-Joy, 427
tools, 147
torture devices, 444
touch, 103, 121, 133, 136, 138, 142, 146, 152, 153, 172, 173, 175, 176, 177, 178, 179, 180, 189, 221, 243, 254, 296, 301, 323, 336, 340, 342, 350, 353, 364, 386, 389, 393, 405, 423, 449, 450, 471, 536
touching your vagina, 393
towels, 106, 345, 353, 454
tramp, 58
translucent powder, 134
treating HIV, 522
treatment
  hepatitis, 520
  Molluscum Contagiosum, 524
treatments, 211
tree, 371
trendsetter, 116
Tribal rugs, 218
trich, 525
trichomoniasis, 514
Trichomoniasis, 525
trim pubic hair, 363
trinkets, 445
triphasol, 134
trivial pursuits, 191
tropical plants, 219
truffle, 492
try new things, 28, 50

trying new things, 43
tubal ligation, 507
tune up, 325
tune-ups, 328, 345
turnips, 479
TV, 323
tweezer clamps, 443
twirl, 146
two ended dildos, 425

U

ultraskin, 449
uncircumcised penis, 256
underarms, 124
underwear, 113, 118, 125, 223, 364, 399, 427, 446
uneven lips, 138
uneventful life, 16
unflavored formula, 457
unfulfilled women, 34
unique body parts, 17
unpleasant odors, 110
unsightly hair, 125
unwanted hair, 125
upper front teeth, 140
upper lid line, 130
urea, 316
urethra, 68, 73, 88, 238, 245, 259, 278
urethral glands, 97
urethral sphincter, 84
uric acid, 316
urine, 245
urine residue, 109
urogenital region, 91
utensils, 136
uterine contractions, 448
uterine tube, 82
uterus., 81

V

vagina, 45, 67, 73, 108, 109, 110, 111, 113, 235, 237, 238, 239, 240, 241, 243, 245, 246, 247, 248, 286, 288, 293, 294, 300, 319, 321, 359, 365, 366, 381, 382, 383, 393, 423, 424, 427, 433, 434, 435, 436, 437, 440, 442, 452, 456, 459, 463, 528
angles, 177
vagina fakes, 415
vagina juices, 319
vagina lips, 383
vagina orgasm, 388
vagina performance, 74
vagina shields, 468
vagina tears, 528
vaginal, 246
vaginal discharge, 516, 525
vaginal discharges, 110
vaginal health, 381
vaginal irritation, 516
vaginal juices, 319
vaginal lubricates, 96
vaginal lubrication, 79
Vaginal lubrication, 74
vaginal orgasm, 389
vaginal simulators, 452
vaginal stimulators, 451
vagina-to-vagina, 434
vanilla, 493
vas deferens, 259
Vaseline, 236, 439, 457
vegetable juices, 122
vegetables, 222
venus lubricant, 460
verbal fantasy, 161
verbalize your feelings, 163
verbally, 44, 161
verbally express your feelings about sex, 26
very private, 459
viacreme, 466
vibrating bullet, 419
vibrating egg, 421
vibrating nipple clamps, 448
vibrator, 355, 359, 361, 363, 411, 415, 416, 418, 421, 424, 430, 431, 451
vibrator dependency, 431
vibrator tips, 431
vibrators, 408, 415, 416, 417, 423, 425, 426, 427, 428,

431, 443, 445, 451, 454, 469, 540
battery-operated boyfriend, 408
vinegar, 128
vinyl cushions, 443
vinyl sex toys, 411
Violet Wand, 468
virus, 528
vitamin B12, 316
vitamin C, 133
vitamin E, 465
Vitamin E, 461, 480
vitamins, 478, 480
vivid virility, 466
voice, 160, 164, 165, 169, 361, 367
voice improvement techniques, 164
voluptuous lips, 135
vulva, 69, 247, 286, 428

W

wand, 442
wardrobe, 115
warm bath, 104
warming lotion, 278
warn women, 303
warnings, 148
Warts
treatment, 523
washing machine, 359
washing machines vibrations, 359
watching reruns, 60
water, 103, 104, 123, 126, 127, 128, 130, 133, 135, 138, 139, 146, 360, 371, 411, 431, 432, 437, 439, 440, 450, 454, 458, 459, 460, 461, 462, 465, 474, 479, 481, 498
water based foundation, 138
water based lube, 437
water lily, 486
watercress, 479, 486
waterproof mascara, 131
waterproof model, 431
wearable vibrators, 416
wearing jewelry, 71
wearing lip-gloss, 137
wearing shoes, 119
weights, 445
wet hair, 128
wet lubricant, 462
wet platinum, 463
what a woman wants, 47
What is sexual healing?, 50
whipped cream, 319, 398, 475
whirlpool, 320
white shadow, 137
white shadow on center, 137
white smooth teeth, 139
whore, 53
why a book on sensuous healing, 14
why a book on sexuality?, 47
Will The Real Women Please Stand Up, 158
wimp male identity, 356
wine, 202, 319, 366, 400, 404, 481, 493
wine, champagne and shrimp, 202
winter fragrances, 147
wipe their anus, 113
woman reaching orgasm, 360, 382
woman's heat, 60
woman's inner spirit, 340
woman's physical enjoyment, 253
women
older, 303
women who enjoy sex, 341
women who refuse to discuss sex, 19
words that begin with the letter "S"., 165
workaholic, 26
wrestle naked, 190
writing books, 45

Y

yogurt, 481
your brain, 494
your lover, 60

Z

Zestra, 464
zinc, 316, 479
ziploc bag, 455
zones of stimulation, 382

About The Author

Ella Patterson is an entrepreneur, sex educator, self-published author, professional speaker extraordinaire and columnist for several local and national magazines. She is Editor-in-chief of Global One Magazine, and Publisher of Global One Travel and Automotive in DeSoto, Texas. She is founder and CEO of Knowledge Concepts Educational Systems, a motivational company dedicated to educating and informing women to accept their sexuality in wholesome, positive, and nurturing ways. With degrees in both biology and health education, she has taught women in five countries to love themselves.

A motivational speaker for more than fifteen years, she has appeared on every major radio and television station in the country. She lives outside Dallas Texas.

Books, Audiotapes, Videos

By Ella Patterson

Order Form

For more information on Knowledge Concepts Publishing
or any Ella Patterson products,
call 972-765-1950 or send in the coupon below.
Please send me information on
books, lectures, seminars or products.

NAME (please print) ______________________________

PHONE ____

ADDRESS ____

CITY ____

STATE _________________ ZIP __________________

Please use ballpoint pen only

Return to: Knowledge Concepts
P.O. Box 973 Cedar Hill, Texas 75106

Ella Patterson

Ella Patterson has made it her life mission to help women believe in themselves, offering straight talk, fun-filled tips, treats and techniques on how to have fulfilling relationships with the person they love.

Available wherever books are sold or at www.amazon.com

At Knowledge Concepts Publishing

Our Mission

Encourage women through our publications fantastic ways to explore life's pleasures without apology.

Our Vision

Empower and educate women so that they can experience strong and healthy sex-lives leading to a positive impact not only in their relationships, but also in their lives overall.

Our Goal

Make it easy and fun for women to tap into a part of themselves that gives pleasure, confidence and higher levels of self-esteem.